BLUFF ROCK

Bluff Rock *is analytical and wise, by which I mean the scholarship and research is rigorous but also committed to the historian's task of making argument lucid and understandable. The book is also impassioned and honest, by which I mean it is driven by the ethical obligation to explore racist interpretations of the past in order to illuminate how racism functions in the words, actions and psyches of our present.*

Katrina Schlunke's book achieves what many of us hope from cultural theory, that through an investigation of language, words and culture, we come to a questioning of history, politics and the treacherous relationship between memory and myth. Her objective terrain is the contested arena of racist war in Australia, but her terrain is also how our ways of seeing race, colonialism, being white and being Aborigine have been formed by cultural forms and expressions that have made us repress signs of both violence and resistance in the landscape.

Christos Tsiolkas

Katrina Schlunke is a senior lecturer at University of Technology Sydney where she teaches cultural studies within the Writing and Cultural Studies Program.

BLUFF ROCK

Autobiography of a massacre

Katrina M Schlunke

Curtin
University Books

FREMANTLE ARTS CENTRE PRESS
in partnership with Curtin University of Technology

First published in 2005 by Curtin University Books
A Fremantle Arts Centre Press imprint
25 Quarry Street, Fremantle
(PO Box 158, North Fremantle 6159)
Western Australia
www.facp.iinet.net.au

Printed by Griffin Press
Editor Sarah Shrubb
Cover design Marion Duke
Internal design Margaret Whiskin
All images reproduced with permission Mitchell Library,
State Library of New South Wales.

National Library of Australia
Cataloguing-in-publication data

Schlunke, Katrina.
Bluff Rock : the autobiography of a massacre.

Bibliography.
Includes index.
ISBN 1 920731 71 7.

1. Massacres - New South Wales - Bluff Rock. 2. Aboriginal
Australians - New South Wales - Bluff Rock. 3. Bluff Rock
(N.S.W.) - History. I. Title.

994.440049915

In memory of my mother Marie, father Bill, sister Megan
and brother-in-law Richard

Dear Robyn + Padmavyuha,
    big love to both of you
    hope that you enjoyed your time in
    Perth, we loved to have you here.
        ♡ Suzanne

Hope you come back soon
                ♡ xxx
                Nandi

CONTENTS

INTRODUCTION

The problem of the past

How do we know the past? We know certain events happened in the past, sometimes exactly when, but we will never know precisely why and how something happened. And yet we shape ourselves through how we think about the past. We tell stories about where we come from and who we are. We change these stories, sometimes minutely, sometimes radically, depending on our audience and our task ... but some stories stay.

I have always known that Aboriginal people were killed as a part of the taking of land in Australia. I learnt this in New England, where I was born, as I learnt to walk. It seems that it was never a shock. I have no memory of a single revelatory moment. I don't know exactly how I knew, but I did. The stories of 'The Bluff Rock Massacre', which you will meet again and again in this book, were stories of confirmation. Passing the place was a moment to retell the story in the company of others — I knew I was never the only one who knew. We all knew.

But knowing that Aboriginal people died is not to know anything at all. That Aboriginal people were killed was another way of saying Aboriginal people did not exist now. There is an echo of the child's fascination with dinosaurs in this. How could something so big, so powerful, not be here now? How could a whole people, a whole way of life, not be here now? Everything I learnt and was told about Aboriginal people confirmed the idea that they were in some way extinct.

But if I knew Aboriginal people had been and were no more, maybe I also knew that that wasn't quite enough.

As a child, I think I displaced that silence onto an un-bounded love of the land. Our land. It was an enchanted place: it was an imaginary battlefield, it was a place to find baby birds and to practise self-dares of travel across the paddocks from home. It was space to escape into and hide within — it prom-ised a refuge from household tasks and sisters and brothers. But this same land, ploughed over, carved up and profited from, could, as soon as dusk swept across the lucerne, turn mean and gape open and swallow you whole. At night things would come out of it. Scary things. There was a breathing in your room; terrifyingly close. 'Out there' transformed your own breath into an alien — gonna getcha gonna getcha. You knew you weren't to call out to your parents and so you willed yourself to open your eyes to take that oh-so-courageous step of seeing if any-thing was coming in the window. Nothing ever was, and now I wonder how much of that fear was a longing for someone to be out there.

But in the day, all that I saw I loved. If we had meant to create our own *volk*, our own white natives, we could have done no more. I had a notion of perfect belonging. This land felt entirely mine. I practised all the natural pleasures of de facto land ownership. I rode up to hills and looked over, and then down to creeks to swim. Our rhythms of sheep born and shorn and joined mingled with crops planted, harvested and hayed. Our lives responded almost perfectly to an anglicisation of time and seasonal order even if the land itself didn't quite correspond to the utter green of a country-lifed Britain.

This imposed seasonality had its moral equivalent. I learnt to do the right thing. Sunday school taught these lessons well. Displays of moral courage were particularly fine if they included some aspect of forgiveness and abnegation. We had to turn the cheek again and again. We could be giving, but we never learnt the courage to say we didn't know, and so displace ourselves from the centre of the moral universe.

So knowing Aboriginal people died did not have the effect it should have. It was not the sort of moral tale that automatically brought forth the 'never, ever again' response. These historical deaths were part of the shutting down of a history, not of its continuous opening up. Without knowing paths from those earlier Aboriginal deaths to existent Aboriginal peoples within my local community, I made no connection — they were altogether other sorts of people. And I didn't know that Aboriginal people fought back. I didn't know about the connections between massacre and stolen land and people. I didn't know to ask how some of their land had become our farm.

I began this book with the desire to paint a bigger picture of the past through one specific event. I want to show you how many ways a massacre of Aboriginal people can be told and used and reoriented.

I 'knew' massacre habitually and naturally as a child, but that is to not know massacre at all. This isn't a complaint about knowing too little — I always knew, but I also always knew *how* to know. But I want to unknit *how* we know something, I want to unravel how stories can both fix ideas (and so our ways of knowing) and intimately and intricately undo those certainties. My hope is that a gap, a space of improvisation, will be found, where stories emerge that speak of how they have been produced but also evoke something more.

And there is something wrong with the title of this book. How can you have an autobiography of a massacre, an autobiography of an event? My suggestion is that this is precisely the way to speak, write and embody the presence of the past.

For this is not an autobiography of a self. It is an autobiography of a past, placed, event. It is an impossibility. A rock, an event, a past, cannot write itself ... and yet it does. To claim such a writing as autobiographical shows the ways in which the past is always emerging via someone in particular, writing a particular past, and someone else in particular creates pasts from that writing. We know we can never know all the conditions that make a particular past possible. Here the spectral 'I' of autobiography offers what is understood in musical terms as an irresolvable dissonance. A dissonance that resonates.

Autobiographies of events create the possibility of an ethical, embodied relationship with the past, not a final story. It is in displaying the relationship between 'selves', time and writer/ reader that we assemble the possibilities of the past in the present, and make a space where the past is a becoming now. The possibilities of what it will become for you and me can be felt, fought over and even momentarily finalised, but the past itself can never be completed — it is neither a sea of infinite possibility nor a reified opposition to ourselves in the present.

The promise of History was that we would know what happened. But there is no single way of 'doing' history, no single way of knowing history. There are just so many stories. But why do only some stories of the past 'work' now? As a beginning strategy for understanding how the past works we can acknowledge how these different stories are circulated and why some are read as truth and others are not. Their context needs to be made obvious, for only some histories are possible at any one moment. And when we look carefully at the stories from the past, some of which are called 'official history' and some of which are called gossip, we see that all stories are personal, while showing that all writing is personal. We see these stories are finely attuned to their sources, while acknowledging that not all sources are available. And when we write our counter-stories, we need to be connected to the possible, while acknowledging that all that was possible is never imagined.

In writing about 'The Bluff Rock Massacre', I am both writing a cultural history, and attempting a model of what writing a history might look like if it were constantly concerned with how the writer was able to write, and how that writing came into a particular form at a particular time. I want to make those productions obvious within what is written, which necessarily questions the idea that anything as straight-forward as a 'past' history exists. Using a number of techniques, I articulate the ways in which particular 'historical' events come to be lived out in people and places who are simultaneously past and present and re-emerging.

But an important part of creating this historical production is the confrontation with narrative itself. To avoid the threat of 'resolution' that narrative has, I have chosen excess. Narratives of narratives, narratives on narratives and narrator and narrative co-mingling so that there is no single home for the writing self. The book employs official historical records, family histories, tourist leaflets, gossip, field notes and other texts to show the multiple ways in which an event both becomes and exceeds its invention. This sort of narrative disorder also has a childhood echo. An order made of disorder, a cobbled-together inventiveness that works for as long as the job requires it to. Dog kennels out of drums, chook sheds out of old doors and history tied up with string. Those mongrels are more like the model for this piece of writing. It is heterotextual.

Implicitly this book is concerned with the ways in which a non-Aboriginal can write Australian history after the many Aboriginal interventions into hegemonic history and the ongoing reappraisal of 'What happened?' This historical figuring is therefore questioning what it is to write 'white' even as this book emerges as white as ever. And written on the terrain of post-identity politics, this text is both queered and performative. You will see.

I apologise to those particular Aboriginal people who will reread in here some of the horrific detail of the many massacres that occurred around Tenterfield, as well as of the Myall Creek Massacre, and wish they had been warned that the deaths of their relatives appear here. I also apologise to all those descendants of the Kooris killed around Bluff Rock who might see in my writing the all too easy slippage into generalisation and numeration. If it reads like that, I never intended it so.

Some might argue that I should have left well alone. That to leave the knowledge that a massacre occurred is enough. That the proper way of respecting that act is to leave it as a single horror which can never be understood and should not be able to be understood ... and I should be clear that I cannot explain massacre to you. But I can show how the story of one massacre can encompass over 200 years of colonial relations. I can reveal the particular difficulty of seeing massacre as untouchable horror when the perpetrators are white like me. I have an investment in knowing them so that I might know myself. And that, I think, is to thicken the description, not diminish it.

I don't know who first told me but I remember the version very well. It was always said that the Aboriginal people were rounded up like cattle (not sheep) and driven over the edge of Bluff Rock. This was presented as a single hideous incident, unconnected to others — isolated. It was all ours.

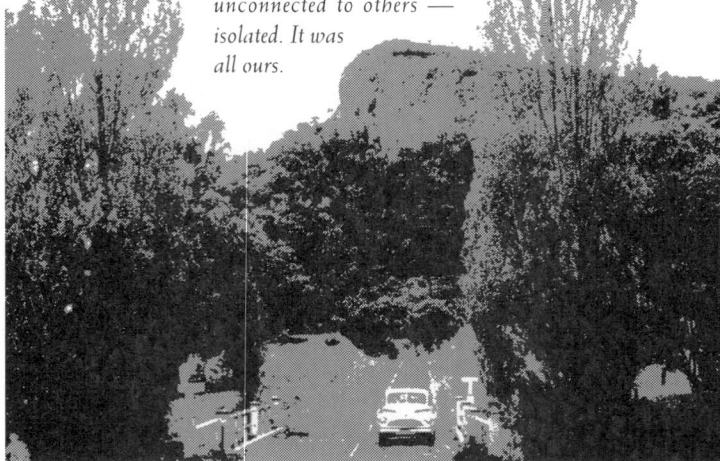

BLUFF ROCK

Bluff Rock sits. Bluff Rock towers. It is the silent main character in this crime cum ghost story – it is always there, it always remains.

There it is before you. It is no shrinking violet, no shy child. It watches and it waits. The scrubby grey of bush around it, and even the bare, plundered hills about it, do not soften its massive, protruding power in this mostly modest, mostly domesticated NSW Northern Tablelands landscape. The eucalypts that try to wash out the bluff's sharp edges fail to diminish its hardness. They scrabble at cracks, they claw within crevices. Their endless task of finding niches, tiny deposits of minerals to nurture their grasping roots and dry seed — that perpetual, Herculean task — here comes to nought. Here there are no horizontals, no soft layers of sandstone, only straight, downward fissures and the simple immensity of granite. It looks the perfect cliff. A cliff that rain and wind and hard New England winters of cracking cold have made inhumanly smooth. Nothing and no one to grip. It is as if over those trees and scrub a giant hand has forced a massive sheet of metal, cutting through each tiny root, each small plant, to leave this unhealable thing.

When there is a rent in the landscape and when that rent doesn't seem to breathe or move, and we can look at it for as long as we like — and as we like, some of us, with our particular fears and our particular prejudices — we can exaggerate its stillness and try to stay it with language. We drag out names and stories in an effort to come to terms with its power.

One of the first white men to own the bluff tried an ordinary name, St Swithin's Bluff, for he saw it on St Swithin's Day in the pouring rain. It is said that if it rains on St Swithin's Day, there will be rain for forty days and forty nights. St Swithin himself wanted to be buried where 'the rains of heaven might fall on him and he be trodden under foot by those who entered the church'. This combination of rain and rock and the figure of a man's body open to the elements and the effect of other men, creates a very nuanced image of that first 'owner'.

But the name never took.

It is the simplest naming by no one we know that has stuck. Bluff Rock. A bluff that is a rock. Both these words mean something that rises out of the land, and put together they tell of something more. A message. A strange angel.

'The Bluff Rock Massacre' is a myth, is a fact, is a tourist attraction, is a national metaphor, is a ...? Here is a short history.

In 1842, Edward Irby and his brother Algernon, plus their servants and supplies, were making their way to Deepwater Station in New England, New South Wales, when they passed an 'imposing bluff' which they named St Swithin's Bluff. It became known as Bluff Rock and became part of the land that the Irby brothers later leased and then owned called Bolivia.[1]

In 1844, Edward Irby, his neighbour Thomas Windeyer and Windeyer's two servants, Connor and Weaver, chased and then lost and then came upon, more by chance than by skill, a group of Aboriginal people, probably members of the Bundjalung or Ngarabul peoples. The Aboriginals had heard Irby's group coming, and sought safety beneath the very rocks Irby and Windeyer found themselves upon. Hearing movement, Irby and Windeyer lay over the rocks and began firing into the trapped group below, knowing that their fire would bring up Connor and Weaver, who joined the slaughter.[2]

In 1925, Thomas Keating, former manager of Bolivia, wrote a letter in response to a query by JF Thomas, who was writing a local history of Tenterfield; in the letter Keating wrote about 'The Bluff Rock Massacre', telling of the armed pursuit of a group of Aboriginal people by Irby and all available station hands. Killing some Aboriginal people near a creek, he wrote, they then chased the remaining members of the group up the back of Bluff Rock and threw them off the top.[3]

During the early 1940s, Norman Crawford, the Honorary Secretary of the Tenterfield Historical Society, tape-recorded stories from Tenterfield citizens and asked many of them about the massacre as a part of those interviews.[4]

And sometime in the 1970s, a local historian put together the pieces of historical evidence of Irby and Keating and produced a tourist leaflet about the massacre.[5] The part of that tourist leaflet text that concerns the massacre is now inscribed on the plaque at the Bluff Rock viewing area, which was unveiled in 2001. This event was seen as 'an act of reconciliation, and a recognition of history'.[6]

But this is not 'just' a local history. Each time a different version of 'The Bluff Rock Massacre' appears, each time it is learnt and known in a different way, an attempt is made to map that moment. Why do we believe this history or that? Who do we become when we know such things? This intense local history lets us touch and feel the shifts in how the past is told.

Radically different ideas about the past and its uses meet in 'The Bluff Rock Massacre'. First, it lets us confront our desire for a certain past made up of certain facts. It is presumed that we need that certainty to 'move on', to make certain we are not what we were before. Yet when we confront instead the babble of the past (all these stories), we might experience an overwhelming loss of place as our own narratives wash away in waves of possibility while we remain in place.

The art of the past is to remember that it is always told in the present. We are not what we were, and we cannot predict what we will become. As new ways of being open to us, so new ways of knowing become available, and these possibilities happen to us here and now, in this small country town in this wary, inexplicable nation. We can become open to what the past might do to us and how we know the past. Once we never thought to think of 'Australian History', as once we could not imagine the 'other side of the frontier', but now we might wonder more intricately and intimately about our own backyards, and our own selves becoming historicised in very personal, always placed ways.

The benefit of being exposed to this thinking in the context of a small town story is that we get to see how important very local stories are for teaching us things that might otherwise be decontextualised into something like official 'Australian History'.

On greyness and granite

Bluff Rock is grey. There are not many rocks that are truly grey. Many may be grey with fallen dust or clearly striped with deposits that have set, but Bluff Rock is all over grey. It is the true grey of a pointillist granite: an illusion, made up of dots of other colours layered over one another — in this case rosy felspar specks, black mica chips and opaque quartz that you would never call white. Up close it is speckled.

Grey is a colour between black and white and has no definite hue. This means that it is not a distinct part of the colour spectrum; it has no saturation and is achromatic. The bluff is the colour of ash.

When the world's people are divided into colours, there are black, white, browns and yellows, but never greys. The only 'Grey' political group is 'Greypower' — a lobby group of people united by their age.

But in photography one uses a mid-grey card as the technical exemplar of white skin. If you are doing portraiture and want the skin tones clear and bright, you first take a light reading of the person, then of the mid-grey card, and then you adjust the aperture according to both readings. This will give you fine white responses, but brown or black subjects with no detailed lines or shadings. The mid-grey card insists on the non-white subject's lack of light. When photography becomes regulated around whiteness via grey, as in the case of British War Office guidelines on how to photograph troops, for example, black faces become nothing but 'eyeballs and teeth'.

'Between black and white' has all the uncomfortable resonance of other points of mediation within a powerful dichotomy. Grey sexuality might be bisexuality — sometimes called 'batting for both teams', as only someone who doesn't know the rules might do; it is an implied treachery.

And yet it is grey that refuses hues. Technically, there are no shades to grey. It disallows any multiple colourings, any fluid identities. Grey cannot be placed as more black or more white. It can't siphon off the privileges of the white and then swim in the authenticity of the black. Grey is grey.

But this refusal of hue is constantly contested. As if to punish its craven neutrality, we employ grey to describe the realms of confusion and disarray. These are 'grey areas'. And those who stand behind and pull strings through another, who don't dare to or can't manipulate from the front — they are *éminences grises*. And the grey market isn't quite illegal; it isn't black, it is merely unofficial. All these 'markets' are of course covered in green.

So we have unfinished business when I call Bluff Rock grey. It is the most constant of colours, and yet it reminds us that it is something that cannot be resolved, that it also stands in a field of confusion.

GRANITE

Bluff Rock is made of granite. Granite is 'a granular igneous rock composed chiefly of felspar (orthoclase) and quartz, usually with one or more other minerals. It is much used for building, and for monuments.'[7] Its second meaning is great hardness or firmness, yet its name comes from *grano*, meaning grain. Its origins are as contested as those of 'The Bluff Rock Massacre':

> With multifactorial generative processes involving different source rocks and operating in different global tectonic settings, and where there are multifarious interconnections, these can rarely be

precisely defined, so that any genetic categorisation must be regarded as a philosophical abstraction; some would say impeding more than advancing understanding.[8]

Granite can be rough or smooth. If it is weathered by water and smooth-ish rundowns form, you can slide down these on a wheat bag, whooshing as you go. But you can climb up the unweathered side and your sandshoes will grip the friction-rich surfaces like sticky sand, tiny motes ingratiating themselves into the rubber treads.

In a government publication on *Building and Ornamental Stones* from 1915, I find the only reference to Tenterfield granite. On page 46 it says:

TENTERFIELD N.S.W. A beautiful porphyritic stone and unlike any recorded granite. The large flesh coloured felspar crystals scattered throughout a grey coloured ground produce a very pleasing effect, and give the stone a most attractive appearance. It is a splendid combination, so to speak, of red and grey granite, and has great commercial possibilities.[9]

The front page of this book has a drawing of two Aboriginal men and their bark shelter, and the words underneath say: 'We replace the Bark Gunya with Stone and Marble Cities.' The infinite possibilities of granite.

You forget that you loved granite. Our creek ran around and through granite and then out into basalt holes where the real swimming happened. But it was over the granite that the little waterfalls ran, and on its curvy surfaces that picnics were held; Lovers' Nook, we called it. Willows dangled into the water and the rocks made perfect islands and imaginary worlds. At my tenth birthday party, we all-girl group took off our clothes and skinny-dipped in the pool below the waterfall. My next eldest sister (by three years) and her friend left on their underpants and trainer bras, as their status dictated. But for the rest of us, what a stew of screams and cries and splashy laughter all rolling over us. But then what an exodus and mad meléeing when one girl found a leech on her thigh and then someone saw my father riding around the sheep on the ridge. Should we dive and risk leeches or dress like mad? I was overcome by terrible guilt. These rocks, this water, was now the site, I thought, of having to say I was sorry for something. It took me a long time to realise that my parents found it funny. Only I thought of possible immorality.

The grains that make up the granite have been brought together through the heat and pressure of the Earth's crust. They were molten magma that cooled, and millions of years later it shows us its tiny cells of existence as flakes and chips — and sometimes beads — of quartz, felspar and mica.

Granite is used in building. But not as some pliable brick. It is carved into slabs and put upon walls and floors in grand hotels and business palaces. In the home it is unforgiving as a benchtop, where the most softly dropped glass shatters on impact.

Now it has also been proposed as a container for nuclear waste. Its impenetrability to water, resistance to erosion and great structural strength are seen as very promising for the isolation of highly radioactive wastes. 'Radioactive wastes placed deep in these rocks are very unlikely to be disturbed by climatic or geological events or by accidental or intentional human intrusion.'[10] Granite is impervious.

And it is used for monuments. A final blanket of granite is placed over graves. Headstones are carved from it and walls of memories are written on it. It lasts. Even unplaned and uncarved granite seems to attract inscriptions. Where there are tors next to roads they are always written on. Most proffer a granular slate in the shape of an elephant's backside. So it's 'Thunderbolts Rock' written over with 'Chris' and a small 'bong on'. Another has had its slate silvered over to emphasise the 'Hi Honey I love you'. And on the other side, away from the sight of cars, right across the elephant's crack, is written 'The Perfect Crime'.

IT HAPPENED
ALONG THE HIGHWAY

Placing the massacre

Bluff Rock stands over the New England Highway ten kilometres south of the town of Tenterfield in the New England region in northern New South Wales. At least that is how I can locate it for you on a road map. Closer to Glen Innes, you might be told it is on the Tenterfield Road; at Tenterfield, it is on the Glen Innes Road; from properties in the east it is in the Bluff Country; and from the west it's up from Pye's Creek. Its situation is dependent upon the position of the speaker and whether they are a local of a particular sort or a passer-by who links the bluff exclusively to the experience of travel along the New England Highway. The bluff is part of the beauty of the place. This part of New England is famous for its European autumn colours, and the way those colours are thrown into light by the tors and bluffs of granite and the grey–green gums smothering the back hills.

There is a tourist leaflet about this bluff.

VISITOR INFORMATION
BLUFF ROCK

Location and History

BLUFF ROCK is situated 10km south of Tenterfield on the New England Highway. It was Edward Irby and his brother Leonard who passed the huge granite rock while moving to Deepwater Station from Tenterfield Station in 1842. They named the outcrop St Swithins Bluff as they passed it on St Swithins Day.

THE MASSACRE The truth of that day remains clouded by many conflicting versions. One time Overseer at Bolivia Station, Thomas Keating, in describing the massacre as it had been told to him by an old man at Bolivia, told of Aboriginal attacks on shepherds and sheep. Keating outlined how men on Bolivia Station were mustered and armed, then set out on the track of Aborigines to Pyes Creek on the western boundary of the property. According to Keating's story the Aboriginals were then attacked at Pyes Creek and they fled across country to Bluff Rock, where they were thrown from the top, killing most and injuring many. None of that tribe, which survived, were ever seen on Bolivia Station again.

Commissioner MacDonald reported that in October 1844 Aborigines on the Irby Station at Bolivia had killed a shepherd, but no retaliatory action was mentioned in the despatch. However, Edward Irby himself, when writing of the incident, describes how Aborigines had killed one of his shepherds, Robinson, and how four men had set out to find the culprits. In these few simple words he described in his journal the terrible deeds of that day:

"The blacks saw us coming and hid themselves among the rocks. One, in his haste, dropped poor Robinson's coat so we knew we were onto the right tribe. If they had taken to their heels they might have got away, instead of doing so, they got their fighting men to attack us. So we punished them severely and proved our superiority to them."

The truth will be forever in the bosom of one of the most impressive landmarks along the New England Highway.

Today there is no evidence of the massacre of nearly 150 years ago, but the majestic beauty of this huge granite rock remains steadfast in its geological characteristics. Bluff Rock and the surrounding area consists of granite rock which cooled from molten magma under the earth's surface about 225 million years ago. Subsequent uplift and erosion have exposed them to the earth's surface. According to geological theory, Bluff Rock stands above the surrounding area because it has been more resistant to erosion, probably due to having fewer cracks along which water can penetrate and accelerate the erosion process. Large crystals of pink feldspar, dark mica and quartz give the rock its speckled appearance.

Researched, written & printed by Tenterfield Visitor's Association, Rouse Street, Tenterfield NSW.

This is the Bluff Rock story that most people know. This is the story that gets set down as truth because it is repeated the most and is formally passed on to strangers and tourists. The leaflet is more like a 'fact sheet'.

Two sentences: 'The truth of that day remains clouded by many conflicting versions' *and* 'The truth will be forever in the bosom of one of the most impressive landmarks along the New England Highway.' These sentences offer two poles to move between: the truth of multiple truths and the truth of knowing that no human will ever know the truth. The information seeker, the tourist, the local and some hybrid of these — the reader — must travel between these possibilities to map the tourist 'sense' of the massacre. Meaghan Morris, cultural theorist cum global worker cum local turned tourist, suggests that, 'A more sophisticated tourist operation would obliterate that [leaflet] immediately.'[11] I know what she means. The message hasn't been massaged. The spin hasn't been spun — the story of a massacre of Aboriginal people quoting the seemingly psychotic 'pioneer' who is well satisfied with his 'superior' slaughter does not have any of the easy pleasures tourists are familiar with (and perhaps require). The story operates too clearly as 'real'. So let's look at what these 'simple' words do. Do they create a new kind of tourist? Tourists who are both initiated into and unavoidably implicated in a past they have not seen before?

A visitor's information

'The truth of that day remains clouded by many conflicting versions.' Here there is a possibility for the tourist to discover the unclouded 'truth'. While history, that unreliable plethora of conflicting stories, has failed to arrive at a single truth, the invited viewers of the bluff can create for themselves their own truths. Their own action in visiting and in viewing, their particular and 'authentic' experience of the bluff as a sight to see, partially resolves the conflicting stories. But something remains. The bluff, brought to life by the leaflet's stories, continues, in its muteness, to be the site of other known but uncirculated counter-histories. It marks the silences of other histories. It resonates the past.

But is this enough? Does the silent bluff rightly mark the inability of historical understandings of massacre to show everything, to know everything? And is its silent looking an adequate response to the many, many acts of horrific colonial violence against Aboriginal people? Or does this silence simply produce the viewer as one more voyeur, one more person who is excused from attempting to engage with the ways in which such a violent history came to be? By becoming attached to a pre-existing series of sights, determined by other Visitor Information sheets, do we ignore the need to know these histories directly? We don't have to know, we are *just* tourists. There are always other things to see, other places to go.

But 'The truth will be forever in the bosom of one of the most impressive landmarks along the New England Highway.' So the bluff itself becomes both site and sight of possibility. The 'bosom' prevents our knowing. Nature's seeming silence won't let us know what happened. Far from being unreadable or hostile, the Australian landscape spreads itself around us as a sheltering blanket of quiet, keeping history well away from us.

The Keating version

The account from the tourist leaflet is taken from a letter Thomas Keating wrote in 1925 to JF Thomas, who was seeking information about Bolivia Station and the massacre for his own records of the history of Tenterfield. Keating's original letter is difficult to read. There are few full stops or capital letters, the handwriting is spindly and sometimes faint, and the spelling and style are difficult to penetrate at times. At crucial moments in the narrative the words are unfathomable. For example, after detailing the pursuit of the Aboriginal people across and up the back of Bluff Rock, he writes without full stops:

> The men got up to the top of the rock and threw the blacks off the rock onto the ground at the bottom the front part of the rocks was a great hite from the ground below a lot of the blacks guh (?) goh and a lot more crippled none of that tribe was ever seen on the station after after that drive but there were a part fixed tribe on the station.[12]

The perception that Keating's memory of another old man's story some eighty years after the event is accurate relies on Keating's localness. It is his being-there-ness, his location, his position as 'one time overseer' that inspired Thomas to write to him, and upon which rests the narrative force of his story in the tourist tale.

Tourism demands that its sites be simultaneously open and closed. Open enough to arouse the curiosity to see for oneself, open enough to insist on a visit, to go there, and yet closed enough that the site doesn't fall into a sea of infinite possibilities where the point of going is lost. Tourism is about managing meaning. It needs to suggest a series of engagements (walking, looking, doing) that can reshape and redeploy themselves around crossecting (crossing and connecting) ideas such as history, identity and place. The guides to these engagements are the written texts — tourist leaflets and advertising material — which help shape these encounters into the pleasures of stopping, viewing and learning.

Of course it is never clear what should be called tourism and what should be called history. But for the moment I am insisting on an artificial separateness which designates tourism as the circulation of particular information leaflets and the active effort to stop and start travellers within tourist spaces, and history as being one part of the possibly shared cultural capital through and around which the tourist will experience the tourist site. Keating's extract intends to motivate the tourist — and possibly the local, now and then — to pause at the Bluff Viewing Area (which has barbecues, toilets and picnic shelters) and look at the rock, but it also serves a number of other functions.

Keating's story as recounted in the tourist leaflet depicts an extermination that is viciously complete. Aboriginal presence is responded to with a colonial power so overwhelming that resistance is impossible. The bonded labour and squatters are made so powerful that they can literally throw the Aboriginal people from their land — 'killing most and injuring many', and none of the survivors was ever seen on Bolivia Station again. This then was conquest, *terra nullius* made manifest. This version of the massacre does not engage with the possibility of Aboriginal resistance, except in terms of generalised attacks on shepherds and sheep which were quickly responded to by this overwhelming white force. Neither does it explore the recorded differences between Aboriginal groups — all have become one. The fearfulness of the attacking whites is never alluded to and the fiction of the disappeared Aboriginal people — so useful to non-Aboriginal land 'owners' — is perpetuated. Is the reader/viewer to be comforted by this? Does it presume a tourist who identifies with the 'settler'? Much more obviously, it presumes a fossilised past, a past that cannot change, a past that we cannot change.

The past is not allowed to creep into the present. You can prove the impenetrability of the colonial past by looking at the silent bluff. Perhaps Keating's story also disavows the authenticity of continuing Aboriginal existence around this land, since the 'real' Aboriginal people who 'really' belonged to this area were all overcome, killed or frightened away. Aboriginal people are granted a place, are named on the tourist leaflet as being there, but then they become part of the all-too-familiar history of vanquished peoples. The leaflet places the tourist in a modern present that is radically distinct from the simple awfulness of the past. As tourists, we cannot be directly connected to those who carried out such acts — we are just driving through. Both the persuasiveness of the idea of 'progress' and the pleasures of 'passing through' become retold and continuously re-enacted within these narratives, and by the act of gazing at the bluff. The divided highway, splitting travellers into directional flows, becomes a fast-flowing band of modernity shouldered by 'history'. Is this transient space a small but perfectly formed representation of Australia's colonial past? Modern Australia as a rivulet of speed surrounded by a timeless landscape that is invoked as enduringly silent?

Keating's version of the massacre, in its simple narrative of horror, hides the stories of both the successful efforts of Aboriginal people to prevent 'settlement' and the increasingly systematised work of 'settlers' and governments to remove Aboriginal people through the use of poison, police and bureaucracy. There is also nothing there of the compromises and sometimes successful agreements (dependent upon exchanges of labour and land) which, while agreed to then, fail to be granted any legal meaning now. These are not links that work within a desire by tourism promoters to have travellers consume the sight — but in a contained, sporadic and isolated fashion. This is a 'history' moment set amongst a range of other tourist moments.

But let us turn back to Keating's letter and what had to be transformed in his original text to make the information leaflet, the tourist map, work. First of all, Keating's 'a lot of the blacks goh and a lot more crippled' as a result of throwing the 'blacks onto the ground' has been translated to a single image of many Aboriginal people being killed by being 'thrown' off. This seems an incredible act for men whom he says were given arms and ammunition and had already shot some Aboriginal people where they were first discovered, at Pye's Creek. Does he mean they were first shot and then thrown? But then what of the 'crippling'? Had ammunition run out? Why thrown at all? Thrown would seem to indicate a superhuman effort of lifting and tossing, except if they were the bodies of children. But perhaps he was meaning 'throw' in a more general sense — perhaps the bodies were rolled off the top. Why not pushed? Is it simply the embroidery to make a 'better' tale? To make incomprehensible monsters of the colonists? To hint at a certain heroism? 'Throw' can be easily mapped onto the bluff if one looks at it from the viewing site. Bluff Rock seems to have a clear and distinct edge from which people could easily have been thrown or pushed. But when one climbs to the top, courtesy of the local farmer, undercliffs break the 'clear' edge, and the spots from which a party might gather to do this are small indeed. The scrub is thick and the ground very rough and rocky. But perhaps this throwing and crippling, with its partiality and incompleteness, points towards the lack of success; why isn't everyone 'simply' killed? The ambiguity in the original needs to be edited for the tourist version to enable a fascination which will stop but not implicate the passing trade.

It is the final section of Keating's original letter that has to be expunged — 'but there was a part fixed tribe at the station'. This means that some Aboriginal people continued to live there; it means that the Aboriginal people of 1844 were not a homogenous entity and it means the massacre was one small part of a complicated colonial system. It suggests a relationship — even continuity — with the massacre that is unable to be assimilated into the design of this tourist moment.

The truth of that day remains clouded by many conflicting versions.

The truth will be forever in the bosom of one of the most impressive landmarks along the New England Highway.

Irby's account

The tourist leaflet then turns, after some introductory scene setting, to an extract from Irby's 'Memoirs':

> Commissioner MacDonald reported that in October 1844 a shepherd had been killed by Aborigines on the Irby Station at Bolivia, but no retaliatory action was mentioned in the despatch. However, Edward Irby himself, when writing of the incident, describes how one of his shepherds, Robinson, had been killed by Aborigines and how four men had set out to find the culprits. In these few simple words he described in his journal the terrible deeds of that day:
>
> "The blacks saw us coming and hid themselves among the rocks. One, in his haste, dropped poor Robinson's coat so we knew we were onto the right tribe. If they had taken to their heels they might have got away, instead of doing so, they got their fighting men to attack us. So we punished them severely and proved our superiority to them."

The description of Irby's account carefully exposes the hypocrisy of the colonial government. The Crown Land

Commissioner (responsible at this time for the welfare of Aboriginal people) only reports that a shepherd had been killed — he says nothing about the retaliation. This suggests several things. First, the leaflet is presenting the idea that there was systemic racism underpinning this one-eyed reporting; second, it assumes that Irby reported the whole incident to MacDonald but MacDonald failed to report the whole thing to Governor Gipps. Either the higher bureaucratic order (MacDonald) suppressed the retaliation in sympathy with Irby's action, or the suppression resulted from his own value system, which saw 'retaliation' as 'not counting'. Another possibility is that Irby never actually reported his actions.

'In these few simple words he described in his journal the terrible deeds of that day.' Here the leaflet is stepping into a surreal Conradian darkness. It having already been established via Keating's account that the Aboriginal people were thrown from the bluff, Irby's words ('punishment') and his boast ('proving superiority') are an impossible fit — they are indeed 'simple' words battling 'terrible' deeds. Since Keating's account leaks into Irby's, it is difficult to read Irby's story of punishing fighting men and proving superiority as anything but horror. How could anyone account for *throwing* people via a need to 'prove superiority'? It is precisely the *writing* and the placement of this account that makes it so effective. If the narrative had been one of a slow descent to savagery, a descent into an other world, the act might be read as some final, dreadful climax, but no, Irby's narrative is rational, making matter of fact and sensible his horrible actions. In a place where 'sense' invented people who didn't count, who could be punished by any means, to whom no rules except the purpose of 'proving our superiority' existed. In these acts we have the invention of a particularly Australian 'other'. This 'other' is an impenetrable nightmare hanging always in the corner, never available to re-readings. Irby is the atavistic threat breathing over non-Aboriginal possibility ... always there, waiting to be us/ waiting for us to be him. The invented chasm between now and then, between the tourist and Irby, is both sustained and gently questioned by this leaflet. What can and can't be said in 'tourist space'?

Yes, 'a more sophisticated tourist operation would obliterate that [leaflet] immediately', but perhaps it is also as Visitor Information that some encounter with this 'other' can be attempted. The leaflet is, after all, marginal and transient, a place where Irby's response will arouse a piquant horror, a nod of knowingness, sharp pain or some other possibility ... then the visitor will move quietly on. It is another 'ordinary' tourist story, like the bushranger and the goldrush. It is a part of the rescued possibilities from the past that might work to stop the passing cars. And true or not, able to be known or not, is it better than nothing being said at all? Is 'bad' history good tourism? Is 'bad' tourism good history?

But where exactly was Irby when he was instigating these acts? How does he fit geographically with Keating's account? Irby writes earlier in his journal:

> We ascended the range near Sugarloaf, crossed Collin's Creek, mounted the range on the other side and saw smoke rising about eight miles away in a north easterly direction ... We made straight for the hill from which we saw the smoke.[13]

Keating, you will remember, suggested that the Aboriginal group was found near Pye's Creek and was chased across to the west. Irby too uses the bluff as a constant marker of his position but fails to do so here, even if we can re-read river to be mountain and bluff to be some rocks. We are clearly in two very different locations. There appears to be no connection between Keating's and Irby's accounts of Aboriginal massacres. They are two separate sets of death and cannot refer to the same one. So what we have is a complicated, hybrid event — 'The Bluff Rock Massacre' generated from at least two violent colonial encounters and a distinctive granite bluff.

What does the Visitor Information pamphlet produce? What do we produce as we read it? What relationship is there between this leaflet and the words of one of the Aboriginal Land Council workers: 'You just have to go up there; the spirits are there. It's a bad place.' And the words of the local farmer who owns the land the bluff is on — 'It's rough country.'

The truth of that day remains clouded by many conflicting versions.

The truth will be forever in the bosom of one of the most impressive landmarks along the New England Highway.

It's rough country.

It's a bad place.

WRITING (AND READING) THE LOCAL

But what if you are not 'just' a tourist? What if the intricately spun webs of family histories also put you there? Because you've always been there? The task of family history seems very different from that of the tourist leaflet. Family histories create simple lines of descent that insist upon our association with a particular past because of the (assumed) fact of our recorded birth. Tourism, however, is different. One travels to and through tourism, but one always travels with a family history. While the tourist site invites spectatorship and temporary association, the family history asks for permanent presence.

Family histories invent a particularly located person who becomes the 'local', who, in turn, intimately brings to life the immediate location. While 'local' is a term that can carry the simple sense of being familiar with a place — 'knowing' a place enough to direct a visitor, for example — it is also a term that denotes a living relationship with that place. A *real* 'local' must be 'born and bred', and more tellingly, must have connections back into the colonial history of the location. These colonial proofs exclude Aboriginal people of the area who, in a bizarre, carnivalesque manoeuvre, are too local to be 'local'. The 'local' is stitched to the place via a series of family movements that work within the framework of a progressive, modernist version of history — the version that tells us we are always moving on even if we remain in the same location.

Locals can be both sorry for those from beyond who haven't known some of their pleasures, and simultaneously long for them. This suggests not the ideas of outside and inside, but of someone who has an unrequited relationship with history and place. 'Local', family histories, particularly those of rural Australia, rarely have a simple connection to the history that says we are always moving forward to something better. Looking to the past normally involves looking back towards seemingly greater prosperity and larger land holdings — after the initial travails of actually 'pioneering' and 'settling' the land. These tales also exclude Aboriginal people, whose land tenure becomes an unmeasurable imagining that bobs uneasily around the edges of all these claims to 'localness'. Their presence must be remarked upon, since this is one more proof of the length of time that a family has been in the area. But the stories are usually tales of loyal workers, 'humorous' anecdotes at the expense of some imagined Aboriginal proclivity, or serious comment on the effects of white ways on 'true' Aboriginals. All of these show some sort of engagement with the range of racist ways of knowing and naming Aboriginal peoples. There are of course many other exclusions, including any real effort to position the 'family' in any broader context. What prejudices did they embrace or eschew? What exactly was their status? How were *they* understood by others?

These intimate histories somehow take you aside, very personally, and include you and initiate you, again very personally, into your family, your place. Is there something vaguely sinister about it? A kind of inappropriate intimacy? Some writers will write their families as something that can stand in for Australian History, but these are not local stories. Local family histories do not place people in something as large

as 'History' or even 'Australian History', because it is understood — without ever being said — that individual 'families',
while producing the occasional public figure, remain unim-
portant in any larger schema. These histories are not truth.
However, they do invent for the present-day family members a
historicised place and person: I become that history because I
am from that history. My links have been carefully traced from
that time onwards; I 'know' who I am. A local family history
privatises history into incomprehensibleness to all but the
'inside' reader. Meaning circulates around a small geographical
area and among a small selection of families. Names of
properties? Ah, that is where grandmother played tennis.
Machinery? Grandpa had the first Ford truck in town. And on
it goes. And so other histories become overshadowed and
sometimes erased by this 'real' authoritative minutiae.

I am interested in the way local family histories in general,
and mine in particular, can be read as parallel narratives to the
one in the Bluff Rock tourist leaflet. But I am also interested in
what happens when this invented person — 'the local' —
comes to read a tourist leaflet.

A pioneering family

'A Pioneering Family' is a small section of a book entitled *Mother
of Ducks*. As the author (who was my mother's cousin) says in
the Author's Note, '*Mother of Ducks* is about people, many of
whom, I knew and loved ...'[14] The book is 'Wholly Set up and
Printed by McMahon Graphics, Glen Innes, 1986'. The local
credentials of this book are therefore impeccable. Like the
tourist leaflet, its purpose is to tell the local, and in so doing
invent the local. Which non-Aboriginal families came *here* first,
how does *here* come to mean historical right, *real* title to place?

The small section on John Eckersley Newbury, my grandfather's grandfather (I am not certain if that is right, I always get these things mixed up) begins with the wonderful lines: 'This is a story of a *family* (my emphasis) who were never to gain distinction in any grand manner, unless it is that they have the distinction of being the first pioneers in that particular corner of New England, their children, the first (sic) to trample the grass in the area.'[15] 'Family', unlike the 'truth' of massacre, is a traceable certainty. Birth and death certificates — the state's and then the individual's means of tracing and retracing legitimacy — carry enough of the idea of scientific 'fact' for this to be understood as a truth, albeit a limited one.

White individuals of the 1850s had European names and existed within a colonising framework capable of turning people into historical figures. Unlike the nameless murdered Aboriginal people and the power employed by Irby (or MacDonald) *not* to report their deaths and so let them enter official history, this family, 'my' family, had every reason to record children, marriages and deaths, as these were explicitly linked to the legal practices of taking land. Children, seemingly of any age, could be registered as owning particular selections, and in this way the legal size of any piece of land could be extended with every birth. The wife, though unable to name land as hers until 1861, could provide the legitimate womb of future expansion. The family therefore does represent a limited truth of colonial expansion. However, to propose that births are an accurate or 'truthful' account of all sexual liaisons is a ridiculous idea. But perhaps this replacement of the usual family tensions and divisions with government records becomes an odd source of reassurance? Genealogical 'histories' are a hopeless starting ground for lesbian, gay and Aboriginal histories, full as the records are of 'unmarrieds' and utter silences.

Knowing that local family history depends upon those silences for its claims to unchallenged truth (and even common sense) can cause us to think again about what a 'family' history does. The very intimacy of its inclusion makes more devastating its exclusions. Those names that never appear in family histories have had their most personal lives disconnected from their emotional and intimate networks and yet the relentless, seamless genealogy still looks complete. Or does it? Does 'spinster' now attract a new resonance? Does 'bachelor' look as if something more needs to be said? If a local family history has been honed down to a skeleton of official records, doesn't it now beg for emotional flesh? For stories that might connect with who and what we are now? Is every skeleton in every family closet another Bluff Rock?

The final paragraphs of the 'A Pioneering Family' story are a record of the lands then owned by some of the fifteen children John and Bridget Newbury raised. These properties included: Green Glades, Paddy's Land, Red Braes, Aboomla, Snow Flake, Mt Mitchell Station, Glen Brook, Wattle Grove, Kookabrookra, Glen Rock, Yuthneath, The Flags, Ryanna, Belfield, Woodland, Bill Meehan's, Braleigh, Fernmount and Ward's Mistake. Paul Carter, Australian cultural (or theoretical?) troubadour and critic, has taught us to look carefully at the way places are simultaneously named and brought into an imagined space — of the picturesque, of domesticity, of nation building, for example — and these properties are no exception.[16] As befits the generation of selectors (who both created and bought properties), most of these property names have pragmatic and personal names. The pragmatism (and implied optimism) is there in the Fernmounts and Brooks and Woodlands, and the reproduction of white presence is already occurring in Paddy's Land and Bill Meehan's. As for an Aboriginal presence and/or history, only Aboomla and Kookabrookra carry it on.

'Aboomla', apparently meaning 'home of the warriors',[17] is an appropriation that conveys both irony and pathos. However, it is the more general naming of these lands as 'properties' that is most indicative of the state-supported establishment of this land in their 'owner's' eyes. Some anxiousness to make this point might be discerned in the 'Paddy's Land' and 'Ward's Mistake'. The latter of these records Ward pegging out a large bit of land only to be told that it was already selected. 'Paddy's Land', which on first reading appears to mark an Irish presence, was in fact a salute to an Aboriginal guide, called (by whom?) 'Paddy'. In very specific namings the particular acts of non-Aboriginal people are given presence and space, while Aboriginal efforts remain generalised (place of undifferentiated warriors) in a translation of a language that does not widely enter the settler population. The meaning of 'Aboomla' is therefore only sporadically understood even as it enters the everyday usage of these 'settlers'.

This same sort of naming is equally visible in the tourist leaflet's account of the massacre. The leaflet refers to 'the Aborigines', but uses an early diary that mentions the name of the individual white shepherd, Robinson, in contrast to the generic 'blacks'. So while the naming of the massacre adds one of the possible acts that are missing from the enormous 'success' of the Newbury children in acquiring land, the leaflet maintains the style of familiar expressions and namings that insist on the shared totality of white experience. The organisation of the Visitor Information leaflet positions the massacre as an act of a squatter, symbolically distanced from the 'families' of the selectors: they came later, after the land was broken up into smaller areas, and were generally poorer — and so, it is presumed, worked harder.

Genevieve Newbury refers to 'The Bluff Rock Massacre' as 'nothing short of barbaric', and writes of other incidents where the viciousness of the ex-convict troopers is displayed.[18] This draws the more familiar line between convicts and all others —

in this kind of history, the convicts are the real root of any cruelties to Aboriginal people. Never the hardworking family.

I remember that my mother told me nothing about Aboriginal people. She told me a bit of family history (her side), took me with 'Aunty' Genevieve to graveyards, houses and ghost villages in the dry backblocks. On this dust our importance was supposedly written. I loved it. Once I remember being put in the far back of our station wagon so that an Aboriginal woman, Mrs Cutmore (who I now know was one part of an important Moree family), could put all her family into the car to be taken to our little church to be baptised. I hope this was Mrs Cutmore's idea. I remember my mother's cooking, the smells of cake, the smells of dinner, but I can't really remember my mother's smell, although I remember being hugged and held in her arms. Family history was a light matter, like my mother's light curiosity. She wanted to hear people's stories; she had no answers; she taught us to be good. Everyone knew her — the ripples of family and association spread all around us. But people must like you: don't go too deep; don't claim truth. It was much more important to be liked than to be clever. This is what family love can do.

A 'family' reconstitutes an extraordinarily uncritical history. Not only can we not judge history since it happened 'back then', but it was also 'we' who did it. This produces in turn the idea that anything that happened in the area is somehow knowable and explainable, and the idea that nothing is ever quite extraordinary enough to become the truth, that is, 'official' history. Local history is 'gossip'. And I use the word 'gossip' not in a derisive way but in acknowledgment of its intimate and productive qualities. It produces local history via the idea of knowing the 'real', much more down-to-earth story, where great imaginings turn into practicalities and local personalities. An example from Tenterfield is Meaghan Morris's account of a local who would 'swear' that Henry Parkes had never given the Federation oration there but simply ridden through the town, relieved himself and gone on his way.[19] These sorts of histories, when they are able to break out of their locality and circulate in a larger system, do challenge, undermine or at least multiply the versions of history available, and no doubt do have the power to be both subversive and playful.

While the family history is able to transform anecdote into truth for its intimate audience, the tourist leaflet acknowledges that real 'truth' will never be known. Both, however, are organised about an idea of journey. To become a 'visitor' and so pick up the Visitor Information leaflet requires some sort of travelling away from home to somewhere else, somewhere where you are not 'local'. The pioneering family, on the other hand, is required to journey towards a home, inventing the 'local' as they arrive. So while both local and tourist travel, it is in opposite directions — or within opposite projects of becoming.

The journeying to New England is written in my family history as a series of anecdotes: 'Also seen were huge mobs of kangaroos which showed no fear of humans' and 'She [Bridget, my great-great-grandmother?] never had any fear of the natives who were often to appear around the early holding at Cooks Creek' and 'On the journey to New England, Bridget cooked in her camp oven and was forced to feed her baby on mare's milk as none other was available.'

A whole tourist region is broken up into a set of sights of interest, just as the pioneering family is broken down into accessible anecdotes. In the journey of John and Bridget Newbury, each stop had its own story, much as, on a tourist map, each town has its own story. But the individualising of towns is publicised, is circulated, while the private placements of Bridget's journey stay, to use a sinister expression, 'within the family'.

The pioneers' journey always ends with permanence, with property ownership, while the visitor continues to journey, having only seen, not acquired, the sights/sites.

However, this 'permanence' or 'settlement' of 'the pioneering family' also shifts. Partly this is because its history remains starkly anecdotal and in part unspeakable. It is a fragment of a non-existent whole. The intimacy of the family anecdote creates a particularly placed and embodied experience of history. It is Bridget's personal lack of fear, it is her taking the milk from the mare and giving it to the baby that demands that we feel attached to this event. This attachment arises not through the 'truth' of public history; it comes through these stories.

In family histories 'our' historically owned characters move between place and situation in a tour that gives us access to a slide show of *our* historical identity. The formation of such historical beings through anecdote and occasional formal photograph, letter or diary will and can invent subjects with claims to a real belonging. But theirs are not the only claims. Within such a small territory the competition for the inscribable surface is intense. We may be told that x and y explorer were discovering to the east, but 'we' know Bridget was already feeding her children mare's milk there the year before. Then of course another family member might murmur in the background that they thought John Eckersley Newbury was in fact a convict, not a remittance man, that in 'fact' *their* grandfather was the first one in town with a car ... and on it goes. The intense struggles over surface within families mean that to speak of the past is to run into other families' business. Therefore all claims to the 'local history' are always contested, often actively. Time, and so also history, are no longer a 'locus or container': we *are* time.[20] Whose family memorabilia gets to go in the local museum? Who gets to make 'first settler' claims? Who is indisputably *from* the area?

History thus unfolds in the present, as imagined time and place, rather than being distanced from the present. Family histories, with their doubtful, obvious purpose and transparent claims of bias, are wonderfully available sites for the invention of particular people. The stories of Bluff Rock read more like family histories than anything else. Complex, hybrid silences and intimate voices amid swathes of national chatter.

To read the Visitor Information leaflet on Bluff Rock as a local, invented (in part) by my particular family history, produces a range of responses and excuses. The first is, I wasn't really there. I was halfway to Germany ...

Liminal (becoming and unbecoming) longings

In my own childhood, my distinctly 'foreign' name (Schlunke) was never understood as foreign — because I was *really* a Newbury. My mother, not my father, centred me there. My Schlunkeness, my 'Germanness', was therefore of an eerily pure kind. Possibly only in such locations could 'German' come to simply mean — as it did to us in our childhoods — music and writing. My father, a third-generation Australian and Second World War soldier-settler, was a part of a new wave who assimilated seemingly effortlessly into different parts of the country. His 'Germanness' explained in part his preference for listening to Bach and reading rather than playing sport; and why he rode, according to my mother, 'like a Pommy'. Germany, when understood as Schlunkeness, gave me access to much more exotic myths than Bridget Newbury and her mare — on this 'side' there was persecution, internment, suicide and (I hoped) the possibility of a castle or two. It breathed an exotica not to be found in New England. This feels now like the most extraordinary misreading. It was as if Australianness had made up something called Germany that was only tangentially related to the country itself. There was no tradition, within my father's family at least, of returning to Germany, so there was no updating, no insistence on a particular meaning of Germany. The Red Baron and Bach were contemporaries of mine. No language, no culture, no time. 'Australia' and being Australian, on the other hand, were sites of active invention, in part because I couldn't be anything else.

There were traces of this ghostly ethnicity in the *kuchen* my mother cooked from my Aunt Margherita's recipe, and my father's two German phrases: *Ich Liebe* and *Good Night*, the German of which I have now forgotten. Perhaps my father was sent to the Pacific rather than Europe in the war because of institutional doubts about the security of someone with a name like that ... and then again perhaps not. Possibly three generations of life in Australia was considered safe enough. Perhaps this is what happens to 'ethnic identity' after too many years? The authenticity of it all just runs away. Constant mutation will not be denied.

My father's parents had tried very hard to establish an ongoing Australian/German identity throughout the 1890s and 1900s, and the established German community had the power to do so. My father had endured whole years with just one annual trip home — at Christmas — while attending Concordia College, the Lutheran school in Adelaide. The long-term plan was that he, as the youngest son, would become a Lutheran pastor. But coming to Glen Innes with no Lutheran church for thousands of miles, he localised to Presbyterianism and grazing.

Away from 'home' I was usually understood first as in some way 'German'. I was often asked if I was born there and, given my New England mythology, I used to find that highly insulting. A German student at university pointed out how she would pronounce Schlunke and I embraced its validity. She could have been wrong. Until that moment there had been constant confusion when I said that Slunky should be spelt Schlunke. Everyone in my family pronounced it differently; it was a private, embarrassed joke. We didn't know how to say our own NAME! How German WAS it?[21]

Away from 'home', people would also ask where the name was from and I would say Brandenburg. Since this was often a polite way of asking if I was an immigrant, this created a peculiar relationship with a then divided region that I had never visited. And given that our supposed village of origin was in East Germany, I was now faintly connecting myself to one of the most xenophobic and violent states in Germany. Brandenburg is now famous for its new '35 strong special helicopter-borne mobile police unit to combat racist, un-German, violence'.[22] Left-wing, lesbian and 'foreign', I stood a theoretical chance of being beaten and kicked if I went 'back' to Brandenburg. I felt something of a fake — a Newbury disguised as a Schlunke.

But access to this ghostly Germanness also presented me with fragments for my conditional keeping. In 1990 the film *The Nasty Girl* came out: its portrayal of the slow discovery of the Nazi history of a small town was not forgotten by me. The need to say something, the requirement to witness, is one gift a German name bestows. This again comes back to location.

I have a friend who is the daughter of a survivor of the

Holocaust. Her mother was, in the vernacular of genocide, a 'hidden child'; that is, she survived by being hidden in a forest. As a part of this story my friend visited her mother's village (then part of Poland) and the death camp that had been set up nearby. She has (holiday? tourist? historical?) photographs of the village and camp. One photograph was of the village cinema. A nice deco building. This had been where her mother went to the cinema, but it became the local gaol where Jewish women were put just before being sent to the death camps. She has a photograph of a man on a bike taken at the ruined death camp, green grass and trees making it look like a park with rail track and wire. This man said he had been a boy at the time and had taken vegetables to the guard's kitchen from the village. He said, 'Oh those silly Jewish women who put on their lipstick' as they got off the train. She has a photograph also from the same 'local' death camp of four small children playing with their dolls, playing mothers and fathers under a tree in the ruins of the camp.

She has another photograph from another place: the Holocaust Museum in Jerusalem. It is a photograph of a monument called 'The Valley of the Destroyed Communities'. It is made of big sandstone boulders organised into a labyrinth, and it has the name — in English and Hebrew — of every town in Europe where Jews were killed and communities disappeared. The photograph is of her mother standing next to the name of her town. What would such a maze/map of Australia look like if it included each town where Aboriginal people were killed, each reserve, each death in custody? It could not be the only monument, since sites of Aboriginal victories in the frontier wars would have to be memorialised somewhere, as would the ongoing gathering places as Aboriginal knowledge is continued and rediscovered, but how could this be said?

Superficial monuments

To drive past Bluff Rock is to see nothing but rock. To stop at the viewing place is to acquire a name and some history. To go to the Visitors' Centre and ask for a leaflet is to be given a story of omnipotent white power. This is not enough. The existence of the leaflet is a gesture towards telling a history that continues to be unwritten on the Australian landscape. That is something. But what the leaflet denies is the possibility of placing yourself in this landscape. Dependent on the silences of the countryside, and as a prophylactic against history, the leaflet denies our continuity with that past: we tourists cannot create our own place within and in response to this country's history and landscape. If the past is a 'fiction' of the present, it nevertheless still requires that those stories emerge from within particular places at particular times. People and their stories need a cultural context. But the leaflet intentionally renders the bluff landscape (almost) sterile — devoid of the possibility of generating people who 'know' the bluff. But remember that '(almost)', because even the most restrictive reading of the bluff, set amidst the speeding highway attractions and trying to catch the passing surfaces of attentions, viewings and transacted cash, cannot foresee how it might be understood. That final lack of control in how this tourist tale might be read, *that* is a superficial monument — indeterminate, contingent, discontinuous and properly dangerous.

WHAT
KEATING HEARD

The letter

West Avenue
Glen Innes
30th March 1925

Dear Mr Thomas,

I have your letter of the 25th of March 1925 asking me
let you have any particulars I know about Bolivia. I will
now send you what I heard about the station before I
took charge & what took place after I took the management of the station over Mr Irby and his brother
bought the station off a man of the name you metion
in your letter, he & his brother Algernon was dead
some time before I went to Bolivia, The black was very
wild and wickat the time Mr Irby took the station over
big mobs of them. They killed two men on the station,
the last man they killed was an old sheppard, he was
sitting on the bank of the river near his hut one
morning early washing his shirt a black fellow sneaked
up behind him and hit him on the hed with a nula
nula, a short stick with a nob on the end of it (*last eight*
words added in above the sentence) the blacks youst carry to

kill thing with after they killed the sheppard they took the sheep that he was shepperding out off the yard & drove (*Page* 2) and drove them through some rough country to a place called Pyes creek on the western bounday of the Bolivia holding as soon as the dead sheppard was found an the sheep missing Mr Irby musterd up all the men he could get together on the station an supplied them with fire armes & amunition the(*n*) followed the tracks of the sheep through some rough thickly timbered country and found them on Pies creek the blacks had them rounded up killing them opening them & taking the caul fat out of them and greacing ther heds with some of it a roaling some of it up to carry away with them they were having quite a jolly time as soon as they seen the mob of men they cleared & as they were acros Pyes creek to get away from the mob some of the men had a running shot (?) at them they knocked a few of them over slit (?) then lay where they fell, the bla (*blacks*) then mad(e) across country to the Bluff rock & the party of men after them they (*crossed out*) the black climbed up to the top of the rock, it was fairly easy to climb the rock on the back part of it (*Page* 3) The men got up to the top of the rock & threw the blacks off the rock onto the ground at the bottom the frount part of the rock was a great hite from the ground below a lot of the blacks goh and a lot more crippled none of that tribe was ever seen on the station after after that drive but there were a part fixed tribe …

Yoursfully(?)

Thomas Keating[23]

All italics are mine; spelling and grammar are per original.

Who are we to doubt this account? Here is the written memory of an old man, in an old hand. This is the original white story. But what kind of story is it?

History and the heard

As we have seen, the efforts of the tourist leaflet are organised around the idea that Bluff Rock is to be looked at. It is the image of Bluff Rock that centres our thinking. When we read Keating, however, he presents us with what he has heard, not what he has seen. In this way his continuing connection to place is established, as is the veracity of his report. Of course his hearings, once they become writing, also become something to be seen and interpreted, but it is the 'heard' which is privileged, which counts.

Keating's letter is also a letter between two locals. Keating is providing particulars of his location, which Thomas presumably wishes to map onto his larger idea of the local. Keating begins the story of Bluff Rock with the idea that there were 'large mobs' of 'wild and wickat blacks' when Irby took over. This is certainly something that I never heard in the 1960s and 1970s. I heard that all Aboriginal people 'came from Moree'. The Aboriginal people of the Glen Innes area had been 'disappeared' between the 1920s and the 1960s, I heard, and yet their actions in the 1840s could still be recalled by Keating in the 1920s. But in Keating's letter they are represented in a very particular way. All non-Aboriginals become 'men' and all Aboriginal people become 'blacks'. 'Blacks' is what happened when you moved away from the known Aboriginal workers on the station to a time when they were 'wild and wickat', something already connected to a heard of rather than an experienced reality. Wild and wicked now carries with it some sense of fantasy, but is perhaps better understood as elemental. I don't think Keating is trying to reduce the presence of Aboriginal people to something outside humanity, but to the essentially uncontrollable. To be wild and wicked is to have the freedom to *be* wicked: that is, to have the power to act against 'men', to be outside *their* control. This does not deny the essential racism of the text, but points to the corresponding fear that produces such oppositions as 'wild and wickat blacks' and 'men'. I wonder too if 'black', like 'white', is being employed in the same way as it was in his past, when 'Australians' were 'black' and 'white'. Perhaps as it will be again.

'The last man they killed was an old sheppard', sitting on a river, washing his clothes, and he was attacked from behind. These are the words of innocence — 'old', 'washing' — and the words of cowardice — 'sneaked up behind'. But more than that, he was the 'last *man*' killed. After this it would only ever be 'blacks' who were killed. Of the two 'men killed on the station', this was the last one. Even after the shooting and the throwing, there is the uncertainty of 'none of that tribe was ever seen on the station after that drive'. They were not the last 'tribe', or even of that 'tribe', although they were not seen on the station; there are no claims to getting 'the (very) last man'. So while particular and distinct white men were killed, Aboriginal people are named by Keating as indistinct tribes and 'blacks'. Later, when this individuation does occur — in some of my non-Aboriginal childhood memories at least — it is in ways other than 'black' or 'white'. (Then there was a boy who always topped the maths group, now he would be a particular Aboriginal person. I was fourth in the same class but now I am non-Aboriginal, and as whiteness works, not all that particular). To be 'local' in the 1960s and 1970s was to be neither black nor white. Outside the school, not very far west from us, the Freedom Ride bus was heading for Moree and we didn't hear a thing.

But who and what were the shepherds of the 1830s and 1840s? Why were they killed? What did they and their flocks mean?

These old, 'innocent', shirt-washing 'men' slept in coffin boxes. A coffin box or night watchman's box was what the shepherds of the Australian 1800s slept in whilst watching the sheep by night. It was a six-foot-something long box with sides of variable height (2 metres by 1.2 metres, say). On some, the sides extended up to four feet and were roofed by bark shingles; others had quite shallow sides and were entirely open above.[24] All versions had two handles extending out both ends — like a permanently poled sedan chair — so they could be carried from sheep camp to sheep camp. This was also the way in which real coffins were often carried at the time, so the journey to a camp always had this funereal echo.

The box usually had legs, but one was reported as having a wheel (so it could be moved by a single person), and others did not rest on the ground at all — they were attached to the moveable fences or folds that held the sheep. If there was only one shepherd per mob of sheep, that person slept in this contraption at night; if there was an established outstation with a hutkeeper, the hutkeeper usually became the night watchman (always cited as a white man, but it is also known that hutkeepers were often women, Aboriginal and non-Aboriginal, and that Aboriginal people were very quickly employed in shepherding) and slept in the box while the shepherd rested in the hut.[25] In New England, the employment of Aboriginal labour as shepherds and hutkeepers doesn't seem to have begun until the late 1840s and 1850s, when labour shortages, due to the reduced availability of convict labour and the attraction of the goldfields, began. Aboriginal people employed as shepherds and labourers with non-Aboriginals were quickly incorporated into station affairs.

What was the relationship between these boxes (and their inhabitants) and the larger colonial project? What work did the shepherds do that one could simply emerge in Keating's account as an innocent who could be killed? The coffin boxes seem to symbolise the dislocation that was the non-Aboriginal's relationship with the land. The boxes' distance off the ground and their occasional attachment to the moveable fences surrounding the sheep spell out a desperate stitching of the shepherd to the only available signs of colonial structure: the sheep fold. I wondered why the shepherd didn't simply pitch a tent, and see in that a refusal to engage with the 'Australian' soil. What was preferred were a few boards of hard wood and legs of saplings which created a known space on a previously unknown but now colonially shaped surface. So these boxes become also a collection of stories about the surfaces of the body of 'Australia', about how those particular material constructions emerged in the fragilely colonised space of squatted-upon land.

For the coffin-boxed individual, the meaning of this space depended upon the task of shepherding. A tent was connected to a series of other endeavours, such as those carried out by soldiers and explorers, where the movement was always metaphorically forward — but the shepherds were much more itinerant. Their movements were back and forth with no firm centre, since the sheep pens or folds they returned to at night were by their nature transportable, and were always being shifted to 'clean' ground. The nightwatch box was built to be moved, and could be placed next to the weakest link of the fold or flock. During times of particular anxiety the box was placed within the fold, with the sheep. It marked off a region of humanness in relationship to the animal even when it crossed the moving markers of the sheep folds.

The more substantial roofed nightwatch box had a peephole at the end which allowed the shepherd to check on any danger. Given the size of the peephole, about 10 centimetres in diameter, and the rectangular shape of the box itself, the shepherd was thus restricted to a very specific area to safeguard. The focus was restricted entirely to the small domain of sheep. The sheep had invented the shepherd's function, the sheep contained their gaze. As with the panopticon (a building in which all interior parts can be seen from one hidden position, such as a prison), the viewer is unseen, but here the watched are disciplining the watcher into the relationship of worker — the sheep, because of their economic value, must be watched. The peephole had no power over the dingoes or Aboriginal people, though: the disciplinary possibility of the gaze — behave, because I can see you and can punish you — collapsed.

Given the restrictions of the peephole, shepherds often also employed a series of bells of different pitches which they attached to particular sheep 'leaders' — if the sheep were startled or left the flock, the shepherd could respond. At night the shepherd apparently came to understand the sounds of sheep contentedness and restlessness and could sleep (or not) accordingly. These boxes, in their naming — coffin box or nightwatch box — signalled their complicated relationship to night and death, sleep and death, and the social hierarchy that literally put convict labour in things that were very like coffins. Night was when the sheep were vulnerable to attack, away from the sunlit purview of the shepherd, and the best means of ensuring their safety was via a sometime sleeping figure in a coffin, metaphorically half dead! It is an evocative image, the figure in the coffin box watching the night anxiously through the sounds of the sheep. Inside the box, then, the sheep imposed an aural and visual regime that invented this thing called shepherd. But the shepherd had other meanings as well.

Shepherds, like Keating's shepherd, were reported as being killed by Aboriginal people. There were many reasons for this. The most usual appears to have been as a countering act to the persistent staying on of shepherds in land that was not theirs and their refusal to conform to Aboriginal expectations of appropriate behaviour. Often there were actions around the shepherd huts, including a showing of force at a distance and sometimes visits by an older male member of the Aboriginal group which could have been warnings; when these failed to be acknowledged or acted upon a spearing or clubbing would usually follow. The killings of shepherds were also often connected with rapes or other acts of violence and/or insult against an Aboriginal person, which brought on a response deemed to be a suitable retaliation. Since the shepherds were intimately connected to the sheep, there may also have been a series of sheep-connected reasons for the attacks on shepherds, given that mutton and flour became two of the earliest recognised currencies for Aboriginal labour.[26]

Within non-Aboriginal and non-shepherd accounts, the Australian shepherd was most often represented as being inherently of doubtful character, and all too powerful. Here is Blacklock, writing about sheep:

> With all its boasted steadiness of climate, bad seasons occasionally occur and lead to sickness among the flocks and in addition to the usual chances of loss arising from this cause in other countries, there is [in Australia] a still more dreaded mischief resulting almost unavoidably from the moral constitution of its society. A convict-servant who has a pique at his master, has it often entirely in his own power to subject the flocks under his charge to some one or other of the serious diseases to which sheep in all countries are peculiarly liable.[27]

He also quotes from Lang's *Historical Account of NSW*:

> The chief source of wealth and prosperity of the colony is thus in great measure at the mercy of the most worthless of men.[28]

The work that the shepherd did was understood in contradictory ways. Frederick of Maitland, writing to the *Sydney Morning Herald* in 1842 on the topic of religious instruction in the bush:

> urged the necessity of this highly important privilege [that of religious instruction] being afforded to those who have left the comforts and conveniences of civilised life and have become half savages whilst following the primitive occupation of shepherds.

However, in Abbott's *The Pastoral Age: A Re-examination*, we find the shepherd understood quite differently:

> If fine wool production were encouraged, since it has a far larger potential market than that of local agriculture, settlers would be able to employ large numbers of convicts so relieving the government of the expense of their upkeep. Furthermore the solitary life of a shepherd far removed from towns and town temptations would hasten the rehabilitation of felons.[29]

So, was shepherding a haven, far from the 'temptations of town', or was it something that turned men around, made them re-enter the primitive state? The idea that shepherding was a 'primitive occupation' that turned men into 'half savages' contains many possibilities. It is in the first instance a salute to the power of the land, and may include an unspecified reference to the adoption of many Aboriginal practices to survive in the bush. It may also have been a less overt hailing of the power of a land which could not yet be lived in by non-Aboriginal peoples without transformative consequences. The naming of 'shepherding' as a particularly 'primitive' occupation may be an invention of colonial Australia.

The pastoral tradition, beginning with Virgil, depicted the shepherd as intimately connected with the gods, though not always to the benefit of the shepherd. It is only when shepherding is carried out within the colonially invented world of the 'primitive' that the shepherd risks a movement back into 'savagery'. Perhaps in the evocation of shepherding as a primitive occupation and the idea of the life of a shepherd as restorative, 'far from the temptations of town', we are seeing two versions of an express desire that shepherding, like convictism, be a world apart, its distant bush location simply extending the marginality of people already marked as such. The power of the bush to both restore and destroy reflects the contradictory ways in which 'the bush' had to be represented: it had to bear the possibility of, simultaneously, containing innocent, noble indigenes in a pastoral idyll and convicts in a 'landscape of damnation'.[30]

The fact that one writer sees the result as a descent into savagery and the other as the restoring of the felon to acceptance may be partly explained by the very real possibility that they were talking about different shepherds. For shepherds in the 1840s were not always assigned convicts. As Edward Irby, the other Bluff Rock 'source', wrote in 1841:

> There are a number of young men, who came out with small capitals, not being able to get into establishments, have remained in Sydney till their money was all gone, and then forced to turn shepherds ...[31]

And a more general comment comes from AJ Boyd, who is quoted in the *Old Colonials*, saying:

> I've been getting lower and lower till at last I became a shepherd. It is a lonely life.[32]

Shepherding became in Australia an unstable social category. It was in the interplay between the meanings of sheep — the regimes of their care and the productive possibilities of sheep rearing — and the convict labour system that shepherds in Australia came to be understood in a particularly Australian way. All these meanings arose within a symbolic system that attempted to reinvent Aboriginal presence as Aboriginal absence.

The meaning of sheep

Sheep were also granted a series of meanings which in turn were inscribed into the cultural meaning of the colony. Sheep, as distinct from their 'savage' and/or reforming shepherds, were granted an almost spiritual dimension when read in relationship to colonial Australia:

> Both the climate and the soil appear by nature intended to produce fine wool and fine animals too, even from the worst beginnings.[33]

And Coghlan's *The Wealth and Progress of New South Wales* (1892) suggested:

> The Australian climate changed the character of the Spanish fleece. The wool has become softer and more elastic and while having diminished in density it has increased in length so that the weight of the fleece has only slightly altered.[34]

Here the sheep is granted a naturalised place in the colonial system. Australia 'naturally', through its climate and land, is able to produce a superior fleece, something it was presumed the convict-based colony could never do. Unlike Australia's Aboriginal and non-Aboriginal population, sheep were able to make natural good out of a land that was often understood as being an other-world and a place of impossible return.[35] Wool, however, returned to its European homeland — and was requested to return — finer and longer than when it left. Finally this place called Australia was making productive sense.

This sense was predicated upon two existing conditions: cheap convict labour and land (pasture). Land that was already being used by Aboriginal people. In New England the pasture land included large areas identified by early explorers as 'park-like' expanse. This expanse was created by regular burning by the Aboriginal users in what was a successful kangaroo-attracting practice. These expanses were then seen and understood as 'most suitable' for sheep. Sheep were unable to share the land easily with the kangaroos: sheep have gargantuan appetites, and eat up to five times as much as a kangaroo; they also crop down the grass so that kangaroos cannot get the grip they need — they have a different jaw structure and need to tear at the grass. But kangaroos may have had some minor bio-chemical defiance as well, because an early sheep management guide suggested that sheep dislike feeding after kangaroos as much as cattle after sheep.[36]

Sheep were killed by Aboriginal people, but whether this was because they were destroying the kangaroo-attracting qualities of the grass (improved pastures rapidly solved this problem), or because they became a useful food source, or for some other reason, it is impossible to say. Many times the sheep appear to have simply been chased off one area of land where their presence was unacceptable to the Aboriginal occupants to another area of land where their presence was tolerated.

The possibilities of the sheep in combination with the Australian climate excited some. In *Australian Sheep Husbandry* (1882), authors Armstrong and Campbell imagined the incipient wool industry thus:

> [T]he immense capabilities which this industry is almost certain to develop become too great and magnificent for human realisation.[37]

So the ambivalently understood shepherd in his coffin/ nightwatch box, and flocks that were erratically at home and away and in a constant process of inventing new centres with moveable gates to return to, were linked to the awe-inspiring possibilities of 'magnificent' production. But sheep and shepherds had to be linked to a more generalised 'standing still' — positive progression, called settlement, which was the antithesis of the invented Aboriginal 'non-productive nomadism'.

Shepherding space

Aboriginal people were represented as in opposition to these the new 'productive' possibilities. Myths were written. One of these myth makers was Richard Windeyer (cousin of the

71

Windeyer who was Irby's fellow 'expeditioner'), who wrote 'On the Rights of the Aborigines of Australia' in 1842:

> I pictured to myself the human race spreading in the hunter state from its nativity in Asia, over the surrounding tracts — the multiplication of the species — the progressive scarcity of game — the increasing conflicts between individuals for the spontaneous fruits of the soil until at length some parent seeing his children pinched by want or some young man able to maintain himself but longing to have a companion hit upon the idea that by rearing instead of devouring some of the wild lambs and kids that fell their way or by planting a fruit tree or grains of corn and preventing their destruction during growth they would obtain a more certain supply of food. But all who had the right of hunting over the land would not give it up. Those who wished to reap the rewards of labour would then join together to restrain the hunter from killing their tamed animals or breaking the fences of their cultivated grounds. Their doing so would constitute the first society.

Windeyer puzzles over why this pattern did not occur in Australia and decides that the 'wherewith to begin, were not'. He continues:

> The kangaroo was perhaps capable of domestication to a certain extent but having no fruit, corn or root to live upon during the process it was impossible for the wild hunter of food to stay long enough in one spot to attempt the task. The possession of a few roots which would repay cultivation is the advantage which has induced the New Zealander to gain the title he has to certain portions of the soil occupied by him. As

it is not to be supposed the Australian ever laboured without an object and we may be certain that he never did what we have seen affords the only foundation upon which the right to appropriate land from the common flock can rest, and that he is, as regards title to the substance of the soil, in precisely the situation he was when driven ages back upon a shore to which nature herself had denied the elements out of which society was to arise.[38]

These writings assisted in the invention of the basic racist myths that both allowed and made necessary the denial of Aboriginal people their right to land. His argument depends upon his 'proven' case that Aboriginal people could not claim 'exclusive possession' of the land since they were not sedentarily occupied with producing food from it.

And Windeyer's polemic has a spatial and temporal setting. In the midst of what may have been, pre-invasion, an Aboriginal cornucopia, Windeyer insists upon positing an Aboriginal incapability in a particularly temporal fashion. The Aboriginals in Windeyer's thoughts failed to stand still, to stop and plant and reap; to 'do' something which would give 'them the soil of the country to our exclusion'. This relates to a history that is necessarily progressive, whereby originally the earth was capable of 'furnishing spontaneously and without culture sufficient support for its inhabitants', but as population increased and resources became scarce the land 'could not have received proper cultivation from wandering tribes of men continuing to possess it in common'. This is the antithesis of an economy of any sort. This was Cook's tale of Australia: a place where all and every need is met without labour or capital. Where nothing needed to be produced. But then, elsewhere, individuals needed to appropriate portions of the land 'in order that they might, without being disturbed in their labour or disappointed of the fruits of their industry apply themselves to render those lands fertile and hence derive their sustenance'.

In this reductive myth, 'settlement' and private property combine to create presence, and the presumed 'nomadic' Aboriginal can only be understood as incapable of economic function. However, this myth was problematic for a non-Aboriginal colonial structure where ownership and production were as dependent upon the ability to 'discover' and 'claim' through a constant moving outwards as on 'standing still'. But white nomadism, particularly evident in the 'work' of the shepherds and the infinite possibilities of the 'natural' sheep — who alone seemed to thrive, without improved pastures, on the indigenous soil — was also productive in its ability to name as 'property' its habitats: it was the shepherd and sheep, mapping out the new meanings of the land as suitable or unsuitable to grazing, that invented the land's 'productive' possibilities.

The shepherd did not stand still, but neither did the shepherd roam. The shepherd moved out and around with his flock of productive possibilities. He moved between temporary encampments that were defined by transitional fences that could literally fold in upon themselves. And the limits of the leased lands beyond the boundaries where the shepherd moved were often unmarked — and disputed — imaginary lines between watercourses and hills. Also, having sheep meant setting limits that disallowed swampy or too stony land or trees with bark that might discolour the wool, so the shepherd's arena was mapped by animal as well as human requirements. (The shepherd managed all these things, since sheep will go anywhere, no matter how dangerous or uneconomic. The sheep were really the carriers of the landowners' rules, and if they were discoloured or wet, the shepherd would be to blame.) In this task the shepherd was liminal: in a state of both becoming and unbecoming, half savage or half saved. Insisting on his labour as 'settlement', as an essentially legal action that underscored the right of the squatters to the land, set up a site of contradiction, a site which was constantly being dismantled by the insistent presence and actions of Aboriginal people. 'Settlement' was therefore a state of 'unsettling', of movement, of shifting meanings of presence and the ambivalent power of sheep, shepherds and Indigenous peoples. The shepherds have gone now, but 'settlement' continues.

Colonial production made a cultural system that could contain the seemingly irreconcilable experiences of settlement and invasion. Production in these symbolic terms is continuous: colonialism therefore never ends, and can only stop at a momentary point before a further transformation. One transformation is Keating's letter.

Mustering up

Mr Irby mustered up all the men he could get ... Muster, meaning to round up or gather together, is one of the earliest technologies of colonial bureaucracy. While it was used in its most general sense to name a census of the entire non-Aboriginal population when all the non-Aboriginal inhabitants were gathered at set locations and counted, its daily usage was in the checking of convict numbers. This led in turn to the 'muster bell', which was used to summon the convicts together. Keating is recounting an event from the 1840s when the men Mr Irby would have 'mustered up' were mostly bonded or ex-bonded labour. This was probably also done by ringing a bell — a bell in 'pastoral' Australia was also often recorded as being a warning system. That is, the bell was also rung to signal the sight or arrival of Aboriginal people, and it became a call to arms. The shift in the meaning of the bell and the muster between urban and rural areas is, I think, significant. In the urban arena (within the limits of settlement), the muster was part of a routine that was creating accountable bodies. At such musters, work and rations were detailed and the convicts were released until the next muster. The muster was also the site around which resistance was organised: escaping convicts would have maximised their success at escape by organising it between musters, for example.

But what happens to these bonded bodies 'beyond the limits' of location — that is, beyond the formally settled regions? They are given over to particular squatters (not yet land 'owners'), into an older order dictated by individuals, the demands of production (in this case sheep and wool production) and the unpredictable actions of Aboriginal people. This scenario is more feudal than governmental. The muster bell is no longer about having their bodies ordered, but is a command that might involve being asked to take risks on their master's behalf and to carry out unexpected work. Their bodies must be able to quickly assume the risk-taking possibilities of armed action. Not in any trained or ordered fashion, but at the whim and command of the squatter, their master. Their punishments were public floggings or banishment to the outer outstations. Are these bodies serfs or governed subjects?

When Keating writes (in 1925) that Irby 'mustered up all the men he could get', the power of Irby's position has remained. The particular 'Mr' that Keating uses for all those above him and the first name 'Tom' that he uses for an old worker on the station indicate textually the residual 'mustership' of the landowner. To 'muster' must have been, by this time, firmly imbued with its use as a term to describe the gathering of livestock. It was the cattle and sheep which would be mustered then, and now, for it is only livestock, not people, that can be so easily commanded. The description of 'all the men he could get together on the station' could mean that there were Aboriginal workers already on the station who may have been included in this 'muster'. Irby's diary and Keating's final comment about the 'part fixed tribe' suggests their presence. This would allow one to re-read Keating's dichotomy between 'blacks' and 'men' as not necessarily being dependent upon colour but as a distinction between 'wild' and station-based peoples. The easy assumption by Keating that they could follow the tracks of a mob of chased sheep even in roughly timbered country may mean that Aboriginal trackers were employed and erased from the text, or it may be a re-reading of 1925's relatively cleared country onto the earlier time.

What is distinctly absent from 'the men' then is any description of the 'women'. Aboriginal women are not distinguished from 'the blacks'; there is no note made of children either. The Aboriginal who is said to have killed the shepherd is described as a 'black fellow', the presumption being that it was a man. But there the gender specificity stops. There are no Aboriginal or non-Aboriginal women in Keating's account. Even in other parts of the letter Keating identifies that *Mrs* (my emphasis) Carr, Irby's daughter, can be tracked through her husband's work. It is a small hint that while the children belonged to the wife and mother in Keating's world, all public trails of women were to be followed through men. He assumes, though, that Mrs Carr (Mrs Irby's eldest) will have the more personal history of her father — in the form of photos, at least. No doubt a part of this separation was the assumption that station 'women' would not be 'mustered up'. He might also assume that there were no non-Aboriginal women there at the time — another historical disappearance. Keating doesn't warn Thomas not to report what he has said, so perhaps either Mrs Carr already knows the Bluff Rock history or there is an implicit understanding that Thomas wouldn't report it to a woman anyway. If we knew such detail it would help explain how this story was sent and received and how and why it emerged in 1925. Of course 'more detail' is just an old researcher's fantasy; as if the text isn't enough. Of course I know the author is dead.

'All the men' presents us with an undetermined scale to this event. I could wheel out the total figures from the archives of those employed at the station in the 1840s, and I could refer to Irby's diary, but what I am trying to emphasise is Keating's intent. How many men did he imagine were necessary to get up Bluff Rock and 'throw'? How many did he hear were necessary then? The text suggests that all available men went — 'all he could get together' — so there was nothing strategic about this venture. No one was left to mind the homestead or supplies (or station women?), which assumes no danger from other groups and assumes (as is borne out by the narrative) that 'the men' could quickly find and take action against 'the blacks'. Perhaps the speed of the actions echoes the resources and landscape of the 1920s, when the familiar eight kilometres to Pye's Creek could be covered quickly enough to discover 'the blacks' killing the sheep.

Fat and jolly

Killing them (the sheep), opening them & taking the caul fat out of them. The caul fat is the sheets of fat that surround the intestine of all animals; it has little connective tissue and can be rendered down very efficiently into lard. It makes a delicious skin for sausages. Keating's use of the word suggests familiarity with what caul fat is, and far from proposing the Aboriginal people's inhumanity or foreignness, presumes some common uses of the sheep. Caul fat has a low melting point, so its use to grease the head (to keep people warm) is a 'sensible' employment of an identified resource. It also points to one sort of translation these Aboriginal people had made of introduced animals. It can be imagined that the need to discover new supplies of cold-deflecting, useable fat would have increased as the larger native species were reduced. Sheep transmogrified into kangaroos? But seeing Aboriginal people 'greacing ther heds' is to see 'matter out of place', some kind of unclean or dirty act.[39] On the head, caul fat is a symbol of disorder and jarring 'otherness'; rendered down on damper it spreads into the prosaic.

'[T]hey were having quite a jolly time.' ('Jolly' is followed by 'middle class', in brackets, in Ware's *Passing English of the Victorian Era*.[40]) Did 'jolly' even then carry that cloying middle-class reduction of pleasure to the contained and restrained? And in this context doesn't the 'jolly' jolt? To describe the disembowelment of sheep as jolly reintroduces an idea of abandon, but this pleasure is about to be discovered and brought down to earth; transposed to actions and repercussions. 'Jolly time' almost suggests a temporal transgression, something occurring outside the conventions that make time — a parallel dimension. In 'jolly time' your pleasure is displacing organised minutes as the indicator of what is happening. It is exactly such types of time which are likely to be interrupted by the sudden menacing presence of 'the men'. For 'jolly time' must always be snatched from rationally organised time, from time where there are no appetites (always primitive, non-rational) to be satisfied. 'The men' come in to reinstate rational time; their task is to disrupt 'jolly time', and so they do. There is a trace of morbid nostalgia here, something like the final feast of the condemned man which whispers in that weird Romantic way, 'They might have gone on as they were' — but is only ever said after it was impossible.

Why else was it necessary that they be enjoying themselves? Had 'the tide of history' by 1925 made Aboriginal people safe enough to be 'curiosities'? Has Keating temporarily forgotten that they were 'wild and wickat', or is this simply further proof? 'Quite a jolly time' belies the sense or seriousness of the event. It could become 'blacks' enjoying themselves at the 'men's' expense, which is a very unsettling description for those barely settled white men. Had Keating never heard that 'men' were afraid of 'blacks'?

Across country to the bluff

[A]s soon as they seen the mob of men they [the Aboriginal people] cleared. The first definition of 'mob' in Hughes's *Australian Words and their Origins* is: '(a) A (potentially hostile) party of Aborigines and (b) An Aboriginal community'. Its recorded use for a group of animals began simultaneously. 'Mob' is itself a shortened form of *möbile vulgus*, the moveable (that is, excitable) common people.[41] In the opening section of Keating's letter, he describes the numbers of 'blacks' on the station in Irby's times as 'big mobs of them'. This follows his description of them as 'wild and wickat'. 'Mob' carries with it some sense of charged atmosphere, the 'excitable', the potentially dangerous. At the point of being seen, 'the men' become the 'mob' and the Aboriginal people begin to try to get away from the threat. This is a momentary reversal, where the Aboriginal people's fear makes them innocent and 'the men' become 'wild and wickat'. Those Aboriginal people who survived then 'mad[e] across country to the Bluff rock & the party of men after them'. 'Party' carries with it the ambiguous meanings of festivities and troop deployment.

The shortest distance between Bluff Rock and Pye's Creek is fifteen kilometres, and no doubt the distance to be covered was greater, given the probability that a running route might not be the most direct. It is very rough country. Coming from any point along Pye's Creek to Bluff Rock means traversing country marked on topographical maps as cliffs, with very close contour lines regularly indicating 1000 and 800 metres — this is steep terrain indeed. It is heavily timbered now and there is no real reason to doubt that it wasn't then. Since there is no mention of horses, are we to assume that 'the men' had already run the fifteen kilometres from the station to Pye's Creek as well as some extra kilometres tracking the sheep before Pye's Creek, making the day's total, at a minimum, thirty kilometres? A marathon (not usually run in this terrain) is forty-two kilometres. And then after the final four kilometres up the steep back of Bluff Rock, 'the men' threw 'the blacks off?' It is an extraordinary claim.

An extraordinary claim

> In order to understand the productivity of colonial power it is crucial to construct its regime of truth, not to subject its representations to a normalizing judgement.[42]

What *does* Keating know? From the time when 'Mr Irby took the station over' in the 1840s to the moment in the 1920s when Keating writes, there was in place a continuous government project of controlling Aboriginal people. While this project had forms that varied from state to state and institution to institution, it was, broadly speaking, a project centred about the continuous dispersal of Aboriginal people. After the terrorism of land taking and initial 'settlement' there was a system of reserves. These were to be temporary staging posts on the way to the eventual complete dying away of all Aboriginal people. When numbers were seen to be increasing rather than decreasing, a more rigorous process of dispersal came into being, with the Commonwealth's Aborigines

Protection Act of 1909. This Act set up the programs that removed children and ran down reserve conditions, and ensured the perpetual availability of Aboriginal lives to the actions and gaze of many government agencies, but particularly the police.[43] These general policies had particular local effects, and form part of Keating's 'regime of truth'. His story of a single massacre might also be read as an allegory of the processes of removal and dispersal which were operating throughout New South Wales from the 1880s, when he went to manage Bolivia, to the 1920s, when he writes.

There is an entry from 1940 in the Historical Society records of Tenterfield that tells us that a reserve was created, but not when or by whom: 'An aboriginal reserve was secured for the Bolivia Blacks in later years on the Upper Mole River. The last of them were Old Jacky and Sally.'[44] Imagining such finality was a direct invention of the reserve system. Allowed onto a reserve because of their 'full blood', or because of their appearance, or because they were known to particular authorities, then named as 'pure' or the 'last' by such a system, their eventual deaths led to such apocalyptic headlines as 'The Last of His Tribe'. Was it the deaths of Jacky and Sally that Keating remembers? Jacky coming back with rations and having to swim a flooded river and dying on the bank, and Sally taken to Tabulum 'to live with the blacks there' — were they the last markers of a system of Aboriginal classification that was directly linked to work and relationships with the large properties?[45] The 'Bolivia Blacks', like the 'Deepwater Blacks', renamed and made final markers of settlement — were these the 'last man killed'?

And might not the energy of Keating's description be fuelled by the governmental power of splitting families up, erasing language and moving beyond geographical recovery — via telephones and advanced postal systems and cars and now the web — the possibility of re-establishing cultural coherence? What happens when we read Keating's letter, written in 1925, along with Margaret Tucker's account of being 'removed' from her family in the 1920s.

Listen:

TUCKER: There were forty or fifty of our people standing silently grieving for us. They knew something treacherous was going on, something to break our way of life. They could not see ahead to the white man's world. We simply accepted the whites as a superior race. Around that particular part of Australia, I feel we were fortunate in having a kindly lot of white station owners ...

Mr Irby mustered up all the men he could get together and supplied them with arms and ammunition.

TUCKER: She went out to her house at the side of the school, taking as long as she dared to prepare something to eat. Her husband, his face going purple, was looking at his watch every few minutes. At last she came in with a tray with glasses of milk and the kind of food we only got at Christmas time. We said we couldn't eat it — we were not hungry — but she coaxed us to drink the milk and eat something. Mr Hill couldn't stand it any longer and said a lot of time was being wasted, and that the police and the driver wanted to leave ...

The blacks had them rounded up killing them opening them and taking the caul fat. They were having quite a jolly time.

TUCKER: Our mother like an angel came through the schoolroom door. She still had her apron on, and must have run the whole one and a half miles.

As soon as they seen the mob of men they cleared. Some of the men had a running shot at them. They made across country. The men got up to the top of the rock & threw the blacks off ... A lot of the blacks goh and a lot more crippled ...

TUCKER: Then we were taken to the police station, where the policeman no doubt had to report. Mother followed him, thinking she could beg once more for us, only to rush out when she heard the car start up. My last memory of her for many years was her waving pathetically, as we waved back and called out goodbye to her, but we were too far away for her to hear us ...

My purpose in reading these terrible narratives together is to reveal the 'nonsense' produced by Tucker, and via Tucker a re-reading of 'The Bluff Rock Massacre' by Keating. There is no real nonsense in Tucker's account, but she makes nonsense of the everyday. Glasses of milk, school teachers, a mother's apron, a car driving off. All these ordinary, 'universal' signs become unstable, and wobble away from their non-Aboriginal, colonially produced meanings when connected to the haunting destruction of Aboriginal living. I suppose it would be clearer to say that it is Tucker's sense (her rewriting, her re-inscription, her effective? ironic? counterpoint) that produces the 'nonsense' of acts of 'normal' life, where a glass of milk now *used to be* something ordinary to drink, not a swallowed-down elegy.

Perhaps it was the monstrous, terrific powers of the state's machinery — and its effects — which produced the all-powerful whites of Keating's letter. Was it the practice of continuous removals and separations that produced the non-Aboriginal Australians' omnipotent imaginings of total Aboriginal destruction, or did it 'really' happen exactly as Keating writes it?

Would the last 30 years of Keating's experience have exposed him to the system of reservations and removal of Aboriginal children (which began in one version in the late 1880s)? If Aboriginal people 'disappeared' around you and if sometimes you caught glimpses of some of the machinery of 'removal' or were actively involved in it, how easy would it be to imagine that the 'blacks' were 'thrown' off, how 'sensible' to understand original colonial encounters in terms of the 1920s governmental machinery of renewed and continuing colonialism. Ordinary 'men', like the ordinary policeman in Tucker's account, when given the power to be one small part of a policy of 'solving' the 'Aboriginal problem', do have the 'super' powers of Keating's 'men'. They did have the power, with paper and reports and cars, to pluck identified people up and throw them down in 'Homes' and hostels and other institutions — and of course some are 'crippled' in the process. A final trip in a Holden? Well 'none of that tribe was ever seen on the station after that *drive*'.

The history of the word 'drive' within Australia is a particularly poignant one. In early colonial attempts at suppression and 'final solutions', 'drives' were envisaged as the ultimate tactic of complete discovery and destruction. The best-known example is the 1830 'black line' across Tasmania, where volunteers and the military formed a human chain across the settled area around Hobart and proceeded to walk: its aim was to frighten out and capture and/or shoot all Aboriginal people. It was spectacularly unsuccessful. In a less organised fashion, individual squatters and workers and official Native Police would organise 'drives' where they would find particular groups of Aboriginal people then pursue these people, on horses, to their deaths — by shooting or being forced over cliffs or some equivalent. But these were sporadic, never completely successful, and of course escalated an ongoing war of counterattacks. But the organised driving away — the removal of Aboriginal children and adults — which took on its most systematic form in the twentieth century, precisely because it was a part of a government which had the power to be systematic, could slice out the connective tissue of Aboriginal families. It was the car which usually made these grabs so possible. The car was a tool of the policy, and it was the speed of the car which enacted the power of the state to remove people utterly, to place them beyond the means of a country public transport system, and so beyond the ability of Aboriginal families to re-establish contact. It presumed the powerlessness of Aboriginal people to follow in any equivalent. Cars, like Tucker's final glass of milk she is given by Mrs Hill, are therefore not entirely 'ordinary' objects. They were part of a machinery of 'removal', another sort of massacre.

MY MOTHER TO MY GRANDMOTHER: Shall we go for a drive, Mum? The McGregors are building a lovely place up in Heron Avenue.

(This was said after Sunday lunch at Granny's. Snailpacing along, we passed other cars doing the same route round the new houses in the right end of town.)

Other letters

Fifteen years before receiving Keating's reply, Thomas had written to Irby's daughter (Mrs Traill, not Mrs Carr [her sister], whom Keating suggests) seeking her knowledge of the event. This is the woman who published her father's and uncle's *Memoirs* in 1908.

Parts of her two replies to Thomas read as follows:

Wirepe
Turramurra
Sept 22nd 1910

Dear Mr Thomas

... The only punitive expeditions I know of were
those mentioned in the 'Memoirs', but we have often
joked with my Father about the Bluff Legend, it
amused him very much — surely some bones would
be there to this day if anyone cared to search ... he
was only a lad of twenty when he came out here, his
brother was younger; I am afraid my two sons of
similar ages have not as much grit and enterprise ...

Dear Mr Thomas

... Referring again to the Bluff Rock episode, the
Blacks were either Clarence or Severn River tribes &
would naturally retreat east or west after committing
murder: they would certainly not go near the main
road which always led close below the Bluff, & of
this I am certain that none but punitive expeditions
were made by the settlers of my fathers day: the
half-caste was right when he said my father fired in
the air, he was not a man to shirk what he deemed a
duty but he was ever ready to give another chance
when justified in doing so ...

I am yrs truly[46]

Initially these letters do not deny the truthfulness of Keating's
account. Keating is clear to point out that the Aboriginal
people were pursued because they had killed a shepherd and
stolen sheep. It was to 'punish' them that they were followed; it
was 'a punitive expedition'. But here we have a struggle with

meanings. To punish an entire group with death seems monstrous and ridiculous. Justice must now be done through particular, autonomous and disciplined individuals. The group must be carefully examined to reveal the leader, the followers, the coerced, the remorseful and the doubtful, and each must be punished according to the valuation of their particular guilt. Making the claim that 'only' punitive expeditions were carried out no longer convinces us. What is considered a legitimate and proper way of responding has now changed, so the failure to recognise humanity and individuality reads like savagery and the work of primitives. The powerful structures that permitted and encouraged the 'punitive expedition' have been resisted and displaced, but the force of their occurrence lives on.

But Keating's letter resists the legitimation of Traill's 'punitive expedition' in another sort of way. 'Punitive expedition' can belong to the matter of law — orderly punishment — or it can be translated via Keating's account into the mayhem of chasing and throwing and shooting. Keating's letter transposes 'punishment' into the key of physical pain, where action has bodily effects: crippled, shot and thrown. Those words jar. Today, 'punishment' is not meant to belong to this world of the corporeal; it belongs to the world of disciplined incarceration. At the same time, though, we concede that all 'punishments' have physical effects, that prisons can induce depression, insanity, violence or love, and so through the spectre of the chase and massacre we understand we are reading the 'real' of inflicted pain versus Traill's euphemistic 'punitive expedition'. But which is the 'real' account of a massacre? Keating's or Traill's? One gives us bloody mayhem, and one gives us the lighthearted touch.

The words 'we have often joked with my Father about the Bluff Legend, it amused him very much …' hang like the proverbial lead balloon. The idea that someone who carried out 'punitive expeditions' could ever have been a part of the

Bluff Legend is here made impossible through the reported fact that it was joked about. These two forms of death, 'The Bluff Rock Massacre' and his 'punitive expeditions', are so far apart, so extraordinarily different that only laughter can link them for Irby. One hundred and fifty years later we see only death, and ponder. Was there another massacre apart from Irby's expeditions? A massacre that no one attempted to legitimate under the title of 'punitive expedition'? Was it carried out by working men, not landed gentry? Did it really happen at the Bluff? What else did Irby do? What else did Keating hear?

On hearing

I will now send you what I heard ... Keating is in his way a revolutionary. He is in the moments of writing this letter radically relocating what was previously an orally shared history.

I will now send you what I heard. What did *I* hear at home? I heard about the little red hen, whom we also knew as the banana lady. It was bad to be the little red hen. It was something to do with babies. Too many? No husband? The wrong husband? Now I'm sorry, because I'm a little red hen too. Then there was Rupert, who lived near the high school. I heard he had murdered someone. He looked as if he might. Later I met him as the quiet man in the sheltered workshop who carried the waste paper to the press. I heard about our next-door neighbour. She walked across paddocks and hid down near a log and took tablets until she died. My mother said they were never happy. The neighbour had once said, 'He can be cruel sometimes.' She was highly strung, I heard. She had a face like a pansy. Soft. There were only eight kilometres of paddocks between us. I heard about the man who came too close. He taught dancing to pretty girls whom he held around the waist. Don't go into his office, someone told me. Maybe it was my sister, maybe not — we didn't speak of such things at the time. I heard that Davros the fruiterer was a drug dealer, heroin. He had an old Mercedes but lived in a flat — nearly proof. I heard that Mr Golstein was a German spy in the war, that he had had a radio. In fact, he was a Jewish refugee who came out after the war. You couldn't send any of this.

If you were taught history you could tell anyone; history didn't hurt. It was all too far away. We didn't *hear* history, we were *taught* history, and what we heard excited us about Europe, but particularly England. 'Local' history was all around us but we couldn't see it. We couldn't hear it. My friends and I were the Youth Group of the Local Historical Society. We dressed in period costume for open days and for the Agricultural Show. We spun wool for exhibitions and had a clubhouse. We cleaned displays and experienced the pleasures of stepping *behind* the mesh doors of the display rooms, but we didn't hear a thing.

But Keating did hear, so he can tell. After 80 years, something can be sent because somebody asked. He was not at the massacre but he was asked; because he was from the place, he *was* there.

Going there

If ethnography is concerned with cultures and the study thereof, then the concentration on the particular and the inclusion of the emotional (pathos) must produce 'pathographies'.

PADDOCK NOTES

(Getting there) *Uralla:* Am trying to coerce Susan, my partner and unpaid research assistant (a historically ubiquitous and difficult arrangement to get right), into writing her thoughts — she seems very unwilling to participate as ethnographer. Where is anthropologist Clifford Geertz's quiet, appearing and disappearing wife?[47] Susan is sulking on the bed with her boots on. The familiar smell of New England coming out of drought is all around us in the caravan park. All damp grass and undercurrents of mud. The proprietor shows us our double bed caravan ($24 per night) and shows us the possibility of another bed that folds out from the table — if we needed it, but obviously not expecting us to use it. Is this simply lack of homophobia? Large family used to sharing? Or is there something wrong with the other bed?

TENTERFIELD, RAINING

We begin going through the newspapers looking for reference to the massacre, deaths of some of the instigators, work reports, police reports, census etc. By 1908 (when Irby's *Memoirs* was published) all the 'savages' are elsewhere: New Guinea and Africa.

D, the caravan proprietor, tells me about the small child who survived the massacre and was brought up by whites on a farm nearby. Campbell had this same story in his article about New England history, which he wrote in the 1960s. T, from the history house, tells Susan about the hail storm interrupting the massacre. This too is familiar to me, but from where?

NEXT DAY

I visit the Land Council and chat with a group of Aboriginal workers there. L says I should just go there, you can feel it is a bad place. Bad country. P says she wishes they would tell the truth: that it was whites who got killed up there, that the Aborigines had tricked the whites into following them without realising the cliff was there. She said she had read something in the archives at the Armidale History Resource Centre. I asked them if they were glad that at least Aboriginal presence is acknowledged, but they all agreed with L, who said, 'We don't want to claim it or anything; we're not like that.' It is not the most interesting thing to them. Their focus is elsewhere. Again I see the non-Aboriginal insistence on 'The Bluff Rock Massacre' as the centre of events when for years (perhaps forever), most Aboriginal focus has been in the opposite direction, towards Woolloo Woollooni and Woollool Woollool. And what is there for any Aboriginal group in this story of massacre, this total destruction? But then what is there in the story for non-Aboriginal people? Supremacy? A hint of the silenced land wars? No one at the Land Council seems to think it happened in the way it is portrayed, but there is no insistent, single other truth.

In the afternoon I talk to one of the Aboriginal tour leaders, who says he doesn't care about the terrible things that happened to his people in the past, he just wants to get on with the future. Points out that he's never been in gaol, never been unemployed and yes there are some Aborigines that get in trouble but if he can just show them that you can live a normal life ... He'd like to leave Tenterfield, though, since his kids are getting older and they need more things to do. The old country town problem.

BECAUSE IT WAS THERE

Finally contact Mr H and receive permission to climb Bluff Rock. It looked easy. You go straight up the ridge and you expect there will be a flat top but there is more and more heavy scrub. Still raining. We occasionally see one large footprint and Susan sees an unidentifiable animal. It is not eerie in the same way that the country near Mt Mackenzie was. This is regrown scrub. There, at twilight, 'trapped in the rocks' among the dieback trees and the grim granite boulders, unsaid history groaned at us. But here, even right near the edge, the bush is dense and the ground uneven; these would not have been easy deaths. Where could someone have balanced to pick up a body and *throw*? Even tumbling an insensible or dead body over would have been difficult. Those corpses would have been 'trapped' on all the minor overhangs. Perhaps at the side, but again, some 'goh', some 'crippled'. How would they have got up? It would have been quite difficult for horses up the ridge but impossible on top, so that at least makes sense, but Irby's trapped under rocks does not. The country is tough and much more majestic from a distance. Walking the stories out brings irritation rather than revelation. I cannot see it, I cannot feel it. More drizzle as we come down and we get slightly lost in the very thick ti-trees. What bloody tree line?

SUSAN'S ACCOUNT

Yesterday we went to Bluff Rock, up an unmarked road and up and down an unmarked track. The rock towers menacingly and the stories we have heard about the massacre hang heavily like the mist and the threatening rain on the nearby hills. 'Follow the tree line beyond the paddock', we are told by the guardians of the rock, the Hs of the closest farm. The first hill is unbelievably heavy going. How could a 'chase' happen here? How could you be motivated to stagger up here, let alone chase your quarry — let alone be chased? Why would you be chased uphill? Wouldn't you divert sideways? The words of Irby along the lines (I'm roughly quoting) — They would have got off if they had taken to their heels but they got their fighting men together. So did the fighting men go uphill in order to gain the upper hand? With a cliff as your final defence? Unlikely, unlikely, I mutter under my breath (what breath? there is none left as I drag foot over foot, requiring the most dedicated, focused effort to continue up). We lose sight of the rock. A moment of doubt with neither compass nor track — where is the rock? Are we heading in the right direction? No doubt really, we know the rock is up. At the top, I see the hindquarters of a strange animal, large cat size, perhaps a large cat or a hare (sighted later, running — definitely not a hare), maybe a feral cat or dog. Sensational and much welcomed view at top. Lots of droppings; sheep, says Katrina. *Sheep?* More and constant speculation about the possibility of the mass murder, fascination with the edge: where is the edge? Where is the cover you would seek by coming this way? But there is none that we can see. Still seems a most unlikely tale. But a spectacular one. A sensational one. The rock is so awesome, looming over the landscape, visible from every which way, sheer, massive. If you wanted revenge, why not the rock as the setting — it knocks one's breath away, it's a darned good yarn. Certainly D and P and Katrina as a child, wide-eyed at the horror of it — it certainly evokes a response from the listener. In the shadow of the rock here at Tenterfield it's a darned good story. Climbing down we lose our way. Where is the tree line? We're in the midst of trees, thick scratchy, dense low ones, ti-trees … where are we? Real moments of uncertainty — will we come to a cliff and have to retrace our tracks and scratch our legs all over again? It's steep and a long haul. Follow the stream, says Katrina, it's the shortest way down. But water falls, down waterfalls Katrina. Come on, come on, you don't know the country, there's no waterfalls here. At last a bleat near the stream, a flash of green and we're back in the paddock, right on course.

MORE PADDOCK NOTES

We go to the Henry Parkes Motel Country Resort in the spirit of ironic postmodern observers, but we are also hungry and want a treat. This is the motel of Meaghan Morris's famous essay 'At Henry Parkes Motel', in which she turns the relationship of modernity to the domestic on its head. I imagine leading small bands of black-clad folk in yet another attempt to revitalise the flagging town through a new niche market – *cognoscente* tourism? While we are meandering along the front flower bed E comes over from the garden he has been working on to talk and talk and talk about his dream of having a guesthouse-type establishment like his family had in the Dandenongs. But this motel is bright pink with blue trim. People are moving in and out with a sort of glee, families of course, children slightly dragging, pleased parents: 'I can afford to give my kids this — at least.' We go into the bright pink palace and are flooded by Meaghan Morris Land. Is the motel hiding its homeness or isn't it? Does the very intractable stature and history of Bluff Rock make this place work in a particular way? Outdoing its 'homeness', does it save us from the 'real' quiet of Bluff Rock? And is it just typical of the small-town girl gone urban that after all the beautiful gardens, I see the vinyl chairs, yick carpet, aluminium window frames and think it is all wrong? And the awfulness of those vinyl clichés being one man's vision, and the way the smallness, the individualness of country towns makes it all so personal and implicate one so. How I long for some sort of easy campness as a way out of this, where I can JUST LURV IT DAARLIIING and leave it without being insincere or unfair. Camp as moral solution. Someone is playing the organ in the ante-dining room/bar. It is *Send In the Clowns* and *Sound of Music*, and she is quite an old woman. It makes me sad. What if this woman is Meaghan Morris's mother? The room is like my stepmother's house. Beige, floral, plenty of plastic wood veneers and pink. Two more dykes come in — is all this pink attracting the wrong types? The food was expensive because we were paying for chicken breast with 'mango sauce' and extra vegetable. It seemed to take a lot of energy to *survive* the night. We were overdressed as tourists and underdressed as locals. The romance of reading great works in the places that inspire them becomes impossible. It's too local for me. I'm worried 'At Henry Parkes Motel' might hurt E's feelings, I'm worried about the woman making beds, who might have gone to school with Meaghan Morris, let alone her mother playing in the bar. Back to the caravan.

Last night I became another sort of racist. I went to dinner. I
didn't know I was going. I arrived at the manager's house of one
of the big stations for what I thought would be about an hour
to check locations, look at the homestead etc., but my maps
were missing a final corner and the manager knew his neighbour had a bigger map, so they rang the neighbour and the
neighbour said he would be over in a while. So C and T asked
me to tea. We talked (as yesterday's killed meat was cooked,
the mash and the gravy microwaved) of who was who and who
had died and where I fitted in in the families of things. The
drought had driven them off their own place the other side of
Glen Innes; they were managing a property now, hoping at
some stage to get back their own place. They had known my
best friend from school and told me her lovely grandmother
was still alive. C had another Bluff Rock story. This one was to
do with the trickery of Thunderbolt's gang, who were famous
bushrangers in the area. When cornered on top of Bluff Rock
they threw their horses over the edge to fool the troopers into
thinking they had gone over, and when the troopers left their
horses to come over and check, the bushrangers made off with
the troopers' horses. ('Black Mary' was Thunderbolt's partner in
crime and this makes me wonder how many Aboriginal
victories through trickery have become the stuff of bushranger
legend.) A big pot of tea and fresh white bread from the freezer
were then put on the table and we ate our way towards them
through steak and gravy and mash. Eventually the neighbour
arrived and we went over the maps and we talked of the
weather and round and flat-boned cattle and kids, and they felt
at home with me and I with them. Suddenly the hospitable and
kindly C said of her eldest son, who is working in the Kim-
berley, 'He's sick of the blacks. They're lazy. The kids and wives
are always trailing along. When you hire someone up there you

get the whole family. Great experience — he's learning toler-ance.' Laughter. I didn't say a thing and I easily could have. If I had said something, I might have seen something better, but I didn't. The description of 'lazy' followed an account of how all the workers up there go for twelve to fourteen hours a day and are paid a lowly $200 a week, but what applied to her son didn't apply to 'the blacks'. Then when we were talking about how quickly a horse could go in rough country, particularly if we could imagine the country of the 1840s, W (the neighbour) said, 'Well they had the Aborigines' tracks already here', to which C asked, 'But wouldn't something happen to them [the settlers] if they did that?' W: 'Well I think that's how they found their way; maybe the Aborigines weren't using them at the time.' C: 'Well I don't know what happened to them [Aboriginal people], but they were gone before we got here.' This said with a sort of humorous finality that didn't let me ask (or so I imagined) how she explained the Land Council office in town or the Aboriginal tours.

Where did I go? What would forever interrupt this comp-licated after-dinner chat, the gossip in the street, this lovingly inclusive thing called (inadequately) racism. I'm sick of the country. I'm dying for a margarita. I'm ashamed of myself. I feel sick and I want to get away from HERE. Do you (did I?) really have to be silent because someone has been nice to you? It would have been so easy to say something. Have I already, at the slightest push, 'gone native'? Or was I being over-polite because I was 'really' a stranger? a guest? a dyke? overeducated? I hate this self they think they've seen. And I know if I see them in the street I'll thank them for a lovely dinner because of course they are more than these few words, of course they are, but what am I? Wholly made of words. I want to get away from here. I WANT A MARGARITA.

LOCAL KNOW-HOW

We need to go on remembering that Keating was not the only one who knew. That the story of Bluff Rock was passed around from local to local, and broadcast through early promotional materials — and that it changed shape in different times and in different contexts.

The major source of most of the following stories is magnificently heterogeneous. It arose from a simple idea: to record the stories of old 'pioneers'. In this way the histories, the stories of some 'ordinary' Tenterfieldians came to be recorded. Norman Crawford was the Honorary Secretary of the Tenterfield Historical Society in the 1940s, and began a process of collecting and typing up interviews and rough oral histories of the older inhabitants of the town. Sometimes these were recorded by him, sometimes by a member of the interviewee's family, and occasionally a correction appears in the margins or at the bottom of the page. Interspersed with sections devoted to individuals are general sections on the local industries, such as the Flour Mill, or large properties, such as Tenterfield Station, and there is also a 1940s tourism brochure. All these different subjects constitute Volume 1 of the Tenterfield District Historic Society Records (TDHSR). The pages are not numbered or titled. I have also included an extract from Norton's 'Reminiscences', which was in the same archive, and a more recent poem (1980) from a local poet. Within all these sources 'The Bluff Rock Massacre' is questioned, confirmed, doubted and rewritten. Its mythical, complex nature as a marker of a certain sort of colonialism comes richly alive. Its role as a theatre of enunciation for every atrocity ever carried out on Aboriginal people becomes more obvious. 'The Bluff Rock Massacre' allows many things to be said.

Making it all OK

Essantee News was a small publication put out by Essantee Switchgear Ltd; it featured the 'many lines of electrical equipment manufactured by the company' as well as 'the scenic beauties and industrial activities of the Municipalities and Shires throughout Australasia'. Published in the 1940s, the issue that featured Tenterfield included a small section on the early days of the area:

> Of the early history of the locality amusing stories may be related; encounters with the natives who did not wholly respect the white men as their superiors, of bushrangers and others. It is related that two distinguished pioneers, Edward and Leonard Irby, owners of Bolivia Station took it upon themselves to lead a posse to punish the blacks for the murder of a watchman at Snake Creek. Dame Nature took a hand in the proceedings, for just as they had cornered the tribe in heavy timber they were thwarted by a sudden and terrific hailstorm, in which 'lumps of ice as large as hen's eggs' gave many of them sore heads, and they retired to cover discomforted. Dame Nature, with characteristic impartiality, dampened the ardour of 'black' and 'white' alike.[48]

This was a publication that was sent to all Supply Authorities, and those supply authorities were invited to send in particulars of 'industrial or scenic' interest which would be put into the next editions. This blend of the industrial and the scenic is representative of a particular current of tourism which may be less popular now but which I remember only too clearly. Whenever we went on a real holiday (one lasting days and including some touring element), we visited dams, big dams. These we never found dull, although there was no interactive educational component; the height of the visit was the walk along the top to look over the spillway and admire the gushing water. The idea of the industrial as spectacle, as tourist destination, was completely accepted, and as spectacle it competed with such natural 'monuments' as 'The Bluff Rock Massacre'. Bluff Rock requires a much more explicit story than hydro-electric or irrigation schemes — they were able to assume their spectacular majesty through their modern enormity. To link the industrial and the scenic as the twin possibilities of interest of early tourism is to see an explicit opposition between the progressive and the historical. The historical here includes the natural landscape; the progressive includes businesses, the industrial infrastructure, small factories and hard-worked farms. Both of these can be presented to the tourist gaze, but in different ways. The Tenterfield population is described as 'a progressive community' whose people 'are alive to the importance that their town has achieved in the commercial world'; it is 'an important trucking centre', and 'there is a large butter and freezer works', and 'its mineral resources have been worked with profit'.

This 'progressive', 'working', 'profitable' and incredibly confident forward march allows the 'attempted' massacre by a (Hollywood western?) posse to become an 'amusing story' that forever belongs to a past that is absolutely past, literally ground into a dust by a progress that allows it no consequence except 'historical colour'. This is something that still goes on. As Prime Minister John Howard said in 1997 of the Native Title debate, 'I think we all agree on one thing, and that is, the sooner we get this debate over and get the whole issue behind us the better for all of us', and then later, 'I believe the time has come for us to fix this issue and to fix it now.'[49] This points to the assumption that in moving forward we leave nothing behind us — we can 'fix' the past once and for all. The past is forever gone and will have no effect in the present. Particular events become pluralised in this set past. The foiled massacre becomes one of many 'amusing stories', since all old stories have been collapsed into 'the past'. How quaint, how odd, how perfectly amusing. Wasn't it Kafka who said laughter was the absence of feeling? We know history but refuse to feel history, refuse to be history, and refuse to become history. Let's look at some of the shapes of this 'amusing story'.

Irby's *Memoirs* include a letter to his mother in 1842 which reports on a fall of huge hail stones, some 'about four inches in circumference',[50] but the story which sounds most similar to the Essantee account is his account of the death of Bonney, a watchman at Snake Creek, in 1845. Snake Creek was on Deepwater Station, and Irby and his brother Leonard were part of a group of ten which also included Collins (Deepwater's overseer, who led the group), Weaver and Westley. They 'came upon the Blacks suddenly about 11am. They had got into a dense mountain scrub, so that we couldn't half punish them.' After a pot of tea and pitching a camp they decide to make another effort to kill the Aboriginal group, and some go back and fire from below while others hide above, in the hope that the Aboriginal group will run out and up and be trapped beneath the guns of those above. It begins to rain and 'some awfully large hailstones fell. Collins had a great lump on his head raised by an immense hailstone ... It was too steep where they had been to do much good.'[51] The only difference between Irby's original diary account and the published *Memoirs* account of this incident is that the original includes the detail that 'It left off raining for a short time so that we managed to get our supper in peace.' So the account in the 1940s pamphlet is a reasonably accurate rendering of one 'expedition', except for its exclusion of the fact that the Aboriginal group had outmanoeuvred the pursuing party. None of the accounts connects this incident to Bluff Rock.

The story of 'The Bluff Rock Massacre' was certainly known in the 1940s, but perhaps even then, at a moment when industry and progress could shape a failed 'posse' into an amusing scene, it could not do the same to the herding of people over a cliff.

There is something relentlessly optimistic about the way in which history can become a series of 'amusing stories'. The tongue-in-cheek description of 'natives who did not wholly respect the white men as their superiors', the unassailable 'distinguishment' of the Irbys, the erasure of the 'posse's' regret that they 'couldn't half punish them' (thereby revealing how badly they wanted to kill) builds a series of stereotypes in a brusque storytelling style that shows us again and again: that was the way it WAS. We are to read this as another sort of time, a time when 'pioneers' could go scurrying off half-cocked after 'natives' instead of working hard and industriously, investing themselves in the new modern project of town development — it is the most extraordinary conceit. And yet in a very subtle way, this is the only version of the many attempted massacres where the particular transportability of the Irbys and other squatters, in their endless small movements between 'properties' and persons, is acknowledged. Implicit in those movements is the ability at any moment to focus on an Aboriginal group and become a band of assassins. A roving primitive force with a modern imagination and capacity to target and destroy.

But the attempted lightness of this story, published as it was in a public relations/advertising pamphlet, lies in its insistence on the 'ardour' of both parties. How much worse to imagine the calm taking of tea, the disappointment in being unable to really 'punish' the Aboriginals, and the relentless commitment to go on with the shooting and poisoning: the industrious efforts at extermination which might echo all too strongly with the 'profit making', 'progressive' community of the 1940s. And so the past is again set up as a place of wild, emotion-driven action, contrasted against the sensible actions of rational work — and possibly (again, given when this was written) also against the warfare of a military machine, where people and killing hardware were organised mechanically and publicly sanctioned.

The saved child

Coming on them on the side of a deep precipice, the avenging party attacked them and wiped them out, with the exception of one small piccaninny. The little chap ran to Bill Bates and clung to his legs and was spared. William Bates kept and reared him (the boy). He was always grateful and useful to him in after years.[52]

The Aborigines withdrew to higher ground until they found themselves between a precipice and their pursuers. The entire group, women and children were driven over the edge — with the exception of one small boy, the only survivor. This boy, incidentally, was brought up very successfully by one of the white men involved. They developed a strong feeling of devotion to each other.[53]

This was also a story I was told in Tenterfield. The story was that the child grew up, and when dead, was buried at the foot of the Bluff. One might see the grave; I found nothing. William Bates' son says nothing about having an adopted Aboriginal brother. Campbell (the author of the second quote above, which is from his thesis) acknowledges no source for his statement; it could well have been the collected oral histories from the Tenterfield Historical Society records (as in the first quote above). There is no supporting objective evidence in the shape of graves or in the shape of adults who have come forward to tell of their unusual upbringing, but the story keeps on being told and written. Campbell's confident assertion — in a thesis, no less — even makes it official history. But if it is not true, why would people invent or believe such a tale? What does this story do?

First, it individualises morality. While a group was chasing and killing, when one child appealed to one of these killers, he 'saved' the child. This same man, we assume, could not and did not wish to stop killing all the others, but he did save one child. It wants to tell us that these men were not entirely monsters; that they also had a fundamental humanity. That close up, when appealed to directly, one man's choice was to save a child. But could we call this 'humanity'? Is this how the sensibility that led to the more systematic Stolen Generations began? When an Aboriginal child was told it was lucky to have been 'saved', stolen up from death, 'rescued' from 'wild blacks' to become 'grateful' and 'useful', 'devoted' and successfully 'brought up'? But if one child could be saved, why not all of the group? One can begin to see why the Romantic imagination strained within colonialism. The innocent child saved but the rest killed — why? The sentiment attached to children frayed and played itself out alongside the raw and unromantic slaughter.

Children were also involved in other massacres. About two hours from Bluff Rock is Myall Creek, where in 1838 (six years before Irby et al. carried out their 'punishment') Kilmeister et al. were slaughtering a group of children, women and men. Some of the perpetrators, all current or ex-convicts, were eventually hanged amidst general outrage that any white man should die for killing Indigenous Australians. They were not found guilty at their first trial, which was for killing an Aboriginal known as 'Daddy', but in their second trial they were found guilty on five counts of the 'murder of an Aboriginal Black Child whose name was to the Attorney-General unknown'. This child had been identified by its rib bones, a jaw bone and some teeth. In *Tales of Old Times: Early Australian Incident and Adventure* (1903), Chomley records Anderson (the hutkeeper) saying about the group on Myall Creek that:

> There was a little child at the back of the hut when they were tying this party; and when the blacks and party were going away, this little child as I thought, was going to follow the party with its mother, but I took hold of it and put it into the hut and stopped it from going.[54]

However, in his first sworn statement about the event, Anderson says the following:

> All the blacks at the station were taken away except Davy and his brother Billy, two Black gins a pickininny [a little boy] and two little boys who saved themselves when the horsemen were coming up by jumping into the creek. The Men left a black Gin with me saying she was a good looking Gin. They gave another to Davy. The little child came from behind the hut when they were taking the

blacks away as I thought to follow them. I put him
into the hut and shut the door — they did not come
back after him.[55]

One of the reasons, then, that Anderson (and Davy) didn't act
to stop the larger slaughter was that they were given women
to do with what they wished. It could also be said therefore
that Kilmeister 'saved' two Aboriginal women — but they
were saved only to be raped? used? by others. There was
another woman 'saved' from this massacre by another man.
She was the mother of Charly, a small boy (noted for his
'familiar and friendly way') whom Davy had tried to save —
but 'he would go along with mammy'.[56] Charly was killed, but
his mother, according to other evidence,[57] was picked out by
John Blake, who kept her, *saved her*, for 'future use'.[58] Like
putting pennies in the bank — this woman was 'saved' as only
the most brutal white economic metaphor can imply. The
colonial rationality of economy. Did this lone woman, the
mother of at least one of the suggested ten to twelve children
killed, imagine that she was saved in any other sense? Was
death by slaughter something worse in her psychology and
cosmology than knowing all her group had been beheaded,
stabbed, burnt? Would it have been better than being taken
away from her country, used by Blake and perhaps others? Did
she think she was saved? Might there also have been Aboriginal
women taken from others of the massacres carried out around
Tenterfield? And were children also used sexually and
economically? What did Bates, of 'The Bluff Rock Massacre',
intend for his 'saved' child? Was the child of Bluff Rock saved
because a dead child had hanged the others who had
massacred at Myall Creek? Had the word come back from the
Sydney — not only don't tell anyone about killing Aboriginal
people, but particularly don't tell of killing children?

This child of 'The Bluff Rock Massacre' had seen (we assume) his closest relations and friends 'wiped out', but he ran toward the legs of one of these shooters and was 'spared'. This little boy ran across and made his physical presence felt to a man holding a gun. The little boy clung to the man's legs and the man couldn't shoot. At that moment the man could have thrown the boy aside and shot him, but at that moment he didn't. And so the story goes that this unnamed boy was always 'grateful and useful' — he had been saved up for later, careful, use. He didn't send those who massacred to be hanged.

> In the early years of carrying to and from the coast the blacks would occasionally raid the teams. When Bates' teams were threatened, this boy would help to defend them and would persuade the wild blacks not to attack, so that his [Bates'] loads were never raided.[59]

And so the saved becomes the saviour on a regular basis.

MY BROTHERS SAVED KANGAROOS

My brothers and the neighbour's boys went spotlighting. It wasn't called shooting, although that was what it was. I knew it was shooting because, dressed in my Annie Oakley fantasy, I knew a thing or two about guns. I wanted to go too. My brother had already taught me to shoot a .22 when held in a stock, and I would have loved to be a part of it all. I may have even helped with the cleaning of the .303s — that was what was used to shoot 'roos. I didn't want them to actually kill anything, but I did want them to bring me a joey if they found one. And when they did bring one home I really thought my brothers had saved it. They had, of course, but by shooting its mother, the rest of the mob and then stopping, I suppose, to pull the joey from the corpse.

I set about raising that kangaroo. When it could look after itself (the test of which was when it decided to jump the orchard fence rather than wait for its enamel mug of milk) it joined a local mob, and then one day no doubt was in turn shot at, or killed, by those same brothers. My father was never a part of these shooting groups, although he would have supplied the bullets and guns. I remember years later (when the boys had left home, I think) that three 'roos had been frightened in the stallion's paddock and one had got its leg twisted in the wire. It thrashed about, caught. It was horrible to watch but we couldn't get close. Eventually it went quiet, fainted perhaps, and my father could get close enough to disentangle it. It lay on the ground with its leg bone jutting out. I suppose others would have shot it, but my father sent me for some plaster bandage which he kept in our 'vets' cupboard, and we clumsily set the leg. The kangaroo was not fully grown, which was why it got caught in the fence — it was too small to have got over cleanly — and so we put it in a lamb pen and fed it. It remained with us for a year or two, until it, too, found another mob and went on its way to be shot at somewhere else — possibly again by my brothers, home from university.

It was the idea of being saved that reminded me of my many pet kangaroos. I am not equating the lives of animals and humans, but I am fascinated by the way that 'The Bluff Rock Massacre' works to inspire and question mythologies simultaneously. On the one hand, it offers us the figure of a child saved, and on the other we see a cheap cross-cultural servant being produced. The story of 'The Bluff Rock Massacre' sets up a massacre of exceptional violence, the driving of people over a cliff, forcing all of them over *except* one child. Does the story of this child carry the longed-for possibility of redemption? Moses in the bulrushes? The single saved boy? Through him will come the undoing of the tyrants, the release of other sorts of prophecies? This child came to love his saviour, which provides a strange sort of moral justification for the massacre: it produced 'devotion' and so love. 'Hard' love?

The story of the saved child fundamentally changes the rhythm of Irby's report. He was shooting because he could, because he had the 'means and will'. And then he rode fast away to report to the Commissioner, being assured by Windeyer that he [Irby] had had 'no choice'. The space between the shooters and the shot, the fast turning away without burial or checking, implies a modern, distanced efficiency. But introducing the possibility of an indistinct line between killers and killed that could be crossed by a small boy suggests a corporeal engagement which Irby ignores. A small boy's hands clung onto Bates's no doubt warm and probably sweaty legs. Did Bates also have stains from arterial blood on him? The screams of the others in his ears? Perhaps for the first time we can now stand below Bluff Rock and have a physical encounter in our minds to contrast with the omnipresent granite. How do we feel? Or does this story of the saved child function as another mirror of whiteness, where the saving of one child proves that it is still possible to claim that the white men were operating in a moral universe? That they were punishing a group who had committed a specific crime ... but of course a child would be saved, at its own initiative or not. Do we believe it proper that such a line was drawn? Does it make these men more like us?

And who was saved? Not a baby — babies were trouble; not an adult — they were all capable of killing; and not a girl child — she couldn't be used as openly and obviously. No, a single boy child was 'saved' — a boy child who would be 'grateful' and 'devoted' to 'The Bluff Rock Massacre'.

The top hat

Was it only ever the top hat? The story is as follows: Edward Irby (or was it Leonard? or Collins, the Deepwater overseer?), while standing atop Bluff Rock, was speared through his top hat by an unknown Aboriginal person, presumably a man. No other figures come into this story as it is told to me by the caravan park owner, by a local historian, and as I read about it in the Norman Crawford records of the Tenterfield Historical Society. Was this the truth of 'The Bluff Rock Massacre'? The starkness of the scene intrigues me. Two lone men on the edge of a precipice. The lack of any connections to a larger picture makes me wonder. Where is Irby's horse? Where are the other Aboriginal members of this man's group? Was he disturbed hunting alone? Was Irby disturbed on some private assignation? Had he walked up to admire 'his' view? But I'm missing the point. This is the 'other' 'Bluff Rock Massacre'. This is the local, pared-down version, the 'real'. It is another local joke on History where the epic slaughter becomes an awkward surprised encounter. One man perhaps startled from his view, another perhaps surprised at the fall of the hat and both aware of their sudden vulnerability, decide to peacefully disperse? And so they went back to their specific sites of security, back to their endangered homes?

But Crawford's version is finely drawn. 'Collins, overseer of Deepwater Station was once attacked by blacks at Bungulla at the gully below the hall and church ... Before he could escape he received a spear through the crown of his hat.'[60] What are the elements of this tale? It is the story of a manager rather than a land 'owner', it shows a non-Aboriginal escaping his punishment not through any greater skill or technological or even moral superiority but because of the style of his dress and the quickness of his legs. Most importantly of all, this is a story of Aboriginal people attacking a non-Aboriginal working man in a gully — the geographical and social antithesis of 'The Bluff Rock Massacre'. Do all myths need the counterweight of the ordinary, perhaps the 'real'? Is it better to understand this counter-narrative as the repressed reality of frightened whites — near escapes and the threat of gullies as places of entrapment — or is it to be read as a further, 'ordinary' justification for the mythic proportions of 'The Bluff Rock Massacre' as revenge?

Tragedy

Mr James Heffernan was born in Deepwater in 1857. He spent 'the evening of his life' in Tenterfield. On the neatly typed foolscap page of Norman Crawford's Tenterfield Historical Society notes there is a subheading 'The Blacks', industriously underlined. Its two paragraphs state:

> Asked about the tradition of the blacks being driven off The Bluff by a party of white men, in the early days of settlement, in punishment for killing a shepherd and stealing sheep, he (Mr Heffernan) said he thought the story was right. It was said that the bones of the killed blacks were to be seen below the precipice and in the caves, but he had never seen any.

> In the early days of settlement on the Mole, the blacks were very troublesome and dangerous. So many shepherds were killed that it was difficult to get men to act as shepherds, as they were in constant danger of being speared. Someone gave the blacks a bag of poisoned flour, and many died through eating it. This incident was hushed up and kept as quiet as possible.

The questioner sets up that familiar Commissioner/Irbyised logical equation: killing shepherd + stealing = death/murder/ punishment. And we hear the nuanced voice of the local — 'he thought the story was right'. But as long as we are able to resist reading the story as a reductive sum, the story is right. It is necessary to open one's ears to the moral structure of this memory. Aboriginal people were driven off, Aboriginal people were killed in a variety of ways. But Heffernan, the old-time local, makes you read those words alongside 'troublesome' and 'dangerous' (echoes perhaps of Keating's 'wild and wickat'?). You must understand that the 'white men' born of these encounters were scared. It is such a little thing, such an obvious thing, and yet the whole meaning of these acts is lost without it. Squatters were driven off Aboriginal land by Aboriginal people. Squatters had already left parts of the Clarence and places further west,[61] and Irby was worried about ruin. Heffernan reminds us of fear. How could The Massacre be written with the remembrance of non-Aboriginal, white fear?

The admission that there was ever a moment when Aboriginal people triumphed over the strangers coming onto their land is hidden by the imagined size of 'The Bluff Rock Massacre' and silenced by the way the story of the massacre grows. Are all these stories of horror — but also supremacy — a transhistorical white noise that won't let that small, quiet tale of successful Indigenous resistance live?

Aboriginal people were not only 'driven off' a cliff in Heffernan's account; they were also poisoned, and following local tradition, they were poisoned by 'someone'. This is an inclusive title. Not a stranger, not a well-known landowner individually named, but the simultaneously known and unknown — 'someone'. Heffernan is not approving, but these things went on: 'this incident was hushed up and kept as quiet as possible'. Poisoning always seems to be able to be hushed up and kept quiet. Perhaps it is the silent, remote nature of poison — something taken away from town centres with no non-Aboriginal witnesses to see the sudden, silent eruptions of death. Heffernan tells us this detail after he is asked about the 'tradition' of 'The Bluff Rock Massacre', and perhaps this is the real work The Massacre does. It allows so many people to talk about silences. For partly through the techniques of silence, through keeping as quiet as possible, Australia was settled. But this silence is no longer a shared virtue — it has become an oppressive secret. By the time Heffernan says his piece in the 1940s it had become impossible to assume that everyone was against Aboriginal people or that you could rely on every non-Aboriginal to participate in poisonings and shootings. At the same time, it could no longer be guaranteed that Aboriginal people would remain silent. Something had changed. Non-Aboriginals could not rely on one another and it was best to keep as quiet as possible because everyone knew that someone, somewhere (quite close) did something.

Ironically, for all the promise The Massacre offers for a final solution to Aboriginal and non-Aboriginal presence — a triumph of the 'whites' — in Crawford's hands, carefully writing down story after story, it never quietens down, is never 'settled' once and for all. The single tidal wave of marauding settlers is teased out and upset by more and further atrocities. Poison was used, non-Aboriginal people were silenced — they become quietly guilty because they knew *something*. And so the 'white' is born out of the truth of knowing 'someone' did something to Aboriginal people and the need to keep 'as quiet as possible'. This idea of flawed 'whiteness' makes the tale of The Massacre intelligible as a tragedy.

If we take three core elements — 'punishment' (but wrongful punishment stuck in an immoral historical moment), chase (the action) and the hideous throwing over the cliff that is murder (the finale) — we have tragedy. This is not the tragedy of a stumble before triumph, since Irby et al. did not hesitate, and within their own terms they did triumph, but they were fatally flawed by their incapacity to see what their violence would go on producing in the nation to come. As a mistaken nemesis, those who committed massacre become the fools of non-Aboriginality. They keep alive a play of silences that tells us something about the quiet of the countryside. But how that 'quiet' about frontier violence is managed in the present also makes for a more Ibsenian tragedy where a society is revealed as stuck or diseased, fatally unable to restore itself.

I understand tragedy to be a morality performance that acts out the possible ways we both encounter and temporarily resolve what is humanly right or wrong in the realm of the emotional and the political. Tragedy also offers a transportability that allows it to be performed for many audiences. In these sorts of ways I see the tourist leaflet about 'The Bluff Rock Massacre' as tragedy. That it exists within the space of tourism is entirely appropriate, because tourism presents its stories to audience after audience. But a tragedy starring a fool who must now perform along highways and in the face of television and historical rewrites can't always be heard. And do we now know too much for the tragedy to be sustained? These kind of pasts don't stay on the stage.

When you attempt to show what really happened on Bolivia, around Tenterfield, near Glen Innes — that is, what happened at 'home' — you discover connective tissue of such detail and seeming pettiness that mine (and now your) entwining with these events becomes unbearable. What begins as tragedy spills into the audience, fills up our pockets, drags us down and dissolves the line between stage and floor. A wild historical melee breaks out. Irby and Windeyer shot so many Aboriginal people and then part of that land was taken up by selectors and then 'Bow Wow' was killed and Tommy started to work for Irby and some of the selectors married Aboriginal women and some of the early 'tourists' raped Aboriginal women and girls and of course some of the men had sex with each other on a 'womanless' frontier and then the postwar migrants came and on the spot where old Fanny died the Greek Café was built and now across the road the Land Council rents and down the street there is the tourist office and the Aboriginal Cultural Tours — we can't walk out. Tragedies end, but an endlessly read and reread history can't. How could this 'tragedy' become testament? We can only hush up and keep 'as quiet as possible'.

Silences can be the trembling of desire for the deeply unsaid, but when does silence become a sustained forgetting? A forgetting so constant that even when you want to speak you find, with a shock, that your dumb fumbling lips cannot say what should be said, never having heard the right words. Are we kept or do we keep 'as quiet as possible'?

Practical demoniacs

There is a popular tale in Tenterfield at the present time that many years ago a large tribe of blacks was driven over Bluff Rock by the white settlers in revenge for the murder of a shepherd. According to Mr Henry Bates this story is untrue. However many natives were driven over the precipice at Demon Creek for committing three murders — one two miles from Bolivia on the Deepwater river and another at Trelongon situated below Mahers property at what was in those days an old Commissioners camp.[62]

They were tracked along the eastern side of the range towards Demon Creek. Coming on them on the side of a deep precipice, the avenging party attacked them and wiped them out ...[63]

The blacks who were camped on the river bank in the bend were attacked at daylight. They immediately stampeded and sprang into the river and swam across losing some of their number on the way. A steep bank had to be climbed on the far side, and numbers were shot as they climbed the bank.[64]

The Demon Creek story inspires a very useful mixture of the practical and the mythical. The idea that a particular massacre (amidst all the ongoing, 'ordinary' massacres of small groups shot in paddocks, trapped in gullies and poisoned near riverbanks) of particular ferocity and spectacular plunges did occur would seem to partially explain the continuing resonance of the story. And it is therefore sensible to suspect that it happened — but not at Bluff Rock. Demon Creek makes a much more practical 'fit' between events. It has the open areas bordered by cliffs to the river upon which mounted men and guns could do the man-oeuvring that would force Aboriginal people over a cliff. The strategic struggle could well have been over the race to get to the place on the cliff that was safe to climb down, a place impossible for the mounted non-Aboriginals to follow. If the Aboriginal people had made it to that point they might have got away, but somehow their escape was cut off, and so we have the same scene, in a different location. Guns, cliffs, horses; the murderers and the about to be murdered. To paraphrase Irby, all that was needed to kill Aboriginal people was the 'will', the 'means' and the 'opportunity'.

But the name 'Demon Creek' also connects this story with the only biblical story I could find about a cliff-side massacre.

Given the power and ubiquity of the Bible in the years in which the massacre story has been told, retold and reinvented, I wondered if it might carry some particular biblical intent or undertow that might help explain its pervasiveness. When I turned to the Bible, however, the only story I found was that of the parable of the Gadarene demoniac.

This is a strange parable. The Gadarene was a raging, powerful maniac who was possessed by demons. When asked by the Lord for his name, he replied:

> 'My name is Legion for there are many of us.' And he begged earnestly not to be sent out of the district. Now there was on the mountainside a great herd of pigs feeding and the unclean spirits begged him, 'Send us to the pigs, let us go into them.' So he gave them leave. With that, the unclean spirits came out and went into the pigs, and the herd of about two thousand pigs charged down the cliff and into the lake, and there they were drowned.[65]

This parable, when mapped onto the geography of its site, also has a problem with 'fit'. The nearest lake to the Gadarenes was eighty kilometres from the mountains where the maniac was found, so the pigs would have had to run miles to drown in a lake, not simply 'down a cliff' — but perhaps anything is possible in the realm of 'possession' (Keating, too, has the Bolivia workers running nearly sixty-five kilometres up Bluff Rock). And it is in only one version of the massacre, involving a creek, that Aboriginal people died in the river itself through drowning. In the Bible, the swineherds ran back to the towns to tell the inhabitants what had happened and Jesus was begged to leave.

In his musing novel *Rings of Saturn*, WG Sebald questions this parable in an aside. Was this:

the report of a credible witness? If so, does that not mean that in healing the Garadene Our Lord committed a serious error of judgement? Or was this parable made up by the evangelist, I wondered, to explain the supposed uncleanliness of swine: which would imply that human reasoning, diseased as it is, needs to seize on some other kind that it can take to be inferior and thus deserving of annihilation?[66]

Did the logic of colonial reasoning also require the 'inferior' who are deserving of annihilation? The colonial allegory provides one sort of translation. What is a 'settler' but a figure possessed of the cultural 'madness' of another civilisation? Trapped in another land, weren't his guns and sheep and stations the unfettered displays of one utterly untranslatable; possessed, perhaps? His obvious, frightening strength insisted that he was given a place through his violent taking of place, and yet he was tormented. Where was this torment finally cast? Into the bodies of the Indigenous. They had to be 'sacrificed' so the colonial man could 'go'/make home. For this is how the parable ends; after being cured, the man begged to stay with Jesus but Jesus said, 'Go home to your people and tell them all that the Lord in his mercy has done for you.' And so the man, the colonial, returns — or perhaps metaphorically 'makes' — a home.

I'm not certain that we can sustain this reading. This is the problem with a parable and, of course, history. It is a story, and as such is open to a certain range of interpretations. As a simple tale of the ferocious need for an 'inferior', for an 'other', 'The Bluff Rock Massacre' (and the perhaps real bodies at Demon Creek) slides into the position of cultural exemplar. On the level of meta myth and psychoanalytical resolution it satisfies, but as a 'history', and something to be lived with, it is far too complete. What does this story look like in its more grounded context? Who was possessed? Why?

In the New Testament story, the demons, having passed into the bodies of the pigs, rushed over the cliff, falling to drown in the lake. But in the Tenterfield story it was the pursuers who were possessed, who rode on and on after the group and — unlike the biblical antecedent? parallel? tangent? — were possessed by possession itself. What energies and spaces must be produced to maintain 'ownership' of stolen spaces? To possess them? The actions are haunted, suffused by original sins; and they are an uncanny putting together of previous spaces that had Indigenous names and meanings, to create new assemblages called 'my place' and Bolivia Station and Bluff Rock. Has some Mephistophelean arrangement been made? Are the sufferings and the torments of those possessed by demons now a necessary resource, an engine of settlement? I don't want to tell this as the making of a symbolic otherplace; that has been done to Australia often enough. This colonial taking of land is a 'practical' rearrangement. There is a need for a judgement of truth and conduct to be made because of who kept the land — the displacement of a particular sort of God happened along the way as mere land-hungry men took up the task of deciding annihilations. And this pragmatism reigned. There are many suggestions about where God may have been displaced, but could I add Tenterfield circa 1840 to the list?

All these Gods and Demons might make this story too 'literary' — available for the invigoration of the dangerous lie of final dispossession. That is why we need to combine the ideas of the 'practical' and the 'possessed' to describe the impassioned, embedded, cultural rituals of massacre. The 'truth' of this event must lie somewhere amongst the circulation of colonial capital and the sharp theatrical rituals of the wheeling horses, the tales told and the shooting, the act of metamorphosis. This event has more than one staging, more than one audience — but exactly who is the audience and who are the players is not always clear. This is not theatre proper, after all, with its staged division between audience and players. Those Aboriginal people who did not escape (and out here, not trapped under rocks, some no doubt did), and those who were killed, were in no position to appreciate these performances. The riding and the wheeling was for the benefit of the murderers, one to another. The stories they were inventing for each other on the ride back, perhaps with the help of extra rations of alcohol — these were the 'speaking parts' that let them live again as 'ordinary' men.

The story of Demon Creek — removed from the Bluff, and from Irby — may place this story closer to the Myall Creek Massacre. The Demon Creek massacre may have been a group of station workers on a hunt, not a landowner on a sepulchral 'punitive expedition'. Some of the motivations behind such actions may have included the fact that Aboriginal workers were doing unpaid work and were therefore pushing down wages. An attack would simultaneously excite the violence and maintain the legend of violence associated with the land 'beyond the limits', and the non-Aboriginal worker could demand higher wages when working there. The freedom for those ticket-of-leave men to move beyond their assigned districts had come through their absentee landlords (and the importance of their labour in these districts), but it is unclear whether or not such conditions existed in the more closely settled New England.

But if a massacre didn't happen at Bluff Rock, why say it did? Because it's there? Because if it's there, there has to be a 'practical' use? reason? for it? It will serve as the site of the past. It fits the bill. As a site of a single, extraordinary massacre, the natural singularity of the bluff is a suitable venue, but as a symbol of the culturally regulated terrorism committed by working men, and of the killing expeditions of landowners, it doesn't work at all. And even an isolated precipice on Demon Creek is too particular for me: once more, the gaze is displaced from those elegant old homes, those cute cottages and well-kept gardens. Sent far from the rich grazing lands and non-Aboriginal back and front yards, to a rough precipice in 'bad country'. How useful and how 'practical' to believe that *that* is where it all happened. And if we do not think of the cottages and the paddocks and the neatly organised cattle, we will never remember the cars and the roads and the reservations and the barristers and the cities which made the systematic dispossession and dispersal of Aboriginal people possible. That is far away.

And perhaps there is a faint unbroken line back to an Aboriginal story that Bluff Rock was always a part of some 'bad country'. Perhaps the earliest killers and settlers, on finding out that no Aboriginal people would go near the bluff, filled in the rest with their own displaced stories — found a gap which could be practically filled. Which allowed everything to be explained. Or is it the old insistence that nature prove the myths of the non-Aboriginal? The non-Aboriginal foundationalist tale that non-Aboriginal people *possess* the land.

A word from the government

Extract from 'Reminiscences During the Fifties', by Hon. A Norton, MLC, read before the Royal Society of Queensland in 1902.

> The only notable places on the way was the Bluff Mountain and the Mole River. Of the Bluff there is a tale of black hunting and slaughter by the settlers. Some people say they believe it. In my own opinion if there is any foundation of truth in it, a grossly exaggerated story has been built from very little.

Exactly. But what is gross, what is little and what is 'truth'?

The local poet

Massacre of Aborigines at Bluff Rock 1844
by Col Newsome (1981)

The rich lands ran enough stock
But the white man wanted more!
The dark tribe met at Bluff Rock
When the whites made open war.
Squatter, settler, herder,   5
Rode out that day to kill,
Rode for rape and murder,
Rode on the devil's will.
But the tribe had danced to a frenzy
In the death corroboree!   10
Oh! Couldn't those pale faced men see
What the sad outcome would be?
The tribe, a death song chanting,
Ran to the Bluff Rock rim,
Where it fell in a cliff, not slanting,   15
Straight down, and its depths were dim.
Decked with daub and feather,
Husband child and wife,
The dark ones leapt together
As they had been in life!   20
Sweethearts, sisters, brothers,
They all leapt hand in hand,
In-laws, fathers, mothers
Leapt for the spirit land!
Did his destruction shock him?   25
Did the white man feel remorse?
Looking down from the crest of the rock rim
Astride his sweat-stained horse
Where the dead dark tribe distorted
Their limbs all twisted lay?   30
The stock horse shied and snorted

And the white man rode away.
A stench rose up to the highway,
All animals left the place,
And the teamsters made a by-way   35
Round the bones of the martyred race.
No sign to tell the violence
Once enacted there,
The white man keeps his silence,
In shame we all must bear.   40
Let us probe no more this mystery
The powers refuse to name,
An event from Australian history
The whites exclude in shame.
Bluff Rock! Clear as glass where   45
New England Highway wends,
A million tourists pass there
Yet none may tell their friends
This tale of words in magic,
While listeners hold their breath,   50
Of the dark tribes' splendid tragic
Noble leap for death.
When you pass there, hold your breath, keep
One brief moment still,
Remember the dark tribes' death leap   55
From the crest of the rugged hill.[67]

Edward Irby, owner of Bolivia Station at the time,
wrote: 'We punished them severely and demonstrated
our superiority ...'

Thomas Keating, in his memoirs, wrote: 'After
shooting some, the men got up to the rock and threw
the blacks off the rock to the ground below ...'

Old hands, including 'Beardy' George Stewart, reared
by the Irbys, said, 'Some were thrown over, others
jumped.'[68]

This poem reworks the massacre as a heroic and resistant leap by the Aboriginal people themselves when faced with the overwhelming odds against them. Thematically it can be linked to *Waltzing Matilda* and *Thelma and Louise*, with that shared desperate bravery of leaping rather than giving the 'white men' the satisfaction of killing (or catching) them. This is a very effective counter-mythology when linked to the following quote from Edward Irby's diary, which writes of the murders as a demonstration of his — and therefore white men's — superiority. Choosing to jump allows the Aboriginal people to be resistant 'forever', proving *their* superiority, and potentially links the Aboriginal people in this white bush poet's terms with the resilient heroes of other unequal encounters, such as the swaggie with the squatter and the farmer with the bank manager.

The murderous white men in this poem are not simply Irby the squatter and his station hands; they are symbolically all white men. 'Squatter, settler, herder' — all classes, all types are collapsed into one by their greed for more and more land. The only white(ish) character that is able to respond emotionally in any way to the deaths is the horse, which 'shied and snorted', and in a much more pragmatic way 'the teamsters who made a by-way, round the bones of the martyred race'. The story of the massacre, while it remains silent and excluded, is understood as creating a shameful burden for all whites to bear, here represented as the 'white man'. But if you can hear it, if you do pass the place and you know, then 'hold your breath', and be still and remember.

'Keep one brief moment still' on the highway. This seems an astonishingly quaint request. Highways are made for the mechanised movement of the car. How do you memorialise and monumentalise a moment within a movement along a highway? Highways are about travel at speed from one point determined by accommodation, food and tourist space to another point determined by accommodation, food and tourist space. At best, monuments on highways are the elegiac plastic posies marking 'Noel's Corner', 'Sally's Place' and too many others; the small crosses marking the car crashes of the past. The Cassandras of those to come. Part of their effectiveness is that we speed by them — the glimpse resonating in a more heartfelt way with what it is to drive than the guided tour with notes. To ask for a moment's stillness on a highway is to ask for a moment's silence — a stop. It makes sense to suggest that if something that stopped the highway tourists, that made them read the history, could be made — a billboard? a large cross? a memorial McDonalds? — *some* of them would fall silent, would reach for the odd comfort of quiet. But this response assumes we know the history, and only the leaflet history is available at the viewing area of Bluff Rock. There the memorial, the silent barbecues and thunderbox toilets do their bit to get us to stop and be still, but if the car did stop and the history was told in the version of this poem, what might be the effects of that silence, amongst so many silences?

I am ambivalent about silence. Its conditional nature is not easily expressed. Silence is so dependent upon its context for its meaning: here it is poignant mourning, there a pregnant pause. Silence is a kind of camouflage, asking to be understood as what it is by where it exists, and yet no one can know for sure that how silence appears is what it is. For what do silent, bowed, heads at Anzac Day *think*? Is a careful litany of rights and wrongs passing through one's mind? I'm not being quiet for the rapists, and certainly not the murderers, or those who built the bomb ... Is my resistant silence noticed? What do we do when our contemplation is organised, to some extent at least, by narrative and natural monument in concert, such as when reading the poem or the history and looking up at the rock? Is this sort of silence an effective space if we understand effective as leading to a change in how 'tourists' will understand this country? Can silence be pedagogical?

The version of the massacre that this poem is asking us to monumentalise, to contemplate in silent attention, is quite different from the versions outlined in the tourist leaflet. It insists on Aboriginal agency, the culpability of white men (which becomes a shame 'we' all share) and the powerful effects of silence, which prevents 'us' telling friends. The poet himself is suspicious of how many Aboriginal people might have actually jumped: 'Perhaps the story of the number which jumped to their death against those slain was grossly exaggerated, to placate MacDonald [Commissioner responsible for Aborigines] who judging by his record, would have enquired.'[69] This version assumes that Irby reported the deaths of the Aboriginal people, but that he reported that they had (mostly) jumped. This mass suicide was a very public event, and the poem suggests it should have warned all the men present that their greed for land and destructive raids were driving Aboriginal people to absolute desperation. As a poem perhaps should, this gives the deaths a social and emotional context that is much, much richer than the 'simpler' tales of retaliation for non-Aboriginals killed. Here the sacrifices are for the 'spirit' of the land, which suggests layers of community and cultural destruction of a mythic proportion. It is precisely this sort of death that invents martyrs, people who die for their beliefs rather than simply because they are 'Aborigines', as the non-Aboriginals (of that time) may have wanted to imagine them.

It is fairly easy to track the invention in this verse of one sort of racist thinking that has been organised around an imaginary idea of Aboriginal people identified as the 'Romantic Passion',[70] or at least a heroically inflected version of that. The chanting, the daub and feather, the frenzy and the death corroboree all contribute to the generic nature of the 'dark tribe' who are able to access particular powers for self-destruction through their exotic practices. However, the Romantic image of embattled Aboriginal people is affected by (1) its position within a poem that begins with the implication that it is white greed that has invented or demanded these reactions and (2) the poem's own existence within a 'bush' genre. The 'romantic' Aboriginal wrapped in 'historical distance' becomes here an additional Aussie underdog whose truth, like that of shearers, horse breakers and other bush folk, requires the witnessing and memory of 'old hands' of 'three or four generations'.[71]

Within the poem itself (ignoring for a moment the quotes that follow it), there is an attempt to grapple with the violence of 'settlers' and their legacy that is not confronted in the tourist leaflet. The forced or chosen leap takes up about half the poem; the rest is a musing on what the effects of those deaths are. The audience is assumed to be non-Aboriginal; 'in shame *we* (my emphasis) all must bear' (line 40). And it grapples with the act of not only saying but promoting to the passing tourists the unsaid act that has led to this shame.

'A million tourists pass there, yet none may tell their friends' (lines 47–48). This poem presents a sort of impossible tourist imagining. A haunted tourism of silences and ghosts and non-Aboriginal shame. As such it is the sayable bridge between simple promotion — 'Visitor Information' — and a desire to know and respond to history as an intimately felt phenomenon. This demand also challenges old ideas of what the rewards of small town tourism might be (for the tourists): not the 'quaint' shops (in Tenterfield, the recreated saddler shop that memorialises the Peter Allen song 'Tenterfield Saddler') and natural phenomena, but a centre and source of creative histories. The financial rewards for this are less easy to be confident about, but tourism always has its intangible side. The first effort is simply to stop the highway traveller; then the demands of human existence will account for the rest in take-away food and motel beds.

The quotes at the end of the poem challenge what is poetry. They demand that you not only read the poem for its rhythm and pacy bush style, but also contextualise it and understand its present currency. They quote Irby — 'We punished them severely ...' — and Keating — 'After shooting some, the men got up to the rock and threw the blacks off the rock to the ground below.' Both are sources the tourist leaflet uses. However, Newsome adds a third: 'Old hands, including "Beardy" George Stewart, reared by the Irbys, said, "Some were thrown over, others jumped."' This third source provides the impetus for the poem, and being a less available but personally known source, is probably considered more truthful by the poet. After these three quotes the poet goes on:

> For years New England tourist promotion bodies have searched our highways for locations of interest which tourists may find fascinating. What a laugh. They have ignored Bluff Rock, which towers majestically above the New England Highway between Glen Innes and Tenterfield. There used to be several signs pointing proudly towards this outstanding landmark. These were, strange as it may seem, pulled down just after my poem depicting the massacre was circulated.[72]

Connected to the poem, Bluff Rock had already become 'majestic', and in tourist terms, when coupled with the poem, an 'event'. Its sheer physical presence demands (the tourist promoters hope) an explanation and a possible route into other of the town's offerings. But the 'towering majesty' of Bluff Rock is not quite clear-cut. It doesn't quite match the overwhelming size of Uluru or even of Woolloo Woolloo — a competing local natural phenomenon — and close friends and even colleagues, seeing it from the highway, have described it as 'a bit disappointing'. I always respond (as residual local? looming marginal subject?) that you should have seen it before the highway was changed, when the poplars framed it and the highway drove straight towards it. As if it was once larger, as if their failure to see is temporal rather than contextual. They haven't learnt how to see it, of course. They aren't 'locals'; they are tourists, with an infinitely expanding vocabulary of comparison depending on what other sights they have seen. Is it larger?/smaller?/more majestic?/less towering? than the Taj Mahal?/Uluru?/Grand Canyon?/Great Wall of China?/Niagara Falls? This does, however, foreground the need for clear signposts to tell people that they have passed something, that it *is* something. Its significance needs the close framing of the massacre. Nature is not enough, but history is too much? *Does bad tourism make good history?*

Newsome is interesting here, suggesting that the signposts point 'proudly'. Town pride? Tourist pride? The things one finds 'highly honourable or creditable', according to the dictionary. Is this true of signposting? When understood in terms of town promotion this would seem to make sense. What local features are chosen to be underlined, highlighted? What makes up the symbolic sense of the town? But when the signs become too particular, too explicitly enmeshed in history (at least according to Newsome), they have to go. The sign becomes too heavily weighted as 'sign', too connected to meanings that might contaminate the local community. Pride, etymologically linked to the valiant and gallant, suggests a judgement that can't be sustained when connected to something more than a mere sight, an untouched natural phenomenon. If it is true that the signs were removed after Newsome's poem was circulated, it suggests that there was an explicit idea of town promotion at stake. Tenterfield must be a 'good' town. It must be a benign site of possibility outside time. This idea of timeless quiet, of tourist sanctuary, is destroyed by an association with 'real' violent history. Or it was then.

The taking down of the signs suggests a lack of faith in the ahistorical possibilities of tourism, in the way it makes things unavailable to be understood in historical terms. Why can't the promotion simply work harder and make this potentially 'fascinating history' work as tourist spectacle? After a brief history of other local massacres and some speculation about why Irby wasn't prosecuted by MacDonald (remember, he assumed Irby had reported his actions — and that Irby's wealth and relation to the Royal family saved him from their consequences), Newsome finishes his notes accompanying this poem with: 'American districts don't hide their history of aboriginal massacres. They exaggerate them. And the tourists love them. Particularly the children.' This has a mournful quality to it. I read it like a long-titled, over-run haiku:

> *American districts don't hide their history*
> *of aboriginal massacres*
>
> They exaggerate them.
> And the tourists love them.
> Particularly
> the children.

These final sentences, at least in my (mis)reading of them, gesture towards the stupendous possibilities of tourism, but also towards the possibly profound dangers of playing too much with 'history'. The poet's vision of exaggerated massacres I understand as a concentrated dramatic putsch. The hundreds of attacks and counterattacks, ethnocentric stratagems and eco-logical manipulations would be collapsed into a single event, called perhaps 'The Battle of Bluff Rock'. I am imagining the noise and dust and stunts of film (perhaps in tower-high Imax Maxivision?) where both sides are temporarily 'equal' and the final victory is made hollow as the Aboriginal people choose to leap. The attempt is to make every audience member (Aboriginal and non-Aboriginal) aware that something was lost to everyone.

But this 'feel good' (reconciling?) 'exaggeration' collapses the scales of destruction. Can the loss of land and cultural links be compared with the invention of 'guilty' historical subjects (non-Aboriginal) who are bound to be cinematically exorcised? And in particular, does this stand a chance when it would have to be motivated by profit, and would therefore become infotainment, with an emphasis on the 'tainment'? Would Aboriginal resistance, while being admitted, become forever fixed as futile, and would the children simply enjoy the stunts, the gore, the play, and make no further connection? If children, as my friends' photos show, are already playing in the grounds of deserted death camps, what could an 'exaggeration' do to 'The Bluff Rock Massacre'?

I am suspicious about evoking children at all. This thing called 'child' has become such an exponentially expanding pile of adult futurism and expectation that the assumptions of their pleasures can only be wild presumption. The ambivalence of the word 'particularly' quite nicely covers the split fears of the 'child' as innocence offended and as guilty savage. Macaulay Culkin versus *Lord of the Flies*. But let us return to 'exaggeration' as a stratagem of tourism, because it is precisely this that seems to be absent from the existing presentation of the event.

Fabulist exaggeration in tourism, via the Big Banana, the Big Pineapple and many others, are comfortable clichés of tourism. Their specific untruth makes their availability as sites of pleasure and consumerist fantasy swell.[73] But the leaflet, the many other accounts and this poem, none of which may fully satisfy the dictates of rationalist and so 'provable' history, nevertheless all have truthful rather than untruthful effects. They can compete as versions of an event, and as such court the difficulties that Newsome has already experienced. Speaking and writing of the event continues to have 'local' effects. The relationship between the actions and the tellings are still actively meaningful — they create meanings here and now that locals respond to and tourist authorities react to; they may not be true representations, but they are effective truths. The most definitive way in which these representations work as effective 'truth' is through their use of evidence from both Irby and Keating. These sources are combined in both pieces and supported in the poem by further (and similar) memories from an 'old hand'. They are primary sources, but located truths. We have looked at the locally circulated hearings of Keating. Let's now look more closely at Irby's more widely available account.

MR IRBY ACCOUNTS

The 'limits of location' were those boundaries delimiting those parts of an Australian Colony within which land is available for alienation. eg. The 1836 Squatting Act ... allowed squatting beyond the Limits, providing a license fee of 10 pounds per annum was made for each 'run'.[74]

The wider significance of the postmodern condition lies in the awareness that the epistemological 'limits' of those ethnocentric ideas are also the enunciative boundaries of a range of other dissonant, even dissident histories and voices — women, the colonized, minority groups, bearers of policed sexualities.[75]

The paddocks there are so wide open
she says you always feel
that the lid has been left off everything.[76]

Bluff Rock was once a part of the land leased and then owned by Edward and Leonard Irby. The holding, as you will remember, was called Bolivia. Edward Irby reports that he and others killed Aboriginal people, but the shape and meanings of those deaths are very different from the many local records in the Historical Society notes, and from Keating's account, and from what appears in the hybrid tourist leaflet. Edward Irby, as diary and letter writer, becomes the second source used by the tourist leaflet, and he is therefore the author of two of what I am calling 'primary' sources in this work.

I'm using the book *Memoirs of Edward and Leonard Irby* 1841 to track how and why the Irbys (and Edward in particular) become people who massacre. This points to a certain fantasy of ethnographic history. That is, I am setting out to 'discover/ invent' the cosmology of the Irbys' world at Bolivia, the 'sense' of their lives. Simultaneously I hope to signal which parts of their experience, and their record of it, allowed them to become the 'perpetrators' of The Bluff Rock Massacre.[77]

I am assuming at this point that you agree with me that Irby's shooting of trapped Aboriginal people is a massacre, but that it does not 'fit' well enough with Keating's account to become the single event, 'The Bluff Rock Massacre'. The question of 'who dunnit?' — the hope of a denouement — now needs to be dissipated, if not abandoned, so that we can begin an engagement with the multiple ways in which Irby writes himself — the always? never? not quite? sometime? massacrer.

The Irbys' account begins with their sail to Australia, but I concentrate on their records from the moment of their arrival in Australia, and focus in particular upon their writings to do with land, Aboriginal people, and their own existence beyond the 'limits of location'. In the first instance I look at the ways in which 'blackness' and 'Blacks' are used throughout this collection of letters and diary entries — there are many ways in which Irby's placements and namings change, and these illustrate his emerging identity as 'squatter'? white? non-Aboriginal? I put all letters first, followed by the diary extracts, but I arrange them in a purely chronological fashion; the diary extracts only begin in 1844.

When we look at the extracts that refer to Aboriginal people, we are looking at the words of Edward Irby. Leonard Irby contributes many fewer letters, and they are usually in a lighter vein. His diary, if he kept one, has not been saved. From here on, 'Irby' therefore refers to Edward Irby unless otherwise stated. That these examples were selected for publication should tell us more rather than less about their contextual importance. My intent is to trace the emerging meanings of Aboriginality as they were written.

I have combined the records of his representation of Aboriginal people with my interpretations and further questions. One of my aims is to show an emerging hybrid (chimera?!) which could be called whiteness or Anglo Australianism (or?), and so remind you of the other parts of the Irby self which emerge along with his process of racial invention. There is no easy reading of Irby as 'developing' or 'advancing' — there is both stasis and change in his writing — but the progressive nature of a diary, the day after day, year after yearness of it, fixes an order that is very difficult to ignore. And if it was precisely this sense of progressive change that enabled the 'settling' process, then it deserves to be properly recorded. But the relentless recording of daily developments emerges as an uneasy, banal background rhythm to the events recorded.

Natives, blacks, Blackboy and Tommy

Edward and Leonard Irby travelled first class to Australia. It was in a barque of 417 tons called the *Flora Kerr*. Their cabin was as large as the Captain's and the Mate's, and of their deck, theirs appears to be the only passenger cabin of that size. While other cabin passengers paid £70, theirs cost £160. All of this was paid for by their 'great benefactor Mr David Powell'.[78] What were they doing there? Of Leonard we know almost nothing, except a granddaughter's idea that he was considered fun but 'unreliable'. Shades of the famed 'remittance man' put under the care perhaps of the older and more responsible brother? He writes in one of his few kept letters that Edward has 'undertaken to write all the sense, and given me the *nonsense*' (emphasis in original).[79] *Australian Men of Mark* (1889) tells us that Edward had been training at the Military Academy in Woolwich when he was 'struck down by a severe illness'.[80] His health was so much affected that he found it necessary to seek a change of climate,[81] and so he came to Australia. This history suggests that Australia was a place, at least in the Irbys' imagining of it, where the climate was good and where something less demanding than a military life could be carried out. This is not a vision of a place that is an 'other world' full of frightening possibilities, but situates Australia as a part of an English whole. An extended version, perhaps, of going to the mountains from the city or retiring from Victoria to Queensland? But early in the voyage it is also the place where Edward promises he will 'live in a steady and upright manner and not disgrace [Mr Powell's] letters of introduction'.[82] This might suggest that Australia was the very sort of place where one was tempted to do otherwise, or it might point to a previous lapse, or it might simply be the offering up of moral conduct as a proof that Powell's money was well spent.

The Irbys begin full of praise for the food on board and with an intention to learn some glees, as all the passengers, 'very respectable young men', are fond of singing. They laugh at anything that goes wrong since it is so much better than 'crying or looking sulky'.[83] Weeks later Edward has decided that there is only one man whom he 'should care to have any connection with in Sydney'.[84] After some rumblings, the crew break into open mutiny and the Irbys are part of a group that capture the ringleaders and quieten the rest. As a belligerent crew member moves towards them, Edward records that it is 'kill or be killed', but the sailor doesn't move; this is a relief to Edward, for 'I was fully determined to shoot him myself if he had moved another step.'[85] From then on they take turns on watch, which they undertake fully armed and, since the prisoners are guarded in two of the steerage cabins, three more passengers come into their cabin. They run into Rio de Janeiro to have the crew charged, and Edward notes how 'enchanting' — after his cadetship at Woolwich — he finds the sounds of cannon, muskets and drums, and the sentries being challenged. And he laughs to find the soldiers using their cartouche boxes (which were meant to carry cartridges) for cigar cases. They set sail again and land safely in Sydney despite sailing under a captain who is discovered to be a dedicated drunkard.

As a journey towards 'a change of climate', one of the traditional upper middle-class roads to improvement, the outward journey must have been an ambiguous success. The spatial status of their double cabin was partially undone due to the mutiny, they had to protect their lives and property through recourse to arms, and they saw in Rio de Janeiro a dirty town with a magnificent cathedral, unreal soldiers who smoked cigars from their ammunition boxes and a bizarre currency which meant one received a bill for dinner of 2300 something! 'Quite a shock.'[86] Sydney Harbour appeared far better. While not as grand as Rio de Janeiro, Edward liked it better — he liked its creeks and islands and 'plenty of gentlemen's seats peeping out'. It *looked* more ordered. Leonard describes it lightly as a place 'infested with rats, babies, dogs and lunatics'.[87]

A NATURAL HISTORY OF THE NATIVES

Irby's first reference to any idea of colour and culture occurs soon after his arrival.

Sydney, April 18th, 1842 (Edward to brother Tom)

[On the dedication of a bronze statue of Governor Burke] One old woman seemed much disappointed when he was uncovered, for she exclaimed, with a look of dismay, "Oh, my goodness, he's a black."

This first reference to Aboriginal people that Edward records is at the expense of an 'old woman' who sees 'a black' as being anyone who was black. This may seem like tautology, but suggests that there was little division between, for example, Aboriginal town dwellers, those further afield and possibly Africans. Even Governor Burke could become 'a black' by having his colour changed. But Irby is writing this as a humorous anecdote. This horror at becoming 'a black' is proof of the silliness of this old woman. Irby knows what the colour of cast bronze is. He knows what blackness is not. In a town where they have been told to suspect everyone, and where the 'leading men' can do nothing for them — their class connections have not worked as they would in England — Irby has declared that he will follow the advice to remain steady. They have been thrown upon their own moral character, and must forge their path in the absence of an obvious class system that would have allotted a set of behaviours and activities to them.

In Irby's first encounter with Aboriginal people, one month later, he refers to them as 'natives', which signals his own foreign status: neither born in Australia nor indigenous to it. 'Native Australian' became a very early source of humour due to its ambiguous meanings of 'indigenous' and 'born', and may have precipitated the early concentration on colour as the distinguishing feature: 'black fellows' versus 'a (white) native of Australia'. The unsteadiness of language.

Sydney, May 11th, 1842 (Edward to sister Fanny)

[While on Richard Windeyer's farm Tomago, near Newcastle] Whilst walking in the evening we met a party of natives, the king of Tomago among the number. His Majesty made us a most polite bow, welcomed us to Tomago, and made his sons throw the spear and boomerang for our amusement.

This image is one entirely of calm and 'amusement'. No fear or qualms are recorded; it reads like a perfect fit between expectations and results. The 'King of Tomago' was no doubt appointed by Windeyer or some other powerful landowner and may have had a brass half-moon breastplate to 'prove' it. The status of such a position was often ambiguous. It usually marked some service to various non-Aboriginal groups and was an effort to map onto Aboriginal people the same order of hierarchies that some non-Aboriginal people lived by. It invented Aboriginal bodies that were systematised — negotiable, and part of a non-Aboriginal state. This is not to suggest that the Aboriginal people who were a part of such namings agreed with the definitions, but it is easy to observe how reassured Irby is by the encounter. He, as a 22-year-old of the right British stock, is amused by the spear and boomerang — it is 'natural' that he is welcomed by 'His Majesty', no matter how ironic the title is.

This encounter with 'royalty' occurs at the very moment when Irby is recording that their capital is their all. Their English education and trainings and their letters of introduction have proved nearly useless, except for an offer from an uncle of one of their introductees. Archibald Windeyer has offered them the opportunity to learn how to run sheep in exchange for their buying 600 head of sheep from him at the end of the year. He will pay them as nominal managers; Irby is delighted to be 'taken in and to gain experience for nothing'. At this moment the welcoming 'natives' have nothing to do with the realisation that their capital is their all. They are no threat to it, at least. Irby did not invent the 'royalty' of the Aboriginal people, but it is a curious moment to become aware of it — just when his own claims to class status have been, in his terms, replaced by the need for capital.

Three months later, the Irby brothers are on their way to New England and the Windeyer property of Deepwater.

Deepwater Station, New England, August 3rd, 1842 (Edward to sister Fanny)

[On the journey from the Clarence River to New England] There were plenty of ducks, pelicans and black swans to be seen, and also natives, to whom we threw biscuits, which pleased them very much. It amused us to see them fishing when we anchored off the mouth of the river ... They sat on a hill about a hundred yards from the river, watching. Directly they see a shoal on the shallow, about twenty run shouting down the hill as hard as they can, plunge into the water, form a circle, and all dip their nets in together, making as much noise as they can all the time. We saw them catch a great many. They then run up the hill again, make a fire, eat them, and then watch for more.

Here Irby appears to be enlarging upon his 'naturalist' appreciation of Aboriginal people. They remain 'natives', and fall all too familiarly at the end of a list of wildlife. Their humanness is not even ironically acknowledged through the self-serving titles of 'King' and 'Queen'. In this example, further from 'settlement' and during a journey where no commitment has to be made to any ongoing relationship, Irby can simply please the 'natives' with biscuits. In this moment it may be he who is the source of amusement, in fact, but his vision is of his bounty and their 'simple' pleasure. It is his eye that then records his own 'amusement' (again) at Aboriginal (Bundjalung?) fishing skills. His pleasure in the 'natives' and their indifference to him is in contrast to his revulsion at the convict and ex-convict workers who travel with them. How will he keep his distance from this group who make sin their delight?

Deepwater, August 6th, 1842 (Edward to sister Carrie [Caroline])

[On the road from Tenterfield to Deepwater] We did not see a single native; they seldom come near a road.

'Natives' who don't come near the road suggests a wild shyness that fits with the 'amusing', 'natural' wonder that is the 'Aborigine' to Edward Irby at this time. There may also have been other stories circulating, even within their small party, but the Irbys' determined separateness would probably have silenced the telling of them. In this journey Irby records how he and his brother talked mostly of 'old times' and played their flageolets, and it is possible that they arrived at Deepwater with a stronger sense of their English selves than ever before. This is a cultural rebirth through nostalgia, and some of its inventive powers are dependent upon these diaries and letters — both of which were sent 'back home'. It is these writings that insist on Edward's sameness with the rest of his family, who are also outside the 'limits of location' for him, as they occupy the original home. These letters become a vehicle of 'locatedness'; they place Irby's actions before an audience of people 'like him' and make available a community beyond the people physically available to him. Irby wishes he had gained more riding practice.

MAKING BLACKS/MAKING CARTRIDGES

Five months after their arrival in Australia, one month after arriving at Deepwater, 'beyond the boundaries', Irby records his first effort to kill Aboriginal people. What has happened to his simple delight in their antics? The sureness of his amusement? Attempting to kill Aboriginal people is never, in his reports at least, the action of an individual. In this instance it is a communal activity that gathers up the workers (two of whom have wives and children) who live in the six huts that surround the homestead or head station. And it brings in the two shepherds and watchman from each of the four outstations, all about three miles (five kilometres from the head station.

Deepwater, September 10th, 1842 (Edward to father)

[When report of missing 205 sheep came in, a party of eight is got together to go after the 'natives'. This account takes up two and a half pages, hence the rolling extracts.]

We had plenty to do the remainder of the evening making cartridges ...

There were eight of us, five on horseback and the other three on foot. We took a couple of dampers and some tea and sugar ...

About five in the afternoon we came to a creek, where the natives had encamped and had two or three sheep for supper ...

[Lose track and spend afternoon regaining it.]

Night came on, and we remained for the night about a quarter of a mile from the Blacks camp ...

[Much more often fruitless tracking until find footprint by chance.]

The natives had chosen a capital place to retreat to, where they had encamped; there were two terribly steep ridges, really impossible for anyone to go down without breaking his neck ... The camp was about 60 feet [20 m] above the gully, but slanted down to it, so they could soon get into it ... There were about 100 of them. They of course took refuge in the deep gully, of which we had no idea till we got to the camp. We completely routed them, and remained in possession of the camp and all their traps. Such a scene I never wish to witness again. There were about 30 fires, and as many sheepskins, also the meat of about 16, cut up in small pieces, half roasted and covered with dirt, nets and baskets half filled with meat ... We found three wedges, a pint and quart pot, a blanket, and a pair of trousers, which we have great reason to suspect they took from a poor man whom they murdered near here about a fortnight ago ...

There were 102 sheep left ... We made a large fire and burned everything belonging to them; we also found spears, skins of opussums, &c &c ...

We got home at 4 pm the next day well satisfied with our success.

This is described as an 'expedition in the bush'. 'Expedition' has always carried the meaning of warlike enterprise, and Edward, with a military vocabulary at his fingertips, used the term precisely. Since the head station is more or less in the middle of approximately 22,260 hectares and has four outstations spread around it, all about five kilometres out from the main station, there are circles of increasing and decreasing 'settlement'. The outer stations are close to the boundaries of the property, which are marked comprehensibly but also ambiguously by hills and creeks. In simple terms, the property of Deepwater occupied the rich, river-fed plain and ended in the foothills of the rough range country on three sides, and on the other side it ended at the already marked boundary creek of the next-door acreage, 'Wellington Vale'.

The expedition works its way through the station's hierarchies, temporalising each position. First the watchman from the outstation (presumably on foot) arrives with the 'intelligence' of the 205 missing sheep. 'Intelligence' gives the figure of the watchman a military air and properly identifies his particular flexibility to move. Unlike the nominated shepherd, who must stay with the sheep, the watchman must take the messages, make the meals and sleep with the sheep. In moments of emergency it is he who moves through the bush to the 'home' centre. Linked with convictism, and not even a shepherd, the watchman is associated with the activities of the night rather than the day, and it is perhaps only within the drama of possible attack that this figure becomes known by his master as carrying (no matter how momentarily) 'intelligence'. There is an immediate response, but it is not the Irbys, nor young Windeyer (not yet of age — nineteen? twenty?), who start out; it is the overseer, Collins, who sets off with two or three men — out of the centre of the head station security, past Three Mile Creek, past the outstations, past Seven Mile Creek and then beyond, into the bush proper.

It is too wet for Windeyer on that day and too wet the next, but when no one returns with any news and Friday 'being a fine day',[88] Windeyer finally sets out. It is as if there is an inverse relationship between reaction time and status. Only someone wholly in charge could wait so long to act and appear to respond only to the weather, not to human-carried news. As a performance of autonomy, of being above events, Windeyer's exit/entrance is beautifully timed. Windeyer's going out is the dramatic finale for the Irbys, who wait anxiously for his return until the next day. As he doesn't return, they then follow him out. Two of them, one of him; they follow rather than lead, for they are, after all, there to learn. The Irbys meet Collins and some men returning. Collins has found a sheep between some rocks, so they are now all aware that Aboriginal people have taken the 205 sheep.

That evening they make cartridges. Where did they make these cartridges? In some large open space or inside one of the small huts in some communal act of preparation? In individual huts? Did all of them make the cartridges? Given the security that would have been accorded to their supply of gunpowder, the careful controls that limited how much of it went into their ticket-of-leave men's hands, it is likely that this was one moment when the careful spaces between people of differing status were moderated. The dual requirements of overseeing the use of the gunpowder and needing all labour would have been met by the making of cartridges together. It is a complex moment within station life. To do the same task together in the same room provides for a moment of suspension when subtle reversals may have occurred. A watchman may have shown Edward an easier way to roll the paper around the gunpowder, or Leonard may have amused all with a joke as he bit down on the end of the paper cylinder and packed it into his leather pouch. Perhaps such moments offered the social space for the usual order to be seen as sensible and right, as something that would re-emerge as the correct way in the morning — or was that order doubted? Was there something particular about the smell and touch of gunpowder and paper that made of this event a sensory otherworld, far from the odours of sheep and gum? Or was it a moment of glimpsed equality? A moment that led to the idea of non-Aboriginal mateship as a means of out-negotiating the existing white(ish) hierarchies? Would the atmosphere have been one of excitement or fear or grim familiarity? The Irbys were probably the only virginal expeditioners. At dawn the next morning they rode and walked out to meet Windeyer and the other men.

Altogether there were eight men, five on horseback and three on foot. If Collins, the Irbys and Windeyer each had a horse, was the fifth given to someone whose status was already established or who was marked as having a particular skill in tracking or riding which suited such situations? Were there rivalries and tensions over such decisions, or was this already an order well established and accepted to varying degrees by all? They follow a trail of sheepskins, fires and marked trees. When they hear the Aboriginal group below them, Collins and Windeyer ride straight down the ridge. The Irbys recognise that they will be thrown off down such an incline and hand their horses over to be held by a man who was already in charge of holding a colt they had brought along (the colt was not to be ridden — they were taken out with other horses to get used to being handled before formal breaking in). But the camp that had looked so attackable from above proves to be more strategically placed than Irby's English military style of warfare expected. Below this camp is a deep, covered over gully through which the entire group of one hundred is able to flee before Windeyer and Collins are down the ridge. And this next gully is too steep for horses and too dense for tracking ... or perhaps they are afraid. They go no further. They are over thirty-five kilometres from the head station, and are between leases of land, in a crack of un-named space.

Their shotguns, loaded with paper cartridges, could only kill up to about fifty metres, and the Aboriginal group had already slipped much further away than that. The technologies of horse and gun which elsewhere might claim spaces that allowed expansive murders were here useless against a competing sense of strategy based on a very different knowledge of the country. The expeditioners stay at this camp and burn all the Aboriginal belongings that remain. The alternatives to a fire would have been the successive snapping of spears and hacking apart of baskets, but they put all into one big fire. Irby doesn't record whether or not 'souvenirs' were taken. Did they make the burning of the camp of about 100 people a redemptive, purifying moment? Their fire was a single 'large' one;[89] they did not use the twenty-nine other small ones.

Theirs was a different use of fire. Unstrategic, destructive, neither covering tracks nor attracting kangaroos by initiating new growth, this was an anti-fire. This one large fire was an attempt to disrupt the communal force of the thirty small fires. The signs of organisation among the group of about a hundred were all around them: the nets and baskets filled with cooked meat, preserved in a layer of 'dirt' (more probably ash) and the signs of adaptation — a pair of trousers, a blanket, a quart pot and three wedges (to split wood).

The expeditioners had only two small pieces of damper each, and yet they would not eat any of the food around them. And so the expeditioners, all except the man holding the horses above them, waited in front of the fire until all the Aboriginal 'traps' were burnt.[90] This is the other moment, after cartridge making, when they are all together, acting in unison, doing more or less the same tasks. Mateship?

As they climb out of the camp, they discover that the man who has been looking after the horses has found the remaining 102 sheep. A tenth of Windeyer's flock has been taken by the Aboriginal group. The Aboriginal group has been able to exploit a new source of protein and fat in an extremely efficient way. Did they suspect that these sheep would not be in the same place when they returned? Could the sheep be depended upon as a new, exploitable food source, or had they merely upset the systems of continuous food harvesting by their temporary presence in places where kangaroos should have been? Were the sheep more continuously there than any indigenous food source, which would suggest a permanency that was profoundly disturbing? If sheep were always available to eat, should one stay nearer them? Should overtures be made?

From this action onwards, the 'natives' become 'the Blacks' in Irby's hand, although not consistently so. It is only after the second night out, and only in his description of the 'Blacks camp' that the word emerges. At this camp Irby is disturbed by the scene: 'such a scene I never wish to witness again'. One wonders what might be disturbing him. Does what he saw this night affect how he will figure the murders he will commit? How he will write and imagine and give moral sense and meaning to them? The moral rhythm of the record of this first expedition is that the pursuit of Aboriginal people was an adventure. Their spirits are high, the 'bushing' (going into the bush) goes well and, after completely 'routing' the Aboriginals, the expeditioners are 'well satisfied with their success'. In such expeditions the authority of the three young managers of the right class invents itself again. Aboriginal people become the symbol around which new constructions of 'we' and 'our' emerge. The ex-convict labour becomes a part of 'our' success and the station begins to become the 'village' that is to be protected from the outside attack of 'the Blacks'. Since these pursuits take Irby into rough and often unknown country, there are also natural hurdles to overcome — and all of this is deadly serious. There is no 'amusement' at the 'native' ways: 'the Blacks are a nasty, treacherous sort of fellow'.[91]

I plot out the approximate movements of these men on a recent topographical map in an effort to discover land — and in particular, hills and cliffs — that might have been the site of such events. When Irby reports that they were now twenty-two miles (thirty-five kilometres) from the head station I draw a large, to-scale circle around the head station. The tip of my pencil runs beyond my sister and brother-in-law's property. They are within the field of possibility. This had not occurred to me. Smaller properties, roads and the cultural traditions of travelling towards the larger town had never connected my sister and brother-in-law with Deepwater Station, but there they are. And so am I. It is not a shock. I feel thoroughly grounded, as if in this discovery I have somehow finally overcome the speculative and the proven parts of this book and seen the ways in which a liminal past is embedded in my present. It is natural that the once isolated sites of massacre will have become someone's backyard, my backyard. The irony of fears of losing one's 'backyard' to a Native Title claim are achingly rich. Isn't something already lost to the idea of 'Freehold Title' when you live over unremembered graves? What is free? What are you to hold? But this twenty-two mile radius of possibility also includes the whole of the current village of Deepwater, a large slab of the New England Highway, miles of prime grazing land, steep rocky hills that are still uncleared except for small inroads made by the discovery of minerals at other times in history, the Japanese-owned feedlot, the city-based QC-owned stations, the struggling marginal cattle growers who try to get some return from those rocky ranges, and so many other communities with nothing in common — all are thus mapped onto what only looks like a shared geography. They are all within the field of possibility.

Deepwater, December 6th, 1842 (Edward to father)

We have not been troubled with the Blacks again, but about a week ago they killed the shepherd of a settler between this and the Clarence, and took his flock, but they regained them all but 50 the following day. The settler had but lately commenced, and he had but few sheep so it is a very great loss to him in fact there is not a single station between this and the Clarence that has not a flock taken off it by the natives since we have been up here, and in two or three cases the shepherd has been killed. [Station currently surrounded by smoke] ... generally supposed that these large fires are caused by the natives dropping their firesticks accidentally and not from any design on their part of trying to burn the settlers out of their station. They sometimes burn the old grass off, in order that they may have a chance of killing the kangaroos when they go to feed on the young grass that springs up, and also when they think they are likely to be pursued they fire it to prevent their track being seen.

... If he [the settler] had that [£1600] he might safely commence because if both Blacks and catarrh attacked his sheep he would still have something to fall back upon; but how would it be in our case?

At this time the 'amusing natives' have become more usually the relentless 'Blacks' who nevertheless still 'accidentally' drop their firesticks. Irby's sympathy now extends towards other settlers affected, no matter what their convict history is, and he begins to draw anxious parallels with his own situation. How would it be in his case? All this is written in an atmosphere filled with smoke, and although his 'steady' response is that of course 'the Blacks' are not intending to burn them out, the atmosphere is literally and metaphorically dark. He has been advised that a commitment to sheep means that you should stay in the colony for life and he worries about the stopping of transportation. 'Blacks' and catarrh (in sheep) are the two greatest fears and greatest impediments to getting on and making profit. Catarrh was thought to be caused by sudden falls in temperature (and/or other atmospheric changes) and/or passed on by other sheep, so the 'native' climate or passing sheep were to blame. Like the actions of Aboriginal people, these factors could not be completely contained by the actions of the Irbys. They had to rely on their shepherds' independent efforts to ensure that the sheep did not experience severe temperature drops, and the shepherds and the Irbys' other workers had to be constantly vigilant as to the passing of foreign sheep or the activities of Aboriginal people. All these fears are now present and personal for Edward. Not only Windeyer's interests are explicitly at risk from 'the Blacks' and from nature; his own are as well.

The Irbys complain that they have to fish without shade and that the overly hot sun spoils all beauty by making everything brown rather than green; the Irbys too would have been turning brown, that sun and wind beaten brown of arms and face. A working man's tan! Even the ability to appreciate the beauty of the rough country of the station, the wild places, is curtailed and ordered by Aboriginal people and the vagaries of sheep: 'And the trees are nothing more than caricatures excepting in the rough country. There they certainly grow finer and you may then also see many beautiful wild flowers but then again you seldom go into the rough country unless it is on some unpleasant expedition after lost sheep and at that time you think very little about wild flowers and scenery.'[92] The Irbys contemplate leaving and returning to England, 'for if a man embarks his capital in sheep, he must do so with the full expectation of remaining in this country for life. Now we could live very comfortably here for ten or twelve years, supposing we should be able to return to England after that period; but knowing we should have to remain here all our lives would make even the first ten years miserable.'[93]

MISSING RECORDS

Within the missing sixteen months of these records, Irby does not leave but takes up a station, Bolivia, next door to Windeyer's Deepwater. What happened in these sixteen months? Were there other letters that were edited out? Did the 'real' Bluff Rock massacre happen in this time and make the Irbys' naturalisation as white Australians complete? What events transformed a moment of literal darkness and anxieties about success to a decision to buy an adjoining property and begin grazing in their own names? What became of the 'firm conviction that we should never be reconciled to the idea of staying here for life'?[94] For in taking up Bolivia they have begun their 'life sentence' in Australia.

WAR, COMPROMISE, PARTICULARITY

Thursday August 15th, 1844 (Diary of Edward Irby at Bolivia)

Tracked the Blacks from Deepwater nearly to the Gap. When I got home, could see the smoke from their fires on the Dividing Range.

Monday August 19th, 1844

... He [Windeyer] told us he had seen our bullocks tearing along the road, one of them having two spears sticking in his side.

Tuesday August 20th, 1844

Feel confident our bullocks were speared by Windeyer's Blacks.

As owners, and so completely responsible for their own stock and station, the Irbys have more formally joined a community of squatters. There is a constant intersharing — sharing and sharing again — of supplies and labour, and the 'outside' is now not so clearly defined. It is now just as likely to bring in someone with much-needed flour or decent tobacco. These exchanges are not always entirely equal, and there is some griping. But these movements back and forth between stations (including at least four others besides Windeyer's) seem to have also included some more careful identification of Aboriginal people. For the first time, a group of Aboriginal people are named as being associated with a fellow settler. 'Windeyer's Blacks' suggests that some rapport has been established. Irby is still carefully tracking 'Blacks', but these presumably are not 'Windeyer's'. The fact that Irby can still suspect 'Windeyer's Blacks' of spearing his bullocks suggests a very loose arrangement with the group. This Aboriginal group, while identified with Windeyer, is certainly not constantly at his beck or call or restrained to his property limits. The circulation of resources that the squatters are practising seems a sort of communicative nomadism where limited resources are shifted about from run to run, perhaps an inverted version of the Aboriginal practice of moving from one resource area to another in an established cycle of care within a designated area. The clear, hard divisions between Aboriginal and non-Aboriginal appear to be getting less fanatical.

Wednesday August 21st, 1844

Whilst hard at work, Mark ran to me to point out smoke from a Blacks fire which was rising from the range at the back of our bullocks' swamp ... Before we had proceeded many yards further, heard some Blacks close to us ... [Irby et al. are seen, and the Aboriginal group flee except for two little boys] ... but I ran after and caught one. He immediately cried out that he belonged to white fellow, so I let him go and the other one joined him ... we heard the men coming along. We coo-ed to them, but they wouldn't come to the camp ... [one] began trying to persuade the boys to leave us, but as we had given them some bread, they were a long time before they would ...

It was very bad country, and, still thinking them Windeyer's Blacks, I didn't like to fire upon them ... As the way we got up was very rugged and surrounded with Blacks, we thought it better not to return there, but keep the most open ground. The Blacks ran along on one side of us, but taking care to keep out of gun-shot.

This is the first verbal encounter with Aboriginal people recorded; it is also the first record of resistant verbal strategies. To say you belong to a 'white fellow' is a way of buying you time, of getting away. It also collapses class and convict/non-convict into 'white fellow' momentarily. How quickly did shepherds, too, become 'white fellows' when forcing? negotiating? bribing? exchanging? to have Aboriginal people 'belong' to them? This extract establishes that the practice of 'protecting' (from whom!) — and so presumably pacifying — some Aboriginal people is known to Aboriginal and non-Aboriginal groups. And as Irby records, the possibility of their 'belonging' to Windeyer does stop him firing at them, even if their distance from him shows their familiarity with the effective distance of gunfire. But again it is clear that non-Aboriginal figures are not solely figures of dread, since the small boys are able to be coaxed with bread: there is no formidable cultural apparatus that frightens the young away from even the thought of a non-Aboriginal person. There is a hint here that some sort of exchange between Aboriginal and non-Aboriginal groups is beginning to establish itself.

Thursday August 22nd, 1844

He [Windeyer] told me he was certain they were not his Blacks but believed they were from the Severn [river], and he, Kelso, and Gardiner [neighbouring squatters] promised to come over the following day and help me drive them off ... [Bates] had seen the Blacks fires all the afternoon on the Gap Range.

Friday August 23rd, 1844

[The party detailed above sets off] Windeyer's black-boy saw a track there but it was too dark to run it.

Saturday August 24th, 1844

... The blackboy got on their tracks, but he hadn't gone many yards when we saw another smoke rising ... We went on this way for about a mile, when the blackboy said he couldn't keep the track ... We felt sure the blackboy could keep the track if he chose, but that they turned up a very steep range to our right, which he had no fancy to toil up ... it was evident the Blacks were going right away, and impossible for us to track them, we determined to return home.

Details begin to emerge of individual Aboriginal people employed on the station. The 'blackboy' becomes a very important part of their expeditions; it is he who allows them to follow other Aboriginal people into country where they cannot see any tracks. The 'Blacks', at least in this instance, are Aboriginal people not known to them. There is no suspicion in Irby's mind that the 'blackboy' might not be lazy but cleverly foiling the pursuit party. These accounts suggest that some sort of territorial readjustment is occurring; there are points beyond which the squatters are happy to let the unknown Aboriginal people go. The 'blackboy's' diminutive title suggest his lack of threat. He is a 'black' but he is also a 'boy', regardless of age. 'Boy' places him in a well-established nomenclature of colonialism/slavery where 'boy' was a native servant and/or slave. While not 'amusing' as Irby's original 'natives' were, the 'blackboy' is ascribed proclivities like laziness — a word which must have bought some comfort. There is no threat from the lazy.

Saturday October 12th, 1844

… The sheep appeared all right, so I did not think he [Robinson] had been attacked by Blacks.

Sunday October 13th, 1844

… Felt sadly afraid he had been killed by the Blacks, and still could hardly believe such could be the case without their taking the sheep.

Monday October 14th, 1844

… He [Windeyer] said he felt certain the Blacks had the sheep in that spot only for their having returned home safe. We had not gone above fifty yards down the river before we saw the body in the water.

... We determined on pursuing the murderers ...

... [Robinson, the shepherd] had been pierced with five spears, had four cuts with a tomahawk on the temples, and one blow from a waddy on the back of the head.

Tuesday October 15th, 1844

Windeyer rode over after lunch. He had been looking over the ranges in hopes of finding some clue to the direction the Blacks had taken, but could find none.

Wednesday October 16th, 1844

... Our party consisted of Windeyer, his two servants and myself. We were prepared for a week's bushing.

... we came upon a place where the Blacks had camped on Sunday and Monday night.

... Weaver sang out that he saw a Black ... We soon got up to him. Windeyer found he could understand him, so asked where the camp was. He pointed to the south east. Windeyer then told him he had killed a white man [Robinson]. He said no, but those at the camp had done it ... We rode about till nearly dark but couldn't find the camp ... [so we] camped about a mile from where we had come upon the Black.

Thursday October 17th, 1844 (Diary)

... We went at once to look about the hill where we saw the black last night. On reaching the spot we found the natives had been there, and must have heard us coming, as in their hurry they had left a fire-stick and two spears ...

... Windeyer soon caught sight of a Black and pointed him out to me ... a glimpse of the rascal bolting down the rocks ... Knowing the Blacks were in the rocks underneath us, I fired off for the two men to join us ... [I] could see the Blacks in their hiding place. Having now the means and will to punish them for the barbarous murder they had committed, we took advantage of the opportunity and gave it to them pretty severely.

Sydney, January 31st, 1845 (Edward to father, letter)

[This is Edward's letter account of the same 'punitive expedition', which Halliday and others put together with Keating's account to produce 'The Bluff Rock Massacre' account in the tourist leaflet.]

For a moment I felt certain the Blacks had been there, but when I thought of the sheep coming home safe I doubted again ...

Windeyer and I consulted for a few minutes, and determined we would pursue the murderers ...

He [Windeyer] had been on the range close to where the murder had been committed, in hopes he should be able to track the Blacks, for we could form no idea in which direction they had gone, but without success. We started early on Wednesday morning, prepared for a week's trip, but with very little expectation of our finding them.

... [I] could see nothing of the Blacks, although it was evident they had but just been there.

... The Blacks had heard us coming, and hidden themselves among the rocks ...

If they had taken to their heels they might all have got off safe. Instead of doing so however, they got their fighting men together to attack us, so we punished them severely and proved our superiority to them … He [Windeyer] said I had no alternative but to act as I had done.

As one more encounter with Aboriginal people, as one more expedition which is more murderously successful than others, this particular occasion — which was used as one 'proof' of the 'The Bluff Rock Massacre' — is exposed as instead no more (or less) than part of a continuing 'settlement'. To read this particular massacre as part of a continuum of warfare is to appreciate its moment in time. People, rather than sheep, are now being killed on Bolivia, and Windeyer employs and can make himself understood to some Aboriginal people. To attempt to track and kill Aboriginal people is now neither a new nor extraordinary event in quite the same way as it was two years before. Four people rather than the eight of the first recorded expedition set out, and there is no detail of the preparations or communal activity.

Robinson was killed without the sheep being taken. There exists in Irby's experience a reasonably established pattern of Aboriginal behaviour, but the death of Robinson does not fit his expectations. This suggests a number of scenarios. The most common reason for an isolated shepherd to begin relations with an Aboriginal group was access to women, so we might believe that Robinson had been abusing particular Aboriginal people, probably Aboriginal woman/en, and that he thus needed to be dealt with according to Aboriginal law and custom. Robinson is stripped; the variety of blows and numbers of spear wounds may point to some ritually sanctioned action, carried out by only those members of the Aboriginal group permitted to do such things.[95]

There are further indications that some interaction between the hutkeepers, shepherds and Aboriginal people was occurring — and between Aboriginals and the 'owners' as well, since Windeyer can make himself understood in their language or the Aboriginal man could speak English. Other reports include another watchman letting 'a few of the blacks' into the hut and giving them food. This may have been going on in fits and starts across the station. There is a possibility, then, that some of the Aboriginal people being pursued may have been known, or even well known, to the workers on Bolivia, if not to those on Deepwater; they may have been strangers to Irby, but not to all his workers. Perhaps the use of Deepwater-only personnel was a response to that suspected familiarity.

So this was not a meeting of complete unknowns. While individuals may not have known each other, patterns of movement and action were beginning to be understood. Robinson's death was probably a marker of another change in what those interactions might be. Shepherds had been killed before, but not on the Irbys' property. And Edward's response here is different from his response on earlier 'expeditions'. For the first time he must account for the killing of Aboriginal people. At other times he may have intended to kill — way back on the boat out he said he would have shot the mutineers — but now he has killed, and not a specific criminal but an entire group of people. The Blacks.

Robinson was Irby's employee, and ex-convict or not, his death requires that Irby take action that he can then account for to the appropriate authorities. Aboriginal people killing non-Aboriginal people is now a 'fact' to report to a government authority. It is his fellow 'settler' who assures him he had no alternative but to pursue and kill the Aboriginal people. The finality of Windeyer's judgement, that Irby had had 'no alternative', immediately suggests to me that he did. But now

Irby knows he can kill Aboriginal people, report the details (possibly only the death of the shepherd is required) ... and he remains 'with no alternative'. He writes 'immediately' to the Land Commissioner. I wonder with what emotion that writing was done. Excitement? Determination? Worriedly?

There is a similar gathering up of peoples as in the Irbys' first expedition with Windeyer. Edward first hears that a shepherd, Robinson — but not the sheep — is missing, from another watchman, Fox. He then sends Mark, who appears to occupy the position of overseer, out to his outstations to have the two other shepherds or watchmen help search for the missing man. In doing so they bring the strangely unmoved sheep in to the head station. The sheep come in, the other men come in, and a letter goes out to Windeyer. When the body is found and the joint decision to pursue 'the murderers' is made Windeyer returns to his home to prepare and Edward and Fox bury the body. That there is no record of Edward's preparation alerts us to the fact that no one from Bolivia except Edward himself goes. Leonard is away in Sydney, but what of the others? Since Bolivia is a smaller holding, with fewer workers than Deep-water, is it simply unable to supply the manpower? Or has Windeyer already been established as the 'best' organiser and perpetrator of such expeditions? Or are the Bolivia workers in some way doubtful? The fact that Irby goes with Windeyer and two of Windeyer's servants marks this sort of massacre as a very different cultural event from the more sustained raids across the land exemplified in official guise by Major Nunn's 1830's campaign of 'sharp measures'[96] and in unofficial guise by the Myall Creek Massacre.[97] And the fact that Irby et al. shot rather than hacked open with swords might support the view that non-Aboriginal people killed Aboriginal people using the rituals that Irby et al. were familiar with.[98] Irby had had military training, so he knew about strategy, surprise and victory, and if his murders look more 'rational' — orderly? organised? — in their careful pursuit and unblinking extermination to us now, that should only expose the class-ridden origins of a civilised death. Think how we accept the insanely neat missile landing on a trapped town, our televisions exposing 'them' as trapped beneath us. As long as we see no blood. Have no suspicion that passions are involved in these acts.

Monday February 17th, 1845 (Diary)

... shepherd of Windeyer ... on his way to the head station to report the murder of a watchman by the Blacks. [The party organised to pursue the Aboriginal group gathers.]

... five of them [the 'party'], besides the blackboy ... Heard that the Blacks had been seen on the ranges close to Bolivia.

Tuesday February 18th, 1845

... For two or three days before the murder he [the dead watchman] had allowed a few of the Blacks to come into the hut, and had given them food ... the Blacks had struck him on the back of the head and knocked him into the fire, they then pulled him outside the hut and finished him off ... [The returning shepherd] came upon six Blacks, who were squatting down apparently with the intention of seeing what the shepherds would do on finding their mate dead ... he fired a couple of shots at them and wounded two, when they instantly made off.

Thursday February 20th, 1845

Came upon the Blacks suddenly about 11am. They had got into a dense mountain scrub, so that we couldn't half punish them ... We determined to make another attempt ... Weaver and I commenced firing, to make the Blacks believe we were all down below ... [This ruse did not succeed, and both parts of the group came together again to camp the night.] It rained all the night, and we could hear the Blacks shouting quite plainly.

Friday February 21st, 1845

... lay by the Blacks fire that night.

The further actions and the further deaths seem to point to an escalation of conflict. It is always suddenly or by chance that the Aboriginal groups are found, even with the assistance of the 'blackboy', and the landowners' and their servants' efforts to destroy Aboriginal people are never completely effective. The weather and the country keep turning against the 'settlers'. At this time Irby begins to record that strategies and ruses are at least being tried by his party. They don't work, but there is a realisation that simple pursuit rarely rewards them; they are being outmanoeuvred, and end up using Aboriginal fires and paths to return by. They have to learn Aboriginal techniques to pursue Aboriginal people. But simultaneously, the 'punishment', murder and pursuit of Aboriginal people is becoming a cultural motif of this tiny society. Such actions are usually shared, and the audience for acceptable behaviour expands to this intimate, active and available local set who reinforce the value of such behaviour. At the same time these 'expeditions' are described in terms that allow for their easy communication to a family audience 'back home' in the diaries and letters which become the lists of knowable experiences. To talk of such things presumably becomes a part of the conversation of 'gentlemen' as well as others. And there is always in the response to what Irby calls violence his refusal to see and imagine Aboriginal reason and culture beyond that of wanting sheep, so taking sheep. Six Aboriginal people waited by the man they had killed. Had that watchman, unlike the shepherd, broken particular rules and were they waiting to clarify the position with the shepherd? Was it Aboriginal people's careful delineations between the shepherds Robinson and Fox which simultaneously made them vulnerable to the crude taxonomies of massacre and enabled their highly successful, manifold resistance across a variety of landscapes and peoples?

Monday February 24th, 1845

... He [son of manager of Deepwater] brought a letter from his father requesting Len and self to meet him next day and look about the ranges, in case there should be any Blacks about.

Tuesday February 25th, 1845

... were on the ranges all the afternoon without seeing any signs of Blacks.

Sunday April 27th, 1845

... Heard that Windeyer's cattle had been rushed by the Blacks.

Tuesday April 29th, 1845

... felt sure they must be our cattle, and that the Blacks had rushed them.

Tuesday June 3rd, 1845

Fox came in just after breakfast to tell us the Blacks were on the five-mile ranges.

Wednesday June 4th, 1845

... came upon the camp, but the Blacks had seen us and bolted. Got an old gin, who had hidden; had a little chat with her, and then sent her after her tribe. She told us two tribes had been meeting; one of them had gone toward Windeyer's.

Thursday June 5th, 1845

Started for the purpose of following the Blacks, who had gone towards Windeyer's; could see no tracks; the old gin told us a lie.

Monday June 9th, 1845

... the Blacks we were after last week passed across the five-mile station on Friday, setting the grass on fire as they went.

At this time Irby must more or less trust his ex-convict workers and the doubtful pasts of his servants — they are working for him and he is dependent on them, and everyone is a long way from what was still called home — so now it is not the convicts whom you cannot trust, but 'old gins'. Again we see Irby's confusion about whom you can and cannot trust in the Aboriginal world. Because he has sought and received information from the woman, he expects that her responses will be sound in his terms.

Thursday July 31st, 1845

... he [Burgoyne] had heard the Blacks, and had seen old Bill, who had no gun with him.

Friday August 22nd, 1845

... Collins sent word that the Blacks were about, and intending to kill a white fellow.

Tuesday August 26th, 1845

Tommy and a lot of other Blacks came over from Deepwater.

Enter 'Tommy'.[99] Tommy is an Aboriginal worker; perhaps he is the 'chief' Aboriginal worker; perhaps he is Irby's first Aboriginal worker. What does it mean to be called 'Tommy'? Irby's other brother is Tom, so perhaps that was the initiating factor. Was it the diminutive of Thomas, so that the symbolic order would be kept? Or was it simply his birth name, indicative of a larger group of 'town' or 'station' Aboriginal people who name their children according to colonial convention? 'Tommy' was also a name given to other Aboriginal people in earlier places and at earlier times, so it may have had the ubiquity and implicit denigration of later names such as 'Sambo' and 'Jacky Jacky'. The name nicely records the variety of intimacies that existed.

Friday September 19th, 1845

Rode over to Windeyer's with George Page; met the Blacks coming here; sent them back on account of my bullocks.

Tuesday October 7th, 1845

... We got four Blacks who were camped here and five of us went with them to look over the ground ... The Blacks said they smelt stringy-bark burning on the distant ranges, which made me almost afraid the wild Blacks had murdered him ...

A new Aboriginal identity emerges: the 'wild Black'. 'Black' has to now be qualified with 'wild' if it is to communicate any sense of threat, since 'Blacks' are now more often recorded as doing useful work rather than posing a threat. This record makes clear that the 'Blacks' doing this work are 'tame' or 'domestic' and that outside there exists a continuing group of the 'wild' sort who remain independent from Irby. Such a seemingly simple dichotomy was probably not the reality, given the number of times various useful bits of the colonists' equipment are found in 'wild' camps, but it succeeds in marking out resistant bodies who are not available for Irby's use. 'Wild' actually serves to textually domesticate 'black': 'wild' has become a descriptor usually used to mark simultaneous difference and similarity, a marker between the known and unknown of the same group. Examples of this from the same period include wild raspberry, wild currants, wild figs ... and now *wild* Black.

Monday April 27th, 1846

Dougherty came in last night to tell us that the Blacks had chased old Bill for his life ...

When I got home it struck me that the Blacks, perhaps hadn't got them [the missing sheep] at all, so I thought I would go by myself first and see for certain if the Blacks had taken them ... I now began to think the Blacks really had got old Bill, and driven his sheep off. I followed the tracks on to the five-mile, and felt so sure the Blacks must have got them ... [After finding sheep on an open ridge] ... I am inclined to think that Bill lost his flock, and made up the tale about the Blacks to exonerate himself from Blame if any should be hopelessly lost.

Now 'the Blacks' have become an excuse that even the old shepherd can use to explain his failings. This action reminds me of the pursued Aboriginal group claiming ownership by a 'white fellow'. 'Black' and 'white' are now used as strategic explications for private needs and claims. But as doubtful as Bill is as an informer, Irby shifts and sways with competing evidence. He can never afford to immediately dismiss a charge against (unknown) Aboriginal people, since they still threaten him, but each report does not necessarily lead to armed pursuit and 'punishment'. And the depth of Irby's settled domesticity deepens: a kitchen is being built.

Tuesday May 12th, 1846

The Blacks came from Windeyer's. One of them said he had seen six men, armed, on the station. Suppose them to be Wilson [a bushranger] and his gang.

'Station blacks' who move between stations now act as (English-speaking?) messengers of danger to the squatters, and if lines can still be drawn, these 'blacks' are now firmly of the station not against it; in rather than out. At this moment the threat is once more from the wrong kind of non-Aboriginal; the Irbys' typologies are crumbling/expanding.

Sunday May 17th, 1846

Came upon a Blacks grave. Saw the smoke of their fire, but no grass.

Wednesday August 12th, 1846

[170 sheep lost] ... Sent all the Blacks out, and went myself but got no tidings of them.

And now it is the (unpaid?) Aboriginal workers who are first sent on any recovery treks. Their integration into station life begins to be more spoken of and their tasks defined. There is no mention of payment.

Friday August 14th, 1846

Rode out with Tommy, came upon the spot where they [the sheep] had been rushed; found fourteen dead ...

Tuesday August 25th, 1846

Sent Black Tommy to tell old Bill to meet me on
Robinson's flat ... supposed Tommy had been too
late to give him my message ...

'Tommy' continues to occupy a textual space outside wild or
station 'blacks'. He suggests another detail of the complex array
of relations between Irby and Aboriginal people — the defined
and/or intimate. Whatever the basis of 'Tommy's' position, he is
trusted and individually named.

Wednesday August 26th, 1846

[Following discovery of Innis's sheep on his run] I
immediately ordered him off, and then rode home
to get out Bates. I sent him [Bates] with two
Blackfellows to carry some tools.

In this final entry the Aboriginal workers assist, albeit
obliquely, in the removal of a non-Aboriginal from Irby's run.
The new perimeters of struggle are being set: squatters will set
themselves against selectors and land reforms, and as their
efforts to import 'coolie' labour fail, they will 'employ' more and
more Aboriginal labour. Aboriginal people keep exceeding the
limits of the categories they are given, and in part this happens
through their productive labour. Irby, meanwhile, takes up
positions made available to him through the increasing
presence of government. Having made one kind of law — the
meting out of death — he soon enacts another: he becomes a
local magistrate.

AND IN PARTICULAR

Edward Irby was not a modern monster. He didn't kill all
Aboriginal people; he may not have even imagined the

category, but he was frightened of and did attempt to kill —
and he sometimes succeeded — 'Blacks' and later 'wild Blacks'.
He worked with, trusted, and no doubt exploited 'Black
Tommy'. He also 'employed', managed and/or was involved
with a range of other Aboriginal people who enter and exit
these extracts, never entirely individuated through names or
constant occupations but always there. Although there are
changes in how he addresses Aboriginal people and pictures
himself, these changes co-exist with a certain structural
sameness — he was always a land claimer. He begins as an
Englishman with an unsteady seat who stays well away from
those with a convict past, and ends up deeply soaked in
convictism, 'Blacks', rural society and 'Australia'. And did he
really begin simply as an Englishman, or was he already made
ambiguous by debt? declining family status? illness or ...? And
perhaps 'ends' isn't quite fair: he doesn't die, but he does stop
writing. His family has no other records of diaries and letters
except for these showing us an exhibit in the circus of settler
truth: Edwardius Irbius, First 'Settler' Man.

These chronological 'clips' are attempting to populate
colonialism's limits and boundaries, to give them some sort of
lived (or written) momentum. What does it mean to say that
Irby was a particular sort of colonial who killed a particular sort
of Aboriginal person? Is this the horror of a 'cultural studies'(?),
postmodern(?), even ethnographic(?) reading where the singular enables a collapse into the schlock horror of relativism?
Does this read like an apology, a 'rational' explanation for his
actions? Does it make him look better or worse? Who are you
identifying with? Who are you appalled by? Me or him or
perhaps 'Tommy'? I am puzzled.

In one way I see Irby's failure to use the metacategory of
'Aboriginal' as preventing a wholesale slaughter — he insists
that not all Aboriginal people are the 'same'. His world was too

small and tenuous for that. But his careful differentiation might be an original form of the intense classification of the 'Aborigine' (to one-sixteenth 'full blood', for example) which in turn led to internments, separations, assimilation, cultural destruction and death. There is, of course, also the possibility that it was precisely Irby's differentiation that was most exploited by the local Aboriginal groups. Was it the work of 'Tommy' and the 'blackboy' and 'Windeyer's blacks' to signal when a raid was safe? Was it they who became the interpreters of colonialism and invented strategies for safe passage, such as 'belong white fella'?

Where Irby saw difference, did Aboriginal groups organise within the larger categories of extended clanship and an emerging (or existent?) sense of 'Kooriality'? I employ 'Kooriality' here to suggest some pre-existing sense of community that was not based on racialisation, as 'Aborigine' was, but on the experience of managing resources in a region now shared by new strangers who had to be managed in particular ways. I question whether new alliances had to be made across pre-existing boundaries to allow for the movements of Aboriginal people associated with the stations? What sort of work might 'Tommy' have had to do to sustain his various roles within the Aboriginal nations and the emerging non-Aboriginal tribes? And if Aboriginal people were organising within a larger entity like 'Kooriality', does it mean the differentiations of Irby read like a strategy to divide and rule?

Perhaps it sounds like the work of the chronically insecure, desperately seeking sameness through an emerging familiarity. He trusts and works with 'Black Tommy' and kills 'wild blacks'. Both of these figurings reduce the complexity of Aboriginal culture to 'good' and 'bad' 'blacks'. One becomes available for work in an ambiguous capacity that rarely included wages and the other was able to be killed — both are 'Aboriginal'. This attempt to 'fix' the 'other' through these usages produces powerful stereotypes fuelled by ambivalence. But does ambivalence invent massacre?

Ambivalence and massacre

Having already looked at the ways Irby emerges as non-Aboriginal and changes his namings of Aboriginal people in a chronological fashion, I now look in a more minute way at how this happens in the two particular accounts Irby writes of the massacre he carries out. What did those words of Irby do? This story is therefore also about how murder is produced through words and thinking that depend, perhaps unexpectedly, upon ambivalence.

The murder of Aboriginal people insists upon an immediate grappling with the colonial world, with its language, its culture — how did it work? How did it make murder possible? The usual response to these questions is to point to the power of the fixed negative stereotype. Examples of this stereotype are easy to find in 'scientific' reports and journal entries, where Aboriginal people are listed as fauna, as animals — a mode of description we can identify in Irby's early naturalistic descriptions. This then leads to an explanation of atrocities as being caused by colonisers' perception of Aboriginal people as simply animals, to be shot and poisoned when it was necessary. A way of 'doing history' is thereby invented where we look for the excessive colonial linkings of Aboriginal and animal and, having found them, relax. Our explanation is proven. It *was* an 'irrational' moment in colonisation and is now dismissed. This sort of explanation fails to engage with the particular ways, the ambivalent ways, in which the colonisers actually constructed and reconstructed 'the Aboriginal' and themselves. How can we explain 'Tommy' as well as 'wild Blacks' and 'natives'?

I begin by relooking very closely at two small textual fragments from a letter and a diary which contributed to 'The Bluff Rock Massacre' leaflet to try to track a process of how these words made up the people who made the massacre possible (and how they made the massacre possible). This forensic textuality might let us see what these murders meant. How they were made particularly possible by these words: that is, how a people that fitted this way of thinking was created. How did that thinking and writing make their murder possible?

THE LETTER ACCOUNT

The first account of the massacre (the one in the tourist leaflet and in other local histories) is from a letter to Irby's father; the second is from entries in his diary. From the letter:

> The blacks had heard us coming and hidden themselves amongst the rocks. One, in his hurry, dropped poor Robinson's [the dead shepherd's] coat so we knew we were on the right tribe. If they had taken to their heels they might all have got off safe. Instead of doing so however they got their fighting men together to attack us, so we punished them severely and proved our superiority to them. We got back the same day. I sat down directly I was off my horse and wrote the particulars to the Commissioner and Windeyer started immediately with it. He [the Commissioner] lives more than one hundred miles from Bolivia. He [Windeyer] said I had no alternative but to act as I had done. Leonard [Irby's brother] returned about ten days after this sad affair occurred. I was of course put to very great inconvenience for want of a man and lost a number of lambs as a consequence, but on the whole we had a pretty good increase — nearly ninety percent.[100]

Irby writes quite simply that they had proof this 'tribe' had been responsible for the shepherd's death, but that even then they could have got away if they hadn't 'got their fighting men together to attack us'. This imagery depends on the idea that there was a hierarchy of warriors and non-warriors. It suggests that the threat posed by such a group made the response of Irby and Windeyer necessary. Whatever images had gone before, at the moment of death this group of Aboriginal people was understood as about to attack Irby and Windeyer and their men, so they were *attacked* back. The 'savagery' of these 'fighting men' has already been reported in an earlier part of the letter, when the body of the shepherd is described as having 'five spear wounds, four deep cuts from tomahawks on the temples, and the back of his head beaten in with a waddy; he had then been completely stripped and thrown in the river'.[101]

Detail like this provides the anxiously repeated vocabulary that invents the Aboriginal people as all and altogether savage. The list of injuries carefully notes not only the three different weapons used but also the absolute nakedness of the victim and his eventual disposal into the river. The shepherd's death becomes a story of crude weaponry and strange ritual which simultaneously produces the shepherd, in contrast, as a simple but familiar and known figure. Irby and Windeyer are enabled by the creation of this opposition between familiar man and 'barbarous' death to consult for a few minutes to determine that [they] 'would pursue the *murderers*' (my emphasis). A crime had been committed.

And yet after days of following the 'murderers' there is a sudden invention by Irby that the group might still have 'got off safe' except that they attacked Irby's party. So there is another shift in the representation of these criminals. They are no longer savage murderers; now they are children who simply need to be scared off to be made good. The effect is to set Irby up as the father of these children — who if only they had run off as they could have done (and were expected to do), would have been 'safe'. But then there is the final imagining: the Aboriginals become 'fighting men' to whom it is necessary to prove the 'white men's' superiority. These shifts in Irby's narrative sketch out the deadly process of creating both an active subject who could kill and a savage/child, ambivalently inferior, who was able to be killed. Through these words and figurings Irby became supra-enabled to kill (some) Aboriginal people.

All around (and within) these shifts is the complexity of the ordinary as it is presented to the parental audience — this was, remember, a letter addressed to his father. The tale of murder moves quickly onto the details of lambs born, and from there until the end of the letter Irby details what letters have or have not been received and ends with a reminder to Fanny (his sister) to address letters to the correct place. But this is still a letter, a narrative creation with a very specific audience. The 'ordinary' is selected and edited. It might be a part of the showmanship of the antipodean colonist to juxtapose attacks by 'Blacks' with stories of lambs born and letters received in accounts written for a non-colonial audience, or it might simply look that way now. Irby's second account of the same massacre is taken from his diary.

THE DIARY ACCOUNT

Thursday 17th ... Knowing the Blacks were in the rocks underneath I fired off for the two men to join us. Before they came up we went on to the farthest projecting rocks and looking underneath us could see the Blacks in their hiding places. Having now the means and will to punish them for the barbarous murder they had committed, we took advantage of the opportunity and gave it to them pretty severely.

Immediately after accomplishing the object of our trip we returned homewards, nor did we stop for breakfast till we had got within a short distance of the Sugarloaf [a hill]. We then spelled for about three hours. We reached home at about four pm. Windeyer determined upon returning the same evening and as he was thinking of going down to Sydney in a few days, I sat down at once to write to the Commissioner informing him of the murder [of the shepherd] and our expedition. Fri. 29th. Commenced shearing.[102]

The diary is an interesting form of narrative. It is assumed in the early twenty-first century that the diary is a private medium, that its lack of audience privileges the information within as being more real, more true to the individual's thoughts. But in the 1840s, diaries, particularly of colonists, were often edited and published, as parts of this one indeed were. We also know of the Irby brothers' practice of sending their entire logs home to be read and kept. There is also the slightly different tradition of the farm diary, where the central effort goes to the tracking of stock and weather conditions and the more personal element is missing. Irby's diary extracts are a mixture of all these. His account of the massacre is followed by the short details of shearing, for example, 'Saturday 30th: Had a thunderstorm last night; were obliged to wait some time before we could get on with shearing. Tuesday, Dec 3rd: Too cold to wash sheep' etc.[103] His account of the tracking of the Aboriginal party and the shooting of them is, however, written in a much more detailed style. This event clearly constituted something other than diurnal detail. What is harder to know is whether that something was colonial adventure or something suitable for possible publication or …

In discussing Irby's letter to his father, I try to track the range of ways in which Irby positioned himself and the Aboriginal people he finally killed. In the diary account, however, there are continuous references to the barbarity of the Aboriginal people, and these are combined with 'opportunity' to explain why Irby committed the murders. There is no mention that the Aboriginal group got their fighting men together; there is no pause where they might have got off 'safe' — here there is simply 'opportunity' to give 'it' to them 'pretty severely'. This idea of 'opportunity' is built up in the previous diary entries, where Irby, with the help of a 'blackboy', had been unsuccessfully tracking another Aboriginal group which continually evaded him — even though each night he would see their camp fires spring up in the near distance.[104] In this instance he was attempting to discover which group of Aboriginals had been responsible for scaring off bullocks. An 'opportunity' then, when Aboriginals were actually trapped in the rocks beneath them, was rare, and to be quickly taken 'advantage' of. But Irby is not simply responding to a rare, chance opportunity; he is also 'punishing' the Aboriginal group and he has 'the means and will' to do so. The means were guns, an established position that enabled him to act in this manner and a group philosophy that allowed him to do so in the company of others. The 'will' was an invention of the squatter who must overcome all obstacles to claim and establish stations in what was understood to be hostile country that was literally beyond the then legal boundaries of ownership. The 'will' of a legalising 'outlaw'?

Is this murdering individual the same man who asks so pleadingly, in a letter of the same year to his sister, for new music for the flute?[105] Here are the shadowy antecedents of philosopher Hannah Arendt's 'banal' evil — she confronts a new form of murder in Nazi Germany, murder that was carried out via a series of systems already in place (such as train timetables) by nine to five 'desk murderers' such as Adolf Eichmann.[106] While Irby is clearly the perpetrator and his actions are not those of bureaucratic order, he still places the murders as part of an 'ordinary' life. Irby's existence as son, flute player, squatter and murderer is performed both continuously and simultaneously. The murderer is a murderer is a murderer is a ... We all now know that murder and music can exist harmoniously within a body via a public/private divide — my aim is to disrupt that whole. The ambiguities of the position of squatter have to be wrested away from premature closure, but we need to also recognise that Irby himself is endlessly trying to contain his own meaning. I suggest that Irby is attempting to control the meaning of the murders throughout his stories by leaving the killings as the semi-final moment in both his narratives. His killing is described in the letter and the diary. But his final *action* is writing to the Commissioner. What happens with this next letter? What does it invent? What does it make possible?

WRITING TO THE COMMISSIONER

The letter is quickly sent to the Commissioner, in this case the Crown Lands Commissioner.[107] Irby's letter cannot be found. MacDonald, the Commissioner, duly reports the murder of a shepherd on Irby's property to Governor Gipps — there is no mention of the massacre. We can only wonder whether that omission was the result of Irby's or MacDonald's action. The reporting of only the shepherd's death, not those of the Aboriginal people, to the Governor denies the massacre entry to official public history. The letter that Irby writes to the Commissioner is most importantly an act of placement: it places Irby's action within a bureaucratic regime of meaning which sanctions and makes sense of the 'settler' defending his property and 'punishing' the (black) 'fighting men'. This writing, like the bloodshed, is a devastating act of 'showing their superiority'.

Writing in this official report form removes the acts described from their immediate context and allows them to be reconfigured in other kinds of spaces. The writing can be classified as a 'squatter's report', re-recorded as a part of the archive of the colonial secretary and reconstituted as a part of 'ordinary' colonial life — for what is a report but the banal flow of modern life?

The act of official reporting therefore becomes a way of making knowledge, a way of inventing the identities of wronged pastoralist and, most effectively, 'landowner' while creating and producing a system of legality based on written evidence. As part of a capitalist economy, these bureaucratic exchanges function as money. They invent and circulate and so give currency to particular colonial identities which are repeated and become embedded within the ways a government creates and continues control. Their purchasing power is immense. The importance that Irby grants the written report is clear — 'I sat down at once to write'; 'Windeyer started immediately with it' — for this, like the murder of Aboriginals, is a constitutive act of pastoralist identity. Writing makes him legal, or at least accounts for the actions in a legal manner. The white shepherd's death becomes all, and reporting it continues the pressure for more police, more official protection 'beyond the limits'.

After writing to the Commissioner, Irby bemoans (in the letter) the inconvenience he has suffered, but he is also able to point to his increase in lamb production and records that shearing began the next day. These economic increases mean that the Aboriginal deaths are also effaced from the material economy; they failed to prevent production, although the 'loss of a man' meant Irby lost some lambs.

The diary account might also be read in relationship to the land economy. Irby wrote: 'having now the means and will to punish them … we gave it to them pretty severely'. These deaths are opportunities in the same way that the land taking was an opportunity that required some means, and certainly will. Irby is not at this moment a landowner. Like all squatters, he paid a small licence fee and agitated for the land to be put up for sale. His tenure depended upon its being surveyed and a licence being paid for each run, but these formalities were rarely adhered to, since surveying meant fees — and one could simply pasture sheep all the while anyway. If the law was interpreted strictly, he was illegal, but his temporary licence and status as a free gentleman gave him 'real' legality. 'His' land lay beyond the boundaries of settlement and, as such, he was limited in how much stock and land he could immediately claim, but these restrictions were generally ignored. And these 'properties' quickly out-produced (in terms of wool and beef) the officially 'settled' regions. Murdering Aboriginals — or more accurately 'disappearing' them, as the murders were usually not officially reported — was a means by which this ambiguous land could be claimed as pacified … and the will to do so established in the process. Aboriginals, as fellow British subjects, were already trespassing on their own land. Production of selves, of subjectivities, was inseparable from the production of 'owned land', of wool and of wheat.

Words like 'will' and 'means' are annoyingly obscure. They contrast vividly with Irby's descriptions of the Aboriginals as 'barbarous' and even 'black' in this context. Irby is able, through the linguistic 'fixing' of some Aboriginal people, to represent them in a number of ways which all countenance his destruction of them.[108] As he swings between often contradictory 'stereotypical' descriptions of the Aboriginal people, he reveals a need to keep on manufacturing versions of the stereotype so that it keeps its power as a basis from which to take murderous action.

They are criminals, they are children — they are particularly available to be acted upon. In these movements there is also perhaps a desire to fix oneself, to become 'unquestioned owner' within a colonial project that could only ever be a constant vacillation between the known and unknown. Action perhaps stops — momentarily — that swinging. Irby has his own ambivalence. He is 'good', he is 'bad'. He is a trained soldier responding to 'fighting men' and an upper-class Englishman becoming settler in part by shooting trapped men, women and children — '[giving] it to them pretty severely'.

Murder may be the most powerful expression of ambivalence. It instantly transforms one set of meanings into another, and is a powerful site of new meanings. 'Beyond the limits' murders simultaneously confirmed and unhinged settlement as they occurred in different places. Hence, perhaps, the waves of violence as various stereotypical understandings of Aboriginal people and of 'pioneers' shifted through the 'settlement' of Australia. It is from sites such as Bluff Rock that the new stereotypes of barbarous squatter and resistant Aboriginal arise. And ambivalence too — of course.

A short vocabulary list

Words change.

Massacre: (OF–Old French before 1400) Comes from *macecler*, to butcher.

1. the unnecessary, indiscriminate killing of a number of human beings as in barbarous warfare or persecution, or for revenge or plunder.
2. a general slaughter of human beings.
3. to kill indiscriminately or in a massacre.

And in particular, in Australia, the 'settlers':

> went 'blackbird shooting',
>
> formed a 'black line',
>
> encouraged and organised 'expeditions',
>
> formed a 'bush party' and
>
> took 'decisive measures'.

None of these definitions gives the sense of a slaughter against unarmed opposition, the sense of entrapment 'beneath the rocks' and the unstoppable 'punishment'. Never a 'massacre' to Irby; always a massacre now. 'Massacre' is the political (and so more accurate, because it contextualises the word's application) renaming of an event. The renaming was made possible both by Aboriginal people's refusal to forget and by the subsequent productions — in the form of books, exhibitions and political acknowledgments — that came out of those memories. This has also enabled further rereadings, or fleshing out of (sometimes) named places like Slaughter Creek, Blackfellows Ridge, Niggers Leap and too many others by Aboriginals and non-Aboriginals. But the incorporation of 'massacre' into history is also a way in which such things become foreign and solidified. This sort of massacre was against a particular people, at a particular moment in colonial history. The waves of racist massacres where vigilante groups swept along rivers and roads through the country seeking out all Aboriginal people were happening concurrently with these much more localised, relatively contained acts. Are they all massacres? Or is it worthwhile to attempt some differentiation? Not to rescue any of them, but to insist on the complicated nature of these regions 'beyond the limits' where only some things could occur. These deaths happened here and happened there, but they did not happen everywhere or in the same way. So 'massacre' remains a difficult term, useful for its naming and power of connection but potentially dangerous in its collapse of events into a single idea of what happened. It is also complicated by my use of it as a construct of a particular event circulated by a tourist leaflet and its most literal usage as the slaughter of human beings. There remain massacres and massacres. But it is useful to keep questioning when precisely these events were able to be *called* a 'massacre'.

Murder:

1. the unlawful killing of a human being by an act done with the intention to kill or to inflict grievous bodily harm, or with reckless indifference to human life.

2. colloq. an uncommonly laborious or difficult task.

Unlawful? Historian Brian Kercher writes: 'The legal position of Aborigines was determined slowly and hesitantly through both physical and verbal conflicts.' New South Wales was assumed to have been organised into existence on the basis of *terra nullius*: settlement of an empty land. Therefore Aboriginal people became legal subjects from the moment that occupation began and should have had access to the protection of the law. But this was difficult, because Aboriginal people were unable to give evidence in court since they could not swear on the Bible, and it was assumed that they would be, according to Richard Atkins, second Judge Advocate of New South Wales (arriving in 1792), 'wholly ignorant' of the court procedures. Atkins then went on to suggest that the only practical course was 'to pursue and punish them when they deserved it'.[109] The fact that Irby and Windeyer were pursuing and killing Aboriginal people six years after the well-publicised Myall Creek Massacre trial points perhaps to the ongoing belief that to kill in vengeance for a white man, even an ex-convict, even a sinful shepherd, was allowed, even if not exactly legal. That the Myall Creek Massacre resulted in the (unpopular) hanging of some of the perpetrators was a direct result, perhaps, of its not having been a 'punitive expedition'. Those massacred at Myall Creek were 'station blacks' attacked by non-Aboriginals from a different area, who, in possible imitation of official campaigns, were riding and shooting indiscriminately across country.[110] Although in legal terms 'there could be no corporal or capital punishment without trial except in self defence or in the heat of battle in a period of martial law',[111] the settler culture seemed to allow that killing Aboriginal people on one's own 'property' in response to a death meted out by Aboriginal people was to all intents 'legal'. The tradition for this began perhaps with the arming of settlers in the initially more isolated regions of Richmond in the 1790s. The Myall Creek Massacre, however, was one of a series of random raids by one group of ex-convict workers, who swept across other people's properties and slaughtered Aboriginal people out of hand, regardless of whether they were workers on particular stations, children or unknown. One of the resulting carnages was reported by a manager who noticed the absence of the 'station blacks'. With the assistance of a non-participating non-Aboriginal witness, he was able to make a case that meant that some of those massacrers were hanged as murderers. No such circumstance made it possible for Irby, Windeyer, Connor and Weaver to be criminalised. Irby, as we know, in fact became an early magistrate, someone who decided what was and was not 'legal'. Someone who continued to decide 'punishments'.

Killing:

1. to deprive (any living creature or thing) of life in any manner, cause the death of, slay.

2. to destroy, to do away with, extinguish: *kill hope.*

At home, that is on our land, my mother would sometimes check with my father whether or not he had put the 'killers' in. These were a selection of sheep (not lambs — far too valuable!) from which my father would select one to kill for our fortnightly meat consumption. Of course it was my father who was the killer and the sheep the about-to-be-killed, but this linguistic irony? confusion? cover-up? is connected in my mind to Irby and the unnamed Aboriginal people as killers. Was the shepherd, Robinson, 'killed' by Aboriginal people or was he ritually punished? Was it the Aboriginal Law that killed Robinson, but fearful, greedy, white anarchy that killed that Law's officers? Was Robinson's death in effect an act of incorporation into Aboriginal culture? This is after all what Irby claims for himself — that these killings were a 'punishment' for murderers, that he was sanctioned to act ... and so the group was posthumously 'civilised'. But the scale of his killings is so much less precise than, so much further away from, what we might identify as the rituals and practices of colonial law. In his lack of discrimination he becomes a killer of the 'innocent' as well as what he may have perceived as the 'guilty' men.

AND WHAT OF MORE ORDINARY WORDS?

Go over the gap
Shove off
Go take a jump
Take a leap
Do all these mean:
Go kill yourself
Before I kill you?

HORSES AND DEATH

What else is going on around Irby and my readings of him? What other kinds of culture, material and social, enabled him to act? And how should I read him so you can see him again and again in his unsettled self?

Transportative colonialism

Horses were important to Edward Irby. Even before signing the agreement to go to Deepwater, he and Leonard are anxiously looking for mares. This is the 1840s, when according to Miles Franklin, 'The whole population took to horse. Wishes were horses from the 'forties onward ...' She sees in that movement the reason why a peasant class never emerged in Australia, for, 'No man can remain a peasant and go a-horse.'[112] All the more reason why Irby must have one.

One arrangement falls through, but with some opportune assistance of a fellow lodger they are able to purchase two, one for £25 and one for £30 — this kind of money (plus rations) was the annual income for a shepherd at the time. Edward notes that they would have cost double that three years before. Leonard provides a description of these horses to his sister Caroline:

> Ted's is a perfect Rosinate; it is what they call ewe-necked, that is, it has a neck like a sheep ... There is such a sink in its back that you might put a sack of flour there without noticing it ... nearly thorough-

bred of course. Mine is just 5 pounds better, so we
have some fine cavalry between us; but they are
both sound and young, so they will do.[113]

They attempt to ride these horses in Sydney and are thrown
two or three times; they noted that their not having had any
practice was a 'drawback' — 'It is very different riding here to
what it is at home, particularly going over great stones and
logs; your horse is liable to stumble every second step.'[114]

Consider the status of the horse at this moment. Carriages,
tandems and the occasional four-in-hand are symbols of the
'gayness and pleasantness' of Sydney. Some of these were
presumably the usual mode of transport for the Irbys. However,
on stations 'beyond the limits' — where there were no carriage
paths, and bullocks pulling drays was the only method of
bringing in supplies and walking (Shanks' pony/mare) was the
norm — the individual on a horse suggested a certain kind of
power. Horses brought into being new colonial formations. Set
upon the thin Australian topsoil, they marked out hoof-riven,
single-file paths; connected to the settler and squatter, they
created ways of imagining distant spaces; and in open country,
spliced to fear and greed, they could run down Indigenous
Australians. The horse is representative of the ways in which
new combinations of being emerged within colonialism. These
new creations tell of a colonialism that was embodied and
desirous: desirous because it created other bodies and produced
new kinds of organisation and new ways of imaging this 'new'
world. I have called this emphasis on what colonialism produces
'transportative colonialism', to acknowledge the ways in which
namings and movements are at its heart. The horse becomes a
vehicle for us, a way we can see how colonialism made new
combinations of horse and man and how those combinations
worried questions of who belonged where, and how.

Individual horses provided the means for separation and ascension. When travelling up with the bullock dray and six others 'we being the only ones who had not been convicts, ... we always rode on with the stockman, who had to get the bullocks in the morning', and while that stockman prepares a fire and hobbles their horses, the Irbys go off to see if there is any game about. So it is not just ownership of a horse that is so significant; it is also how that is understood and brought into relationship with other bodies. This becomes more obvious in the diaries, where Irby records constant movements via the horse in circles of sociability as well as utility. Variously named workers have horses taken to them for particular tasks, and are sent to catch the horses for Irby's use — but to Irby, horses are as ubiquitous as air:

> Rode over to Windeyer with the Cream of Tartar
>
> Rode after the bullocks
>
> I rode off to look over the run again ...
>
> Rode out to the shepherds
>
> Rode after the bullocks
>
> Len rode over to Robertsons
>
> Rode over to see Windeyer
>
> In the afternoon rode to the gap but no sign of the sheep ...
>
> Rode over to pay Robertson a visit
>
> Rode out early to tell the shepherds to keep away from the road ...
>
> Len rode over to Kelso's for some seed corn
>
> Len and self rode over to Mackenzies to eat strawberries

The horses make possible the network of communications which makes the station productive in Irby's terms. This includes social and economic exchanges with the other squatters. One of the ritual exchanges is the gathering together of a 'party' on horseback to pursue a group of Aboriginal people. Horses, particularly before the employment of Aboriginal trackers, were an important tactical vehicle. Horses enabled the squatters to cover open ground quickly enough to prevent the Aboriginal groups reaching the protection of denser gullies or rougher higher ground where the usefulness of the horse was minimised. Horses and guns were the speed and weaponry that made action of Irby's 'will' to 'punish'.

These units of death had names: Smudge, Skipper, Speedy, Boxer, Blazes, Wildfire and Crib. When Skipper appears lame a sprain is suspected. Her deteriorating condition is noted over the days and Irby laments that he does not have the medicines the horse needs. Skipper is bled, and then help is requested. Irby plus an unnamed worker put a rowel (a piece of leather or such inserted beneath the skin to create some sort of discharge, usually blood) in her chest and a 'drawing plaster' on her heel. Finally Irby records, 'Skipper much better.'

The horses are also a source of humour. When recording how he shot a turkey, Edward notes that the sound of the gun also 'shot Speedy as she was quite asleep'. This is the care of a necessary resource, and the affectionate sentiment and anecdote of the familiar.

This domesticated creature is an emblem of transportative colonialism, of movements of all sorts, particularly on stations 'beyond the limits'. First, there was the transportation of convicts, which provided the cheap labour which enabled the labour-rich activities of shepherding. And then there was the 'transportation' of pick-pockets into shepherds (they were reported as making the best shepherds) — for this, the spaces and movements of colonial structures had to be wrought personally and particularly: individuals had to be made different. 'Transportative' implies the conveyance of sets of cultural mores as well: one could be 'transported' to something beyond — a capitalist nirvana, or death ... Or one could remain in a state of 'transport', a magical paralysis of mother country culture which keeps the colonial in a state out of or 'lost in' translation.[115] To 'transport' was also to kill, and when Irby, Windeyer, Connor and Weaver kill the Aboriginal people they have trapped under the rocks, they are 'transporting' them first to a state of imagined barbarism and thence into a death of 'punishment'. Then Irby and Windeyer ride away.

The Sentimental Blokes

That riding away, that transportation, of Irby and Windeyer might suggest a constant lack of care for the dead, but this was not the case. When Robinson and Westley die, Irby is careful to bury them properly. (These are the shepherds Irby reports he had to allow into his kitchen due to a very heavy downpour of rain — he would not normally have had anything to do with convicts or ex-convicts. When he found out a man they had sailed over with and had become friends with had been in gaol, he wrote to his father that he would not be having anything to do with him any more!) Westley's mate commences the coffin and Irby begins the grave, and then 'we consigned the remains of poor Westley to their last resting place'. Days later a fence is put around the grave. The 'melancholy business' of burying Robinson, who died further from the head station and on very hard ground, difficult to dig, is soon over, but weeks later Irby writes that he rides out to 'see that the native dogs hadn't disturbed poor Robinson's grave'. This was a time in which death was understood in western culture as 'Thy Death'.[116] This was, as described by cultural historian Philippe Ariès, a shift from the focus on 'one's own death' to concern for and attention to the deaths of others. A part of this was the invention of cemeteries and tombs that could be visited by family and friends. Ariès also identifies the rise of hysterical (transported?) mourning in this period. Only a very scaled-down version of these behaviours was possible on Bolivia, the Irbys' station, but we can see that adequately accounting for the remains of the dead was important. There was always a burial, and always a protective fence. These modest graves were to perpetuate the memory of the deceased — they created a place entirely given over to the dead person's memory, a place which might be an inspiration to those who passed and which might also inspire the romantic, overblown melancholy of the 1840s. It may also indicate the cultural uneasiness with the idea of dying alone (far from home, perhaps, but particularly without extended family, village, workmates and for upper classes, servants). In Europe, a lonely death — a death without family — was a marker of poverty, but here, 'beyond the limits', anyone from any class might die relatively alone (although it was much more likely to be the shepherds and nightwatchmen). Family was much more understood then as synonymous with wealth of varying kinds: even a very poor family had, in its many children, real income-earning potential. Family was as much an economic as a sentimental unit.

Crib, a horse that dies, is also buried, as are the twelve sheep killed while they were being washed. Even these animals are too close to the 'inhabited' heart of the head station to be simply abandoned to rot. Was it because of the smell, the risk of disease? Or was it the simple aesthetics of order that would have been disrupted if these creatures had not been interred? Although these burials are of a more mundane nature than

Robinson's, the fact of them is a sharp contrast to the ways in which the bodies of the Aboriginal people are treated. Their remains, their bodies, are abandoned, even though Irby recognises that they had their own graves and burial system. Irby 'transports' their bodies into a record about the death of a shepherd in a letter to the Commissioner. A report to the Governor's representative fills the space of mourning and interment. Their burial happens via a primitive bureaucracy.

Killing Aboriginal people suggests that many cultural frameworks are at play, some of which may have been greed, theories of racial differentiation, expediency; failing to bury the bodies shows the complete absence of an inclusive human sentiment. Death was able to transport the looked-down-upon shepherd to a 'poor fellow' whose grave fence is fussed over, but the murders of Aboriginal people are ridden away from so quickly that the murderers don't stop until they are on the 'home' runs. When finally they do stop, they eat quickly and Irby goes on to 'write immediately' to the Commissioner. The horse-driven speed of these events is underscored by his final diary entry for that day, which is, 'We have indeed been very lucky in getting back the second day, we fully expected to be out a week and the chances against our coming upon the Blacks at all appeared very great. Fine. West.'

It seems trite to suggest that Irby lacked 'sentiment' for Aboriginal people, or at least those he had categorised as 'wild blacks', but perhaps it was this lack of incorporation into the sentimental, combined with the speed of settlement and the space of 'beyond the limits', that allowed Irby the Damoclean 'freedom' to murder. Even as corpses, 'wild blacks' were unable to be accounted for within Irby's system of ritual except as bureaucratic detail (the nature of which we can't be certain of). Irby as man/horse becoming colonial can move quickly and violently into spaces which are far enough away from his domesticated head station for him to never be confronted with the need to touch, bury or mourn those he has murdered. Another historical marker fails to come into being; more Aboriginal people are 'disappeared'. A Historical massacre.

But this transportative power was not unlimited. Within these newly belonging bodies and bodies of knowledge were bodies that hurt — membranes of mortality.

The fragile body

Five days after the killing of the Aboriginal group, Irby writes that he '[w]as seized with violent spasms, took a dose of Rhubarb and Magnesia but found no relief from it so took an emetic which gave [him] some ease, at night took some catechu and laudanum.'[117] This is not the first or the last time Irby reports being ill. Twice before he records bad headaches and being taken badly by dysentery, which keeps him unwell for two days. And many months later, intermittently, he has several days in which he is 'unwell', but there is nothing at any other time as dramatic as 'violent spasms'.

What does it mean to be transported, to become squatter? colonial? murderer? Beyond the 'limits of location', within the possibilities of transportative desire, what becomes of the so-called human body? Veronica Brady, writing about the violent settlement of Australia, quotes South African-born writer JM Coetzee's description of space stretching out in front of the white man in a hot colony:

> The operation of space is thus: the five senses stretch out from the body they inhabit, but four stretch into a vacuum. The ear cannot hear, the nose cannot smell, the tongue cannot taste, the skin cannot feel: the sun bears down on the body, flesh

and skin move in a pocket of heat, the skin stretches vainly around, everything is sun. Only the eyes have power. The eyes are free, they reach out to the horizon all around.[118]

Brady suggests that the non-Indigenous, within the vast spaces of Australia, 'loses any sense of limit', and that the experience of infinite space in turn provokes 'a kind of nihilistic violence'.[119] The emotional — and to some extent physical — experience of being 'beyond the limits' of one's cultural location and beyond one's spatial sensibility is nicely sketched here, but perhaps it suggests too much. Coetzee's description is of senses overwhelmed by landscape, whereas Brady's evocation of a nihilistic voyager assumes the overwhelming power of these 'settler' experiences. It is an easy step by a clumsy reader of Brady to see these white men as nearly gods; yet their bodies, even when joined to horses, hurt. Individually and corporeally they had to struggle to maintain their new order. After shooting the trapped group, Irby contains the meaning of his actions through the writing to the Commissioner and through the reassurances of Windeyer, but later his body is in 'violent spasms'. This reminds us that although he is God-like in his capacity to institute official silences, he is also never entirely in control, never able to expunge the effects of being a body.

His method of controlling his violent spasms is first to take rhubarb and magnesium. The rhubarb is to make him purge his bowels and the magnesium is to then settle his stomach. But the spasms continue, so he takes something to make himself vomit, which helps a little. At night he takes catechu, which settles the stomach and contracts the tissues and canals of the body. He combines this with laudanum, or opium — the main ingredient of laudanum was opium (and sometimes laudanum was just another name for a particular measure of opium). The current translation, according to the doctor I spoke to, would be a serious dose of morphine. This would have relaxed all his muscles and probably put him to sleep. He is still 'very bad' the next day, but is 'rather better' the day after that. He sticks to the catechu and laudanum. Thereafter he is back cutting the lambs (removing their tails and testes), and visiting 'poor Robinson's grave' to check that the native dogs have not disturbed it. The fragile limits of the colonial body have been temporarily re-established.

The murdered, the unspoken-of corpses, the efforts to make himself shit and vomit, and the re-ordering of his body — putting it back together again so that it would look and feel the way it did before the attack of illness — through laudanum are rich in possible meanings. His self-induced vomiting and shitting can be understood as protecting himself from the corpses, and from his own capacity to make those corpses, and from the possibility of becoming a corpse himself. To paraphrase philosopher Julie Kristeva: he expels *himself*, he spits *himself* out, he abjects *himself*, and within the same motion he establishes *himself* as a coherent colonial body, as differentiated from the wild? the colonial? the Aboriginal?[120] The corpses he has created have instituted a space beyond the locatable limits of location for him. He is without borders. He has the borders of his corpses oozing and writhing, sucking him out of himself, but then he vomits and shits himself back into existence — or does he? For three days he is in a laudanum hollow, a place where the body moves only haltingly at your command and where your world shrinks to small actions that you can minutely observe. Your own limits shrink back to the lifting of cups and the slow drift between sleep proper and daytime fug. The bowels and stomach retire and there is stillness … Little by little he moves out again. But it is not all OK.

Irby's conflicted body may be able to temporarily establish some beachheads, to ambiguously fortify self and Other, but he remains horror to me. His murders disrupt the idea of linear, progressive time — of growing up — and they pollute place. They last, they haunt. They have become a part of my childhood; they question the future. Irby's shadow is long and pervasive. I must not become him. What is the point in saying, 'I just wouldn't have done it, I never would have done it.' What sense of self, informed by what, do I have that didn't also inform him? What keeps me apart from him? Nothing but writing it, thinking it differently so that such a certain self is not possible. That's why we write our books: to save ourselves — they are spider threads of life, fragile imaginative strings.

Taking it personally, making it personal

So how do you write 'The Bluff Rock Massacre'? How do you write Irby? Dear Reader, let me marry him. He is my husband; I am his wife. Our unnatural fucking, through insuperable history, makes us both strange. We are the supposedly extinct night parrot — that strange returned creature from poet Dorothy Porter's 'Scene from a Marriage II': the night parrot that wreaks 'rebellion, havoc and birdshit in immaculate boring places' and who 'whispers seductive nightmares'.[121] We need the night parrot, Edward and I. Menagerie à trois. How can I write about this intimacy? How can I explain how his legs smell like horses and his hands like ink? How he writes down our life as if we never meet. He has built a new hut which he calls, in his wry, fey way, the 'garter gunya'. In this way, he can prepare his 25-year-old man/monster body and then walk across to me just as he remembers the sounds of his father's steps moving along the corridor to his mother's wing. This is fine; it leaves me time to be with the night parrot, coming as he does to keep us alive — his arrival is indicative of a world turned around, a world where the extinct return to connect the living to the dead, the past to the present, to speak, to haunt. Edward is ashamed that my feet have to touch the ground, coming as I do straight from castle to carriage, which is how he imagines the Hebel brick house and the 1982 Pulsar. But he hopes I'll have time for my prayers and has begun building a chapel for me to sit in. He's bringing me into myself. He's complaining about the land under threat, that he won't be able to hang onto it all with the town and the Governor muttering loud and louder about splitting it up, letting 'selectors' come. He's dreaming of more cheap labour and he likes the word 'coolie' — it's fresh on the breath and sounds fine for the country, for growth, for his enterprise. He can't see my great-great-grandparents coming down the hill. He can't see Bridget feeding mare's milk to her baby. But he is making it all possible. I'm coming out.

They won't know the sort of fear he has. Every fire in the hills is another sign to him to mount up, to load his gun, to thunder off. But almost always to no effect. The Aboriginal people not attached to the runs as workers or trackers or in other unspecified occupations have their own systems for attack and retreat, their own ways of getting what they want from what Edward seems to offer, but it makes no sense to Edward — everything is an attack to him, because he is not in charge of the meaning making. But Bridget and John Eckersley Newbury will find only Aboriginal people used to very hard work for very cheap rations, and these Aboriginal people will be soothing balm to the Newbury fecundity. It will be Fanny's (the Newburys' Aboriginal servant) and others' 'faithful' black hands in the suds of petticoats and stockings that nourish the incipient respectability of the twelve, thirteen, fourteen Newbury children, who outbreed Edward teddy bear's lot in perfect ten to one ratio. Every Newbury Mass followed by another action-packed propagating afternoon.

No one dares to point to our hugely reproductive families —
our own white flood, when we bred like rabbits because we had
God on our side. Scientific breeding programs will be practised
on Fanny's people and we will look away, sorry for the loss of
cheap labour and oh how we loved her children, 'their quiet
dignity, all their own'.[122] It is Edward making all this possible
for me, and yet he is awkward before my questions. He doesn't
like to think a woman could be here.

I sneak away to the shepherd's wife to drink beer and suck
her breasts; Edward finds her later, drunk, with bodice agape,
and notes that he must speak to Bates about his wife stealing
beer. This is only the third time (in three years) he has had to
mention a woman who works for him. I'm not counting the
women to whom letters are sent or from whom letters are
received; they are altogether other beings. Breasts form no
connection in Edward's mind between me, who steps from my
carriage, and the doubtful beer-drinking wife of a convict,
whom he does not speak to. For the moment it is only I who
see the possibilities. But Bates's wife is no slave; it is often she
who lunges first towards me. Her name is Mamuk, Scottish for
a bird no one has seen, and I see what she means, but her touch
is real enough. Bates is her third husband. 'They don't last,' she
says. She always has to be looking out for others and for
something more. The tricks she practises upon my body she
learnt from her mother's lover, who was in the 'factory' and was
queen of the cats. She never asks me to stay, and she knows she
will be leaving before me. 'When you're out you can't stop
moving,' she says. 'I should know,' she says and laughs. Is she
also the night parrot?

It is the night parrot that keeps oiling Irby and me so that
we slip an' slide into one another, so that we cannot forget that
we fucked. His clotted ink stains are inside me and my silicon
chipped nails leave torn shreds of membrane in his arse. You

cannot deny this connection — history explodes every time we touch. Can my little Howard, my prime mistress (ministress?), imagine an armband like this? A sinuous coil that writhes into an avenging clitoris rising higher and higher, rubbing harder and harder? But sometimes the night parrot comes to take me away into a void, past the cranky freedom of celebrated, academic Histories and history to a place where I can't hear myself, where words fail, where one cannot imagine oneself and where the histories of the night parrot become impossible. Too many trips like this have made the night parrot extinct.

THE BRAIN FARTS

Here, like everywhere, there is space for your own readings, and here, like everywhere, I am hoping you will compose whole scores out of this pap gone rotten. But I have the penance to write. As writer, as irritant, I am called on first to prick my own balloon, to let out the energy of effect into the ether of intent, theory, reading. What do I mean? What am I trying to do? Let's begin with the night parrot. Taken from Dorothy Porter (who wouldn't thank me for the accolade — 'not another academic wanker', I imagine her saying), the strength and the horror of the (almost) extinct night parrot suggested to me the raw, moving liminality of imagined histories. I wanted to do at least two things. The first is to insist on the intimacy of both History (as officially documented) and history (as a fiction of the present) and the effects of both on live, real bodies, on us now. In particular I need to show that Irby's diary is ongoingly productive, that his words and actions are still assisting in the making up of culturally marked bodies. The experience of reading him, going there, living there, growing up there, means I experience his words through my body, my childhood, my intimate selves. When conservatives suggest that academics and others are subscribing to a black armband version of history, it is not the fatuousness of their columnist-speak that so irritates me; it is the crime they commit on their own possibility. The flimsy armband is not an adequate metaphor for history of any sort. Removed from the heart, three-quarters up the arms of action — this is no place for any symbol of history to lie. To insist on this inertia is to attempt to misplace history and reinforce History. It powerfully circulates an expedient knowledge that has to be engaged with over and over again, since repetition is a convenient moving, standing stillness. H(h)istory is always speaking, and no one can stop us becoming, but each insistence that Aboriginal history is not a current effective History results in an increasing limitation on who 'we' can be. Is there room to be queer? to be 'woman'? to be? when over and over again your public possibility is endlessly rehearsed as only ever non-Aboriginal or Aboriginal?

To know the past in the present is to be in a state of metamorphosis. As we know the past now, we become aware of a world of excessive possibility. How will we show care for this past except by using it carefully, allowing ourselves to be moved to new states of being? (Marrying Irby is a demonstration of thinking differently with a rethought history, acting differently, writing differently, in not-predictable ways. The past can't offer a single truth and neither should the present — the task is to reflect the excess of the past in the present, not reduce that past.) Marrying Irby was just one possibility. Of course Irby was not married at the time he wrote the diaries, and 'naturally' he wasn't married to me. Here is not even the slightest consistency between writing and appearance. I am inventing, not telling 'truth'. I am, like Margaret Tucker in the story of her 'removal', writing sense, but our projects are very different. As I have suggested before, I understand Tucker's writing to be a fundamental challenge to the 'sense' of colonially invented language and structures. Hers is the sort of history that challenges the material effects of History and makes us question every ordinary detail of so-called ordinary life until we can see something like that final glass of milk as a certain kind of evil. To write that history is to write the sense, the underlying assumptions about a shared past and shared values *out* of official History, to expose the carapace erected against difference. It would be easy to suggest that if her history could become Australia's History I may not have to write the way I do, but there are a few things wrong with this thinking. The first is to recognise that the struggle to write out possibilities of becoming is not necessarily going to be applauded by any Australian History, no matter how heterogeneous, since it is always an insecure project, related to but not solely born of a particular nationalism or commitment to place. The second is that the ongoing rethinking and reorganising of histories, institutions and governments that has already been necessary so that we can hear Aboriginal voices will surely continue to invent histories unlike others — my inventive technology may not be adequate under those conditions.

The sense I am writing, then, is a struggle of nonsenses. Partly produced by the 'sense' of colonialism, the same 'sense' that disables and denies Tucker's history, the arena of my struggle is marked out. Without Tucker's experience, without her history, I can perform only within the theatre of colonialism's nonsense. My sense also seeks to make nonsense, but through excessive sense. The many histories which I have some access to open up the routes of my possible encounters with Irby, but material reality insists that this is a marriage rather than a love affair. I am not a 'free' spirit.

Secondly or simultaneously, I am struggling with the textual omission of women. I *am* there in Irby as much as I am in Bates's beer-stealing wife — but how can I insist on that? There are clear reasons to do so. The first is part of a wider and more obviously historic project where 'women' are reinvented through the fragments and detritus of Historical formations that privileged the keeping of a variety of 'men's' reports and thoughts and replicated the material conditions that meant many more 'men' than 'women' would write and that their writings would become History. One resistant possibility that arose from that constellation of effects was the category 'woman'. This is now as unstable as any other category, but it still has, I imagine, writerly effects when I flesh out imaginary bodies for a simple sentence in Irby's hand. What I mean is, I think that you as reader would figure this character differently if it was gendered male. I don't care what those figurations might be, but I don't want you to forget that it was at least these possibilities that Irby is unable at this moment to express.

His inability — or his choice — does not, however, affect my ability to invent all over him, since he, as much as anyone, has made me queer. To write of queerness is not the same recuperative project that I refer to with regard to 'woman', although I have no doubt that women were sleeping with, making love with, sexually exploiting etc. other women at the time and quite possibly at Bolivia. No, what Irby has done to me, which I am now calling queer, is that (out of history but of this moment) invention where the imaginary line between past and present ... and so future ... becomes imagined body on imagined body, a limit at which we produce our own located-ness. This state is both transportative and within the realm of the abject, operating between past and present in a way that denies the stability of either.

A final point to make is that reading the intimacy of Irby's writing is an 'emotional experience'. These wonderful words, with their banal resonances from the mouths of Hollywood stars and New Age devotees, form an intriguing cliché. Can we have experience without emotion? Can we have emotion without experience? I have taken, I am *taking* Irby personally, but what does this do?

Closetting: hidden histories and the erotics of silence

The closet is a contested, relational space. Once imagined as a corset? club? moving car? tunnel? that one was either in or out of, it now has to be acknowledged that 'out' means many things to many people, and the power of heterosexual expectation and queer groove can constantly locate you as 'in' or 'out' whether you are or not. The closet is a magicked space, a strategic cloud and a mad idea. The idea of a final emergence, a totally coherent knowable identity, is something that haunts history as well as our 'selves'. The closet, a powder room of preparation, invents a persona that can emerge historically knowable, a certain, queer, shade of white. Were the impossibilities of being lesbian connected to the impossibilities of acknowledging Aboriginal presence?

Perhaps I didn't fuck Irby, but truly, I did make love. I made love as if I had never known what love was before. Perhaps I hadn't. No-one's parents asked where we had been until four or five in the morning; our positions were so well established — we were the girls. And yet we knew absolutely that we could never go back. We had moved forever to another country where nothing was as we expected. Lips didn't feel the same, fingers were extraordinary things and we were sucked out, heart first. Our desires were antipodean. Were these the pleasures of being 'white' and becoming postcolonial? Was this 'entry into an arrangement, an assemblage of other fragments, other things, becoming bound up in some other production'?[123]

And wasn't a part of those productions the silences of homo-phobia and the scratched-out racist routes that meant we never saw and never considered? Were these sexed intensities following the well-worn colonial paths of opening us up to the new, investing ourselves in spaces and places — always into country owned by no-one else?

Because some were rich, we always had drugs. Usually marijuana but later speed, so we could slow down and speed up, enervate and proliferate with each line and each puff. We spent two summers on the bizarre edges of the Bachelor and Spinster Ball circuit. We drove to Gunnedah, Black Mountain, Wagga Wagga — excited, high, everyone's fantasy of getting out and off on it. We didn't notice the absolute non-Aboriginality of those gatherings. Our out-of-itness was on long stretches of scrub and Bundy-soaked halls where we collected stickers saying Got Ripped and Rooted at the Dundee B&S and put them next to our Feed the Man Meat sticker. And then I flew out again.

I didn't meet my old high school friends on the plane at the end of the university term (AUSTUDY paid an airfare if you were more than 24 hours by bus or train from your home address). They were in jobs or in relationships that kept them in the cities — they had relocated. Neither did I meet people of colour nor distinguishable queers. But I loved this flying back to the country, the complicated connections from Mel-bourne to Glen Innes that always required a minimum of four hours in the airport bar and then a sudden readjustment to the small, rickety twelve-seater that marked the final passage back home. Once my return coincided with my by then ex-lover's parents' 25th wedding anniversary party. Everyone on that plane was going up for that party. That was the sort of set they were: cosmopolitans, which meant they knew the same sort of people whether they lived in Watson's Bay or Moree. They had access to a circularity of sameness that I never did.

Glen Innes and the countryside surrounding it was our shared place: the moneyed, the semi- moneyed and the poor, the black and the white, the straight and the queer. But we all used very different maps that only occasionally crossed over — at the bar of the local Agricultural Show for a moment, maybe. We knew the rivers to swim in, we knew where to go, we were goddesses of locomotion. She and I lost our lesbian virginity on blankets near a creek. It rained at the end and the truck cabin was filled with the sweat of sexed bodies and wet wool. Some sort of primal settlement smell. We saw no 'natives'.

I see the parallels with Irby's constant locomotion. The money and the time and the class and the whiteness and the drugs that were necessary to be. Were these bodies colonial or postcolonial? Were these pleasures queer or historically inscribed? Did knowing of 'The Bluff Rock Massacre' change any of this?

It couldn't have happened without Irby and dear Windeyer. The intense silences of the country began with the murders of Aboriginal people. They are the magnificent edifices of whiteness. This was not the silence of not saying or not doing — after all, Irby did both — but rather the power to disappear people, to 'understand' so completely that nothing was ever said. We 'lesbians' too had been disappeared, even though we were still there. We were 100 per cent somebodies who couldn't be seen. The technique of vanishment was perfect for them and for us, for in the interstices of its silence we discovered another sexed self.

We could never really come home. And yet Irby did. He lived here, murdered other possibilities, stayed and prospered. Our exclusion from his sort of country wasn't all bad. I found it quite warm on the outside. I was glad to get rid of Irby, wanted to step out of Bluff Rock, but where did one go? Back to a beginning?

The original diaries

I'm sitting on my single bed in a pub with a six foot barbed wire-topped fence surrounding the beer garden, which is the only open area. We have passed various groups of Aboriginal people on the roads but there are none in the pub. On our second night I see one Aboriginal man drinking quietly in the corner, completely alone, but this is obviously not an Aboriginal-friendly pub. I am scared. Susan and I are given a 'twin' room. We don't make a fuss. In this place a 'twin room' is a single room with another single bed put in. There is room between the beds for Susan to lie down to do yoga — just. The bags have to go on top of the cupboard. Since we asked to be furthest from any noise, we are right at the very end of the curving corridor of this worn-out, forties? fifties? building. It is a long weekend, but no one else is staying here. Later it turns out that their usual guests are the road or Telstra workers who stay for the week. I think I am glad to be in single beds. They are a convenient, desperate sign of our normalness; this was no place to kiss your girlfriend at the garden gate. Love is blind but this town ain't. I am scared and depressed. There is always the hope that 'research' will lead you to some obscure place that is an undiscovered gem. The researcher as tourist. Perhaps a big old pub with verandahs all around, cheap rooms with home cooking ... and work and holidays mingle. But here, along a highway that is cut every time there is heavy rain, is not quite like that. It feels, I feel, trapped. Tomorrow we start on the original diaries.

THE NEXT DAY

The owner of the original journals and her husband are very welcoming. Their little fibro cottage with its antiques and studio out the back is a haven. We have very formal morning teas and when invited for dinner we know to dress up as much as we can manage. We 'fit', you see.

READING THE ORIGINAL DIARIES

Irby's original diaries provide the most extensive opportunity to engage with, invent and read the culture that enabled the recording of the killing of Aboriginal people and which emerges from the perpetrator's own hand. But what happens as you carefully read and write (and eventually record into the tape recorder) is the development of an excited enthusiasm. It is like falling in love. You become part of a tiny, exclusive, world. You are the civilised, who cares for these documents as thousands haven't, and then the content begins to throttle you. You want to annihilate this history and this man; he and his friends are the original act of classed white male bonding: pack murder. But I am a true researcher. I spend hours and days trying to do it right, and the fantasy of one definitive story of 'The Bluff Rock Massacre' returns. I will work out how he thinks; I will discover the original sin. But of course much of the material is familiar from the published *Memoirs*, and the detail that has been edited out is the daily weather patterns, the endless records of riding here and there and receiving x and y. The most obvious textual difference between the *Memoirs* and the original diary is the removal of the adjective 'immediately'. Too many times for his editing daughter, Irby *immediately* saddles up, *immediately* sets out and *immediately* sends! Too much immediacy? Did Irby imagine himself so? As utterly immediate — without culture or language and existing only through his actions?

I am back in the grind of details and contexts that tease and refuse to satisfy. The earlier journals, which provide an account of the brothers' voyage to Australia reveal two men who love to sing and joke and play their instruments but who are anxious about missing a Sunday service and how best to deal with a mutiny. The later journals, the ones I am most concerned with, are duller in their details, and when he tells stories of any length they are to do with tracking and sometimes finding and murdering Aboriginal people. Irby is available as a player and perpetrator of 'The Bluff Rock Massacre' because he wrote and because he was published. What these original diaries and his *Memoirs* suggest about those actions is the absolute presence of movement and form: horses and death, people and stations, and an immediate past in this present. He's somewhere very near me.

THE DISAPPEARING
WINDEYER

Who was the Windeyer mentioned again and again in Irby's letters and diaries? Windeyer was also a killer of Aboriginal people. He initiated and participated in many 'drives' and 'expeditions', including one of the incidents that is set up as 'The Bluff Rock Massacre'. It is Windeyer who is sent for as soon as it is suspected that Robinson, the shepherd, is dead, Windeyer, with Irby, who 'determined on pursuing the murderers', and Windeyer who assures Irby after the event that he (Irby) had 'no choice'. Windeyer is the seasoned 'expeditioner'. Yet the tourist leaflet ignores him, and his public coupling with the event is almost completely shrouded. Who was he? What was he?

One of my early interests in Windeyer came with the discovery that in the very year that Thomas Windeyer of Deepwater was mounting expeditions and organising the deaths of Aboriginal people, his cousin, Richard Windeyer, was expanding his legal practice, joining the Aboriginal Protection Society and writing 'On the Rights of the Aborigines of Australia'. At first these read like two opposites: the educated and urbane Richard and the murdering, perhaps less educated Thomas. But their fathers took up Deepwater together, at least in name, and in many ways, as I attempted to show in the section on shepherds, Richard's myths of a particularly Australian situation that denied Aboriginal people a right to land provided the 'rational', 'historical' arguments which, when joined with the tactics of massacre and warfare, set up a paternalistic, genocidal system. Richard had also been a part of the defence team for the Myall Creek Massacrers. But Richard Windeyer belongs to another story; it is the far more obscure Thomas Windeyer whom I am trying to 'discover'. Why and how did he disappear from 'The Bluff Rock Massacre'?

The man and his men

Windeyer, Connor and Weaver: these are the names left out of 'The Bluff Rock Massacre', and so they should be. If the scale and spectacle of The Single Massacre is to be sustained, the idea of a mass of men hurtling after a single group of Aboriginal people has to be perpetuated. Admitting Irby's account, which states that there were only four in his 'expedition', paints a different picture. 'Our party consisted of Windeyer, his two servants [Weaver and Connor] and myself', and when he finds himself above the Aboriginal group — 'I fired off for the two men to join us.'[124]

Thomas Windeyer was 24 years old at this time. He died five years later, on another Windeyer property, in northeast Queensland. This was 'Juandah',[125] on the Dawson River, close to Hornet Bank Station, which became notorious after Windeyer's death for the Hornet Bank Massacre. Was this a coincidence, or did Thomas bring with him a style of interaction, a set of beliefs through which a culture of massacre could continue?

At twenty-nine he accidentally shot himself in the thigh while mounting his horse. His father carefully reports in his diary that although Thomas was shot on 6 August 1849, he lingered until 28 September 1850, 'when it pleased the Almighty to take him to himself. He was buried at the back of Mr Stephens Hut and the Grave fenced in.' This means that Thomas 'lingered' for over a year. If in Victorian times people from the wealthy classes desired a slow death, in the company of family and servants, throughout which the almost departed could reflect on their life and prepare for a deeply religious exit (as Ariès[126] suggests), then Thomas got at least one thing right. I wonder who nursed and comforted him? An unnamed Aboriginal servant? And if he reflected upon the deaths he caused, did he ask forgiveness or was he another sort of man altogether? Why did he linger so? In the end, the elements of his death seem to hold within themselves the quiddity of colonialism: staying overlong, the horse, the gun and the final fence.

Thomas Windeyer's position at Deepwater Station is in loco parentis. He is a son-in-waiting and a squatter in the making. He was not the manager or overseer. This position was occupied by Collins, whom Thomas Windeyer's father, Archibald, advises not to take his family to New England. This is some indication that Collins was considered to have a family of some sensibility — in contrast to the labourers (as evidenced in the reports of extra rations for their families, who were living with them).[127] Collins, however, was not a clear or entirely literate writer, and in comparison with Thomas's well-scripted station diary entries, could be considered illiterate. One of Thomas's main functions was probably therefore to provide to his father an account, clearly written, of what happened at the station.

White writing

The station diary attributed to Archibald Windeyer but which must have been written by Thomas, who was actually continuously there at the time, begins in 1845, one year after the massacre that is the Irby source of 'The Bluff Rock Massacre'.

But this was still a time of bloody reprisals and skirmishes. What happened to previous diaries? What do we learn of Thomas Windeyer from his entries? In the three years covered by the diary there is no mention of Aboriginal people except to write as part of a list: '" so " so blacks employed'.[128] This is the Windeyer who Irby reports could understand and make himself understood in the language of the group they were pursuing, Windeyer of 'Windeyer's blacks' and Windeyer who responds so quickly to Irby's request for help. But in this diary there is only page after page of money, work and weather:

> Engaged Connor and White to Shear,
>
> Collins an order for one pound ten to pay Herring for horse, John McPherson 12- per week to take Stephen Fury's flock Samuel MacMillan washer 10- per week in the meantime,
>
> Frank Smith Died. Took possession of his horse saddle and bridle to pay the Doctors bill and other debts to the station.
>
> Buried Frank. 1 chest of tea returned from Bloxsomes w(ith) 89 pound owing 13 pound.[129]

Is there no need to mention the horror since it is all about him? Are Aboriginal deaths and engagements so expected that they have become the ordinary? No need for Windeyer to mention the raids and retaliations he organised since they were such a part of daily life? Or is it a matter of form — this is a *station* diary, so there is no place for organisational detail, even day-to-day activity that didn't have a particular cost, monetary or labour, attached? He does record the building of a bell: '6th July — At the side of the woolshed put up the bell post and bell'.[130] This bell is recorded by others as being particularly used to warn of Aboriginal attack: 'at Deepwater station the hasty clanging of a bell denoted that the watchman had spotted aborigines in the vicinity and generally the sound of gunfire during the day was taken to signify an aboriginal attack'.[131] But there is no purpose given here for the bell, simply (!) bald detail after bald detail. Did the larger operation that was Deepwater (compared with Irby's Bolivia), with its extra workers and families, not demand the same attention to every possibility of Aboriginal presence? Did Thomas Windeyer have reason to be less fearful of ruin brought on by Aboriginal people? Was he being banal or strategic?

There was an 'official' massacre on Deepwater some months after Irby's. Commissioner Fry (from the coastal region, not New England) and three troopers tracked a group of Aboriginal people he held responsible for the murder of a shepherd and dispersal of a sheep flock up from the Clarence River to Deepwater, where in a 'deep brushy ravine' they shot 'five children, four women and seven men'.[132] This was reported by Fry to the Colonial Secretary on 15 April 1845;[133] Thomas's diary begins in October 1845, some six months after this event. So there is never a particular massacre or 'expedition' recorded by others which allows me to show spectacular oppositions between Irby's or the Colonial Secretary's records and Windeyer's. These other reports do, however, suggest very clearly a time in which there was a very active Aboriginal presence and resistance, and yet day after day, for *three* years, there is only a single entry from Windeyer. This is a point of high frustration. Silence is a part of this project, but this blunt silence, amongst so much minor detail, is galling. And although there is an erasure of Aboriginal people, it is not as if Thomas himself disappears. Many of the entries have a deliberate gentle humour that supplies something of a mood or atmosphere of the day.

20th May '46 — raining all day, very miserable, took to our pipes

13th Jan '46 — Mrs Weaver increased her family at precisely fifteen and one half minutes to one, ten o'clock pm

19th Oct '45 — Offered them (Connor and White) 9/4 perscore [to shear] said they would consider about it 'ie' will not take it

So it isn't really fair to say that this is bald detail. Perhaps in the same way that Irby erases the wives and other women associated with his workforce, Aboriginal people disappear from Windeyer's account — except for the single moment when they are employed, and even that appears to be close to unspeakable, and incomprehensible to the reader.

25th Feb 1846   " so " so blacks employed.

I've given this a separate line — I want you to appreciate its importance to this book. Let me try it a little bigger:

25th Feb 1846   " so " so blacks employed.

and bolder:

25th Feb 1846   " so " so blacks employed.

This is all we have. Irby wrote enough to let us see something of the shifts and changes involved in becoming a 'settler', and we see how he shaped his stories to his different audiences. But Windeyer simply reports. And this report has no space for story, for narrative, for the failures or 'successes' of trying to contain Aboriginal people. This could be deliberate, keeping a careful eye on the elderly parental audience, or a sensibility that meant his many encounters with Aboriginal people simply did not matter here.

These certain entries establish a curious constancy for the new and uncertain station. There is no real disturbance to Windeyer's watching and recording of resources going in and out. We might see each entry as an effort in daily forgetting that drives Windeyer again and again into the present — even yesterday has been lost except as something to look back upon. Yesterday was only when Connor first owed some tea, or when the wages for shearing rose. I wonder about this ritual of forgetting Aboriginal people and its relationship to those other moments of absolute present presence, where mentally and physically he must have been totally concentrated on his body and horse as he hunted Aboriginal people. Can we think that his silence suggests a saturation in Aboriginality that could not be spoken of until their difference could be known enough, could be translated into almost workers, 'employable' types? After all, what kind of account book could speak of those other Aboriginal people? And so we have omissions and the unsayable … and what Windeyer writes:

25th Feb 1846   " so " so blacks employed.

This entry follows a list of the full names of non-Aboriginal workers and the exact rates at which they will be paid. The ditto marks are therefore referring to an impossibility, because Aboriginal workers were not paid. The marks are not repeating the conditions of the previous entry, but it looks as if they are. Does this 'mask and pervert a basic reality' or 'mask the *absence* of a basic reality'?[134] The unspecified number of 'blacks', and the absence of detail about their wages and set tasks, makes this a very different entry, and yet the effort is there to make the entry *fit*. If you are killing people, if you are taking their labour but not paying them and if you are doing this on a reasonably large scale, not just to isolated individuals, what are you doing? Perhaps you are a slave holder and can enter their names in your stock books. But what if these same people refuse to stay under your control, arrive to be 'employed' at certain times and then move back or away? What if their wholly autonomous lives have incorporated just the bits they want of you and no more? You are in an unspeakable, unwriterly relationship to them. You are not in an 'equal' relationship; that word has no meaning in this terrain, where, unlike them, you are refusing to move back, or away or simply on. And how could equality account for your fears, your bell erection and the murders you commit? You attempt to taxonomise Aboriginal people, you recognise that your treatment of this particular group has some similarities at certain moments with 'employment', but you can't quite complete the movement, you can't name them, you can't list their tasks and you can't itemise their payments. Words fail because your system fails — you are not actually employing them; you are approximating a category of worker that is changing beneath your hand.

Why does Windeyer take this moment to include Aboriginal people at all? What is it about the repetition, the toting up, that prevents him excluding them? Does the listing, the item-isation, carry its own insistence on completion, its own totalistic ethic? It is useful to contemplate lists.

Lists were the lifeblood of the squatter-devised community. The entire station's sustenance depended upon the correct detailing of what was needed until the next dray brought supplies. The stations constantly borrowed from one another, as Irby too records, and they were in a continuous relationship of paid and owing with one and other. It is the record of these small exchanges that incorporates these stations into a new community 'beyond the boundaries'. Upon primitive lists non-Aboriginal society arrives. But can you list everything?

Windeyer seems to have personified 'the station' in a particular way. Remember that when Frank dies, it is not Windeyer who is owed, but 'the station'. This is indicative of Windeyer's situation as *son* of the 'owner' rather than *the* 'owner'. He is running an account, and that account is the station. But this doesn't really help explain his minute admission of Aboriginal labour, because even if they were merely being paid mutton or flour or bad tea, these payments would still have been important enough to record — these commodities were common currency and had real repercussions for supply lists. Could these Aboriginal workers have been forced? Paid nothing in kind but granted some non-material good, such as freedom to travel or ...? Might this Aboriginal group have assisted because they were asked? Might they have assumed some sort of reciprocity? Protection? It is easy to see why Windeyer disappears from 'The Bluff Rock Massacre' — according to his words, how could he have been a part of killing Aboriginal people who were never there? Except for a moment, when they were almost employed as something like workers.

DEEPWATER STATION

Deepwater Station was the home of Thomas Windeyer. When he was there, he and the Irbys initially lived in a small hut of two rooms. But now it is a station homestead with empty workers' cottages that gesture back to a time when it was the cynosure of a local aristocracy. Deepwater, the village, some five kilometres from the station, has a population of 300 and is closer to Glen Innes than to Tenterfield. Its postcode was found by the last census to have some of the lowest incomes in New South Wales. There is an excellent primary school and a general store that sells the best fruit around. There are small and large farms and poor and rich people, and you can choose to drink at the top or the bottom pub. The children of the village leave home for university, or a job 'in town' or any city. Smallness is not togetherness. Smallness is not sameness.

Weaver and Connor

And what of Weaver and Connor, Windeyer's 'servants'?[135] Their opportunity to write themselves into 'The Bluff Rock Massacre' is limited. Weaver couldn't write. His mark is recorded in lieu of a signature in the diary of Archibald Windeyer (Thomas's father), beneath the conditions of employment:

> David Weaver is to pay half his passage money as per agreement, 10 pounds of which I charged him now, the remaining half he is to pay next year
>
> 1 years wages Dec 1838 20 pounds
>
> Gratuity I give him voluntary & a promise for good conduct 5 pounds
>
> I advanced him for clothes, boots, washing and friends passage[136]

So Weaver had been on Deepwater Station since the very beginning of it. He was not bonded labour; he may have been known to the Windeyers in England, and he was invested in by Archibald Windeyer. Weaver also had a wife and a family. We don't know their names, but we have Thomas Windeyer's entry from 13 January 1846: 'Mrs Weaver increased her family at precisely fifteen and one half minutes to one, ten o'clock pm'. How could a birth be both at ten and at one or did he enter it at ten o'clock? And Connor? Connor was 'engaged': 'Engaged Connor and White to shear'[137] and 'Engaged two other men' (one of whom is Connor).[138] Another squatting neighbour, Robertson, records in one of his lists:

| Connor 2½ days | 11 shillings and 3 pence |
| Black boy 2 days | 9 shillings 0 pence[139] |

A near neighbour therefore appears to be paying at least one 'black boy' what looks like equal wages while denying him a name. Connor is not listed as bonded labour, but neither is he mentioned as having any particular arrangement with the Windeyers, so he was probably a free immigrant or ticket-of-leave man who worked about the area during shearing and was otherwise more or less attached to Deepwater. I'm not certain if there was a presumed intimacy in Irby's description of Connor and Weaver as 'Windeyer's men'. Irby refers to Weaver as Windeyer's servant but to Connor as 'his man'.[140] Does this suggest that they were particularly chosen by Windeyer for this task? Moments before the massacre, Weaver and Connor were left with instructions to tie the horses and to 'follow in case they heard us fire, we promising to return in case they fired'.[141] When Irby knows that the Aboriginal people are trapped beneath the rocks on which he is standing, he 'fired off' for the two men to join him. Weaver and Connor come. The not-too-many meanings of gunfire. One shot in the air means come, sustained shots means slaughter. If I told you to stand in the middle of the road, would you do it? If I shot in the air, who would come? At one shot, Weaver and Connor come up. They haven't seen the single Aboriginal man run down; they are not among the 'natives'' dogs; they have to start shooting as soon as they arrive at the spot, firing their shots into a group of people trapped below them. Windeyer's men.

The case of the disappearing whiteness

The idea of whiteness, sometimes a shadowy presence, sometimes explicitly addressed, has been a constant subtext of all the writings so far. I have been very careful to employ the expression 'white' only on certain occasions and in contexts which I believe are relevant. In most of the texts and contexts that I am looking at the division is much more clearly Aboriginal and non-Aboriginal, rather than black and white. Naturally, these temporary folds can't prevent the incessant spillage of naming. Within the boundaries of the term 'Aboriginal', do I include 'wild blacks' and 'Tommy'? And what of the 'black trackers' and Native Police who assisted in the capture of other Aboriginal people? Are they a new sort of Aboriginal person, or non-Aboriginal, or ...? Should there be a colonial nomenclature dependent upon who was shot and who wasn't? If we did this, bushrangers, some Aboriginal people and escaped convicts might form a group to be contrasted with the Native Police, other armed forces, pastoralists, farmers, farm labourers (which always included Aboriginal people) and so on. If we expanded this to include hangings, we could include solicitors, judges and legal systems. 'Black' might be useful as a means of acknowledging early relationships that were formed between Anglo-African convicts, Massacarans and Aboriginal people, but what of Johnston the 'black' or mulatto convict who was hanged for his role in the Myall Creek Massacre? Wasn't he much more a settler or labourer than 'black'? I am making this judgement because he killed and was hanged on that basis.

Does killing with others invent an especially virulent identity? Is that how one became a settler or labourer 'outside the limits'? Or does murder place one within the meta category of terrible 'killer', as the Myall Creek murderers' inclusion in the *The Chronicle of Crime, or the New Newgate Calendar being A Series of Memoirs and Anecdotes of Notorious Characters* would suggest? And don't the oppositions of 'Aboriginal' and 'non-Aboriginal', 'black' and 'white' continue the erasure of the immense diversity of languages and cultures that existed and continue to exist within those strange, metastasising headings?

Looking at the 1840s but writing on the postfeminist, post-colonial wordscape, I want to present whiteness as a partial solution to the problem of Windeyer. Windeyer's diary textually disappears Aboriginal people, but he also reduces himself to the advancer of monies, the recorder of debts and the smoker of pipes. He makes himself a system, not a race. He makes himself a neutral recorder, not a colour. This reminds me of sociologist Ruth Frankenberg[142] and her familiar experiment: when individuals are asked to write down the ways in which they would identify themselves, they invariably list the things that mark their distinctness — lesbian, black, woman, working class, for example — and fail to identify middle classness, heterosexuality, and whiteness. Those categories are so power-ful that they have created a seemingly natural landscape within which we imagine ourselves at home. Being 'ordinary', we claim we cannot see the privilege these things grant us; they are naturalised. (And look how easily I plunge into 'we' — are you all white or middle class or heterosexual? I hope not.) And of course the nature of this privilege is itself invisible. There are no funds called 'white' funds (and yet most money goes to whites), no Minister for White Affairs (and yet most ministers are white). My privilege is my anonymous whiteness.

Can you be white only when you disappear? Perhaps in 1845 you wrote explicit narratives only if you occupied a particular position of cultured certainty that depended more directly upon education and class than on whiteness. Did you take time off white to write, perhaps? Did not saying anything about anyone perhaps make you really white? Did being 'white' rather than 'non-Aboriginal' mean you saw no point in describing what was happening about you because you were so implicated in that system? White is nothing, and yet it's everything. Whiteness is unlike other categories because of its very mobility. Here it couples with middleclassness and abled, there with lesbian and professional. But its mobility is not only as one part of some concatenation; it is also in the way it passes as process. It can be a legal system, a way of working, a dress code, a bank or a library. There is nothing to which it *necessarily* refers. Context is all — or is it?[143]

'In order to understand Windeyer, we need to read him through the systems he invents, as he seems to read and write himself. A smoker of pipes, a recorder of monies, a character put in recordable control. What might this suggest about whiteness?

THEY DO IT WITH MIRRORS

When thinking about the ways in which whiteness works, two particular images come to mind. The first is a Leunig cartoon I saw years ago which has a figure contemplating the first glass-clad skyscraper, then another and another skyscraper is mirror-tiled until every building is a mere reflection of other mirrors, with only shadowy lines between them. The second image is that of mirrored fish scales. The more light is thrown on their scales, which act as tiny mirrors, the less they are able to be seen. My suggestion is that whiteness works in at least these two ways.

The first point is the conceit that 'white' is not a colour but is best understood as light. The invasion/settlement of Australia, the coming of 'whites', was not represented as one colour meeting another, which would inevitably lead to some mingling of the colours (which of course did happen), but rather as the coming of a metaphorical *light* — which was variously called massacre, invasion, civilisation and (sometimes) religion. Unlike mere colours, light was itself responsible for colour. It invented, distorted and reflected what was seen.

'Settlement', government, economy and education were the mirrored tiles with which light reflected back on itself. There were so many tiles that it was impossible to find the original source of light — it had long since been multiply reflected and refracted. Light reflected not only the good, but also the bad, in its multiple images, and when an injustice was seen, further light would be thrown upon the subject, until it too reflected the right colour or aspect or goodness. An example of such an effect might be the Westminster-informed legal system. But while good and bad, justice and injustice, could be seen on the tiles, the more light was shone, the more the tiles themselves disappeared, and what was light and what was tile became confused. Within whiteness, white people became institutions and systems — they represented the presumed basis of a normal functioning society. So-called ordinary (white) language became smooth and 'representational'. The task with Windeyer's diary is to attempt to wrest 'whiteness' away from its normalising effects. But what is white and what is patriarchal? What is white and what is imperialism?

Have I reached my own end point, where I simply can't see what he does because I do it, or have it, too? Am I writing white? This is the ahistorical threat of whiteness, its all-encompassing power to get me, to give me something I may not even want. I can't see the white except when it is contrasted with its own shadows, but there is often too much light for shadows to occur. I can't quite believe I *am* white.

Chorus moans: *GET REAL!*

EVERYONE IS BLACK AT A DISTANCE

Does this happen to everyone? Is there some point when the writer loses control of the point? At this moment, in trying to write about Windeyer through whiteness when whiteness is something that right now, right here, needs to be constructed, deconstructed, run over, pulled about, and finally revealed — I fail. My idea of openly making the past in the present has come

home to roost. Irby was so identifiable. Our mutual textuality permitted our relationship, but Windeyer simply *is* in a way that I 'simply' am. It is a crisis of excruciating self-consciousness, of grisly overidentification. I sit and write in a world removed from others. I drink quietly on my verandah. I can list what I do. I can show you my bank account. Windeyer has left me a way of life. The ordering and the recording, the white patterning, are all here in *my* head. But my white patterns record how land was taken, my white patterns show how my own overblown love of the land I grew up on is now doubtful and ugly and undecided. When I write down how much I am paying, it is never enough. When I think of the nation/station it will always be in debt, always owing. This is the list of lists. But now I'm thinking of myself as a boat listing over on the water, nearly drowning. And now that image of the tragic boat, alone on a vast sea (make it dark as well), looks so stupid, ludicrous, so sorry for oneself — *Get ON with it!* But I can't without imagining, and everything I think seems wrong. I am a secret agent, I am 007, about to blow up whiteness. I am a good mole, I'll travel far, I'll carry bombs — I am not afraid. But all this action stuff sounds like another list of what I'll do and where I'll go. Beginning, Middle and End. Action lists. Narration lists. I can't act outside of them. I will sit in my room and hold my finger on the key forever, something soothing, something that won't offend, something like this
zzzzzzzzzzzzzzzzzzzzzzzzzzzzzzzzzzzzzzzzzzzzzzzzzzzzzzzzzzzz
zzzzzzzzzzzzzzzzzzzzzzzzzzzzzzzzzzzzzzzzzzzzzzzzzzzzzzzzzzzz
zzzzzzzzzzzzzzzzzzzzzzzzzzzzzzzzzzzzzzzzzzzzzzzzzzzzzzzzzzzz
zzzzzzzzzzzzzzzzzzzzzzzzzzzzzzzzzzzzzzzzzzzzzzzzzzzzzzzzzzzz
zzzzzzzzzzzzzzzzzzzzzzzzzzzzzzzzzzzzzzzzzzzzzzzzzzzzzzzzzzzz
I've just opened my eyes and I see the zeds starting on the new line. I wanted them to start right after 'this' but the computer reads them as a single word and insists that as a single word it

just won't go. These crappy, crappy, zeds — they are so straight, so utterly straight, so incredibly neat. They even look as if they make sense. They bring me unexpected joy. The lines look neat — they contain letters, but THEY HAVE NO MEANING! This is a triumph. This is a legal system that can't make 'sense' of forced removals and massacres, which insists it can still justify the taking of land if one connection was broken; it can't believe in renewed connections or old connections. These are the zeds of a government who can't say they're sorry, of a ... But what do I mean has no 'meaning'? Everything has meaning. This is one of my credos. This is the fascination of 'The Bluff Rock Massacre': it means so many things. But that is the problem with the zeds. They are over-attached to their zedness, they insist on themselves until they become nonsense. And this is what 'white' law does: it over-attaches to the single meaning of itself until it stops doing what it once imperfectly did, which was to stand for the possibility of justice. But what about Windeyer? What about his sense? His zeds are his entries, which insist on their own ordinariness to the point of madness. It is not only Aboriginal resistance and Aboriginal 'writing back' which makes them mad; it is also the many ways in which people wanted to be white. It is Irby who makes Windeyer look most strange.

EVERYONE IS BLACK AT A DISTANCE (MARK II)

I am sitting in a restaurant in Chinatown (Sydney) with my white partner, my brown nephews and their white mother. The Australian Chinese (?) *maître d'* comes over and asks if things are fine and then says, touching the head of one of my nephews, 'Lovely hair — where did you get them?' I have no memory of what we actually said in response, but the uncensored version would have been — 'He "got" them from my sister and brother-in-law, they are a part of me/him, you turkey', etc. We probably said their father was Zimbabwean. But I was furious. Aunt rage? Race rage? How could anyone so simply draw a line where there was none? And on the basis of hair or colour? There was no intention to offend that I could see. The man may have intended a less loaded 'Where are they from?' rather than the capitalist acquisitiveness implicated in his use of 'get'. And what did it mean to be experiencing this in a 'Chinese' restaurant, when the Chinese were a group against whom the fears of miscegenation and cheap labour were given full rein by an ungrateful nation? The work of cultural theorists Rey Chow[144] and Ien Ang[145] warns us to never be complacent about who and what might constitute 'Chineseness', and at the moment of this event, in a stark choice between 'white' and 'black', what was I? What was he? If there was a colour to my Auntydom, was it black?

This conditional 'blackness' is very different from Windeyer's 'blacks'. In his case it is not the colour but the plural which unquestionably indicates that he is referring to Indigenous Australians and not other labourers with black skin. His father had in fact employed at least one convict with black skin[146] who may have worked at Deepwater, but he was not a 'black'. 'Blacks', therefore, always meant more than colour. In Windeyer's case the word meant labour, threat, people he could shoot, people to be possibly paid. It would be tempting to suggest that in the categorisation of Aboriginal people as 'blacks' we also have the creation of all others as 'whites' (even if they were black). In this way there could be an argument that Aboriginal people, through people like Windeyer, invented 'white' Australians. But as Irby's differentiations show us, there was never anything stable about the category of non-Aboriginal or Aboriginal people. Windeyer, however, disappears Aboriginal people from his text, and in his lack of differentiation, in his failure to admit any particularity, isn't 'white Australian' born?

IT IS RIDICULOUS

(EVERYONE IS BLACK AT A DISTANCE) (MARK III)

When Richard, my black Zimbabwean brother-in-law, arrived in Australia he did not leave his Erskineville squat for a week. David Gundy, a completely innocent, but most importantly for the purposes of the police, Aboriginal man, had been shot dead in his home. The police knew, you see, what an *Aboriginal* man looked like. Richard thought that what had happened in his original home in South Africa was happening again here. When my sister told me, we were sympathetic but we hmpphed. Of course there were occasional injustices, gross injustices, but the system, *our* system was OK. We did not believe Richard was vulnerable to attack here. He was black, not Indigenous.

And then one day at afternoon tea, Richard began to talk about the KKK Sauna which he had passed in Anzac Parade. How could they have something like that? I bet you won't find many black people in there etc. I was certain *this* was nonsense. I vaguely knew it to be a gay sauna — and therefore not only OK, but good. A gay venue surviving outside the ghetto; the name referred to something else, for sure. But what?

My girlfriend at the time was the daughter and grand-daughter of white liberal South Africans. At a time when we were all trying to free Nelson Mandela, she would occasionally do her impersonation of an Afrikaans accent. We laughed and laughed — it was so ridiculous. Richard said 'They are cruel people.' He didn't see the humour. They were not ridiculous to him.

A few years later it was my turn to be with Richard — there were several of us taking shifts to cover all the hours it might take. He was in a coma, part of the diaspora of HIV, and I was waiting with him. I was holding his hand and watching him breathe, taking breaths with him, when his breath got a little more even and he died. There was nothing as noisy as an angel

231

appearing; there was a complete, touchable silence. Our hands felt utterly united, completely alive. The whole room was pure stillness. How had this happened? How did it come about that this man, miles from where he had grown up, should find me at his death? And why should I have had the gift of that atmosphere, that extraordinary room? It was ridiculous. Death wasn't black at all. And neither was it white.

Death by implication

Windeyer's records are the mark of a man at work. The expected nineteenth century sentimental response to death is absent. There is no feeling, no emotional cost, no curiosity — simply death and tea. One of the first fair-dinkum laconic bushmen?

> 24th   Frank Smith Died. Took possession of his horse saddle and bridle to pay the Doctors bill and other debts due to the station.

> 25th   Buried Frank. 1 chest of tea returned from Bloxsomes w(ith) 89 pound owing 13 pound.

Frank Smith's death is barely given a full stop. The fact of dying is absolutely conjoined with a series of actions. Selling his possessions and paying his debts are as textually significant in this entry as the final expiration. Windeyer has learnt to record a human life in terms of debts and dues. Assigned labour was partly paid in rations. Exact amounts of flour, mutton, moist sugar, tea, soap and tobacco were given according to the number of children or the presence of a wife, and in exchange, a predictable amount of labouring energy was required. Why couldn't Windeyer write, 'Blacks killed, 45 cartridges expended'? Or given that Irby suggests that he was mostly unsuccessful in his pursuit of 'wild' Aboriginal people, why couldn't he write, 'Rode after blacks' or anything that showed the presence, friendly or otherwise, of Aboriginal people. But we have only '" " blacks employed'. One answer is that Windeyer was not responsible for Aboriginal people. He was not their master and their lives could not be accounted for within his system of ledgers. He had no set rates of exchange for the labour their bodies produced, and he had no recourse to the magistrates when they disobeyed him. He couldn't demand they be flogged or fined or ... But perhaps his ledger style offers one sort of translation he might have understood:

Land taken from Aboriginal people to make 'Deepwater': 54,400 acres

Destruction of food resources: 1 shilling per acre

Refusal to obey laws of country, treason, perjury, trespass etc: 1 pound per day of offence

Water: " " per acre

Pasture: " " per acre

Culture " " per acre

Murder: " " per body?

Employment of Aboriginal people: " " per day

But what an enormous entry this would have to be. Windeyer owned as far as the eye could see, and he had power over as much as the hand could write — he could punish labourers but not hang them, and he could write requests for various other kinds of power. Frank Smith died, debts and all. But no Aboriginal people did, not by Windeyer's hand; thick ink on thick paper.

The rock on the edge of my skin

As a monument to Windeyer — to what wasn't recorded, to what wasn't, can't be, seen — Bluff Rock seems very appropriate. There is a warning in its silence, as there is in Windeyer's diary. If I understand my position to be wholly stable, able to be simply listed and recorded, I will fail to articulate a sense of whiteness that continues within my volatile self. I understand myself to be always embodied, and always in a state of becoming and connecting with others. But those possibilities exist within an environment of systemic whiteness. 'White' endures in a way that other categories or ways of knowing do not, but 'white' is also a kind of silence written into how we know the past and how we see the land around us.

If I listen and see, I can show how I have been shaped by the colonial experience and implicated in the destruction of some Aboriginal people, but how I have also been given the possibilities of mutuality and connection. Windeyer, even more than Irby, is 'The Bluff Rock Massacre'. He is the single storied silence of that tale. He has invented a monolithic whiteness, whereas I acknowledge its instability and contextuality amid its frightening endurability. We both belong to Bluff Rock. But in my belonging I am trying to live, as feminist critic Minnie Bruce Pratt suggests, 'on the edge of my skin'.[147]

I have arrived at a familiar point in postcolonial, post-feminist, thought — at the invented, historically contingent meaning of an identity like 'white', or 'woman'. As one summary puts it, 'Women (as a unified category) don't exist, but it is (sometimes) useful (strategically) to believe they do.' There is a post-liberation politics committed to the self always expanding, always attempting the limit experience that makes new identities, new ways of thinking and being, possible. This idea of constant expansion is also how colonialism was imagined, though expansion was there formulated as a straight, progressive path.

Only with Bluff Rock do I feel the desire to question the connection between becoming and being. That is, when looking at whiteness, whiteness seems to do the opposite of what I expect it to do. The very mobility of how and what 'we' can be — lesbian, woman, man, middle class — seems to hide the endurability of white. Is the theoretical framework that supports the possibility of 'becoming' so embedded in whiteness that that once-celebrated fluidity simply perpetuates the privilege of whiteness? Is it that white doesn't exist, but it is strategically useful to believe it does? Or does it sound more believable to say, 'White exists, and it endures, but it is strategically useful to believe it doesn't'?

And somehow a limited movement of atonement doesn't entirely work either. To say I am sometimes racist, to point to parts of this book and write, 'I acknowledge the racist assumptions here', to say, 'But I am not always this way; I am also anti-racist', 'I have worked in this book against the subtle powers of race', 'White is only one of my positions' ... yet yet yet ... no longer seems enough. And neither is it enough to say we are all constantly becoming, for although that displaces the power of particular identities, it does not displace or expose the light of 'white'. To do that, a much more radical fracturing is called for, which in Australia must begin with the undoing of 'settlement' — and so also of History as we now know it and do it.

When writing Windeyer, it is important to keep pointing to the particular moments when something we might want to call whiteness is able to appear, because whiteness is so often dependent upon its capacity to disappear. Describing a list, such as Windeyer's lists, as a technique of white power reminds us of the ubiquity and enduring raw force of racialised writing. My claims to knowing Windeyer are based on 'going there', reading him and placing him within a particular historical context. If I am to challenge the awful banality of his records, which seem to efface murder, I must also acknowledge that my techniques of knowing him may be a problem. In our claims to 'know' something or someone through evidences and styles of research we can reduce them to 'same', thus destroying what is different about them and (usually) maintaining our own singular completeness.[148] In looking at Windeyer I need to be able to show you both his difference (from me) and his familiarity (to me). I need to be able to suggest the ways in which Windeyer's world pulls me towards it, but also why I am intent on translating and acknowledging that pull, showing its purchase in my life and my ways of knowing him. In doing so I am hoping to let you see a set of records as a kind of living creature that has a force we still need to reckon. That force is hopefully frayed by working along the fracture lines of whiteness. But I must also admit that while writing this critiqued whiteness I might be the last to know that I am reproducing its less obvious forms.

MAKING ENDS MEET

Land, God and longing

I am walking down Penrith's High Street, in the western suburbs of Sydney. It is the walk for reconciliation. I thought it was the rally in support of Native Title. There are differences in politics and attitude between these. I cannot find a university banner to walk behind. I had assumed that there would be one, but today universities have been replaced by Health Networks and Christian schools as the carriers of community conscience. It is hot and I find friends, individuals, from uni who have also found others to connect with. At the end of this bitumen-sticky, gentle walk we arrive at the rally proper, where almost every speaker has a religious calling and we are thanked and preached to. Some of the balloons say 'Justice, mercy, compassion'. Mercy and compassion for whom? Helium-filled longings from non-Aboriginals for them or Himself to have mercy on 'us'. This is Christian shorthand for something I don't quite understand.

There is a performance by a Christian primary school of a rainbow dance; all the colours are necessary (it says) to make the world work. I realise I'm lonely. I want the sisters to be there. I want that loose alliance, that feministy, leso, gay boy, lefty crowd to be here and they're not. Is it too far west? Have those loose collections fallen into some final, fragmented dance party? And while I applaud the preachers and the speakers, I am thinking — at each mention of God — that this is no place to hold your girlfriend's hand. But these are strange times, when 'mainstreaming' (unisex gyms, no women's studies subjects, because we are all equal now) is still considered a strategy. So what if I feel a little out of place, if I don't feel addressed by this crowd — a little alienation isn't a high price to pay if the Ten Point Plan could be overturned, if land could be distributed, if the full possibilities of Mabo could be expanded and put in place. But you see the problem: so quickly I'm thinking like an old comrade — things will be better, just a few adjustments, just a few million dissidents, just let us institutionalise the queers, starve the Ukrainians … and things will be OK. But why not the rhetoric of the Church? After all, it has the words — 'compassion, mercy, justice' — to temporarily overarch all difference. It is a magnificently fragmented, transcendent universal that might just hold all this together. And suddenly I understand the appeal. Who else could form a ring, hand in hand, around Bluff Rock and overcome the past in our hearts? Who has the right? Please God grant us non-Aboriginals compassionate, merciful Kooris. Forgive us our trespassing as we forgive those who trespass against us. Forgive us for the taking of your land as we will forgive those of you who refuse to forgive us? But who would take on the burden of forgiving or being forgiven? What was it that God said to the Rabbi when he asked for His words amidst the Holocaust? I am tired, tired unto death. Are we allowed partial, fluid Gods? Gods that give us the hope, but not the necessity, of resolution? Gods that are contextual and strategic? Gods that will welcome lesbians and gays one day and forgive the past another? God never died, he just became one more strategy, one more political possibility.

When Aboriginal people were murdered, was God waiting in the homestead? Shining His boots while waiting to lead whom to the gates of salvation? Aah, but this is a different God, a bright, shining, just God that never did any of that. This God could walk right through Bluff Rock and all mica crumbs of deep despair would drop away, clean as a whistle. Just as suddenly as it bloomed/loomed, my love affair with Christ is over. Botched-up, mixed-up 'history'/cultural studies with no offers of truth or redemption at least puzzles and engages — I'll take Bluff Rock after all.

Placing an end

It was in part the experience of walking over Bluff Rock that made me doubt it as the site of a massacre of Aboriginal people. Walking out the textual body of Keating and Irby's accounts, with all the other stories in my head, didn't make the fit I was looking for. In the end, this landscape had a logic of its own which kept interjecting. I kept thinking that Aboriginal people who lived here, who would have known this country so well, would never have let it happen like this. They would have got away; they would not have run up to a cliff and there wasn't the open country for the squatters on horseback to force them into. The Land Council worker's story of Aboriginal trickery makes more sense.

Or was I simply so intrinsically non-Aboriginal, so caught in my desire for another sort of history, that even looking at the rock I still couldn't see destruction like that? I know Aboriginal people were massacred — usually, according to my readings, by grisly shooting parties, and in ambushed or snared groups. They were massacred by Windeyer and Irby when trapped beneath the rocks. They were massacred 'officially' in a gully near Deepwater. They were probably massacred somewhere else near Tenterfield as Keating described (perhaps along Demon Creek), long before the machinery of removal and reservations and missions. And even the total of all those tiny fragments can never be the whole of the story. There were too many massacres. For the single event of 'The Bluff Rock Massacre' to be true, and for me to go on being witness to its truth, would be to be a good, educated white. My father (in particular) and mother would have been proud. My grandfather would have done the Anglo equivalent of spitting in my face. I would be nicely placed as speaking for an injustice to others. I would be a hero of sorts, almost a sort of Judith Wright (without, unfortunately, the poetry). But the truth I found was grubby and unrecognisable. As a lesbian, wanting to get out of town, I found I was sick of being Bluff Rock.

When you go back to your childhood for work, some strange things happen. In the first place, it wasn't quite home. The towns of Glen Innes and Tenterfield are sixty kilometres apart. So I could visit Tenterfield, particularly under Susan's influence, as an almost tourist. We wandered up beautiful country lanes in romantic mists and lived out this version of an area that my own small-town geographer would once have construed as simply the wrong end of town. Run-down cottages and paddocks of mixed cow breeds, once sure signs of the disorder of poverty, became quaint and scenic, the inhabitants safe and unrecognisable. We did things no one ever did in my childhood. We citified, yuppified, middleclassed, arts studented, lesbianfied, outsiderfied the landscape with our ritual exercise and dusk drinks at lookouts. With our questions and tasks and insouciant naivety we were not afraid; things could be said, questions could be asked. We played table tennis after dinner.

Writing up

Writing up. Even the words are hopeful. From a mixture of journal entries, readings, primary sources, leaflets and different visits I have written up what 'going there', doing this, was all about. Like 'talking up' a bad proposition, I can inflate the quality of my insights, expand, through careful selection, my growing awareness, my located-thereness. I can now write down the coherent theorisation of what happened. Instead I find my self writing to you. You, my reader, were not an imagined presence at the time. Then I really was 'just' writing down, just tracking, just disciplining myself to record. Now I am chopping up, sautéing, broiling those records to invent (partial) stories for you. And although the 'I' is still writing, I'm not the 'I' I used to be. And what a convenient catch 'you' are, my invented ears that hear this speaking out. But I'm writing too fast. I can't keep going back and taking away; something must be left. I loved this place. I'm running all over my parents' lives, I'm shitting on the hand that fed me, I'm school captain gone grunge. I'm mucking up. I'm scratching out the things that people died for. I'm writing too fast. I can't see or hear, my sisters are dead, and I'm just writing too fast. There's nothing to witness, nothing to say. It's snow-dry country with no animals in sight and I'm writing too fast. It's dying all over their feedlot cattle, it's dying all over the quick-buck crops that blow the brains out of the soil. That's my country, Jackie (Huggins)[149] — see why I can't go home? But I write real fast. I'm keeping my toes tingling and my tongue twisted so high in the air that I'm making a place of my own up here. It's not much, but you come visit. Any time.

Conclusion

Bluff Rock is an uneasy past. It is presence and present without immediate voice and yet it is a provocation to speak; a space where accustomed thought stutters.[150] It demands a life's story, a live speaking; this is one of its many possible auto-biographies.

The autobiographical of this past present presence is a bodial haunting. Bodies of knowledge, bodies that hurt, and administrative bodies reveal the spectral selves that write into current flesh in a weird arrangement that produces 'now'. The comfort of the historicised past is disturbed by the fleshy immanence of this past, as stories spill over stories in disjointed efforts to spit and whisper this ghosted skin, this stammering tongue, this Bluff Rock. Tourist leaflets, gossip, collected data, published diaries, letters, me and you, him and me, poems and pictures ... together they refuse the seductive known of 'a story about the past' and leave in its place this wash of reactive possibilities.

A part of this place is death. Bluff Rock remains as the invisible past deaths of Indigenous Australians remains. A fact, a present presence, ultimately untellable but remaining — always. This is not something to 'get right', to 'correct' or resolve for non-Indigenous Australians. It is something to live properly, personally and politically with. Bluff Rock teaches us that, as generations of Indigenous activists, intellectuals, elders and writers have done in a more immediate way.

'The Bluff Rock Massacre' as a story in place, as a situated narrative, is a mother. A mucilaginous substance that has let other stories ferment. It is sticky stuff that brings other words forward to show what colonialism still creates. Its shape was that of a fable of annihilation and the resultant certainty of non-Indigenous presence, but it could not contain, in this place, what it produced. And because of what it produced its own shape changed, and those of us who use it still know that its slimy stick is working with the colonial within us to make up something more.

Bluff Rock in its abiding presence, 'The Bluff Rock Massacre' in its textual performances, in its half-remembered connections to someone we know who did something to

Indigenous peoples, and both in their deeply localised ephemera and their national importance, are places and ways of making up now. Bluff Rock lets us say, do and think in a complex, productive way as long as we think the past and subjectivity, place and time, simultaneously, while granting a space to the unknowable.

That some of what is said might be a tourist tale, a muttered local truth, a plaque, a queer book, a new sense of hope or a bush poem might seem strange. They all might seem inadequate, wrong or weird. But that is right. All of them become efforts to actively but gracefully cohabit with Bluff Rock.

And finally

Susan and I are on our last 'field trip'. We have my two nieces and nephew and we are going on the recommended experience of the Tenterfield Tourist Office — we are on the Woolloo Woolloo Aboriginal Cultural Tour. We are picked up by a small bus at the Tourist Information Centre and set off in the opposite direction to Bluff Rock. We pass the homestead of Tenterfield Station (where the Irbys went to eat strawberries), which is pointed out to us, and the story is told of how McKenzie was one of the first 'whitefellas or gubbas'. Our guide points out the erosion brought on by the intense clearing and says, 'Well, we would have done it a bit different.' And then we are shown bush foods and Thunderbolt's cave and we climb Woolloo Woolloo, which I once knew as Bald Rock. We learn a little bit of the Bundjalung language and eat a good lunch and learn to throw a boomerang. The massacre is never mentioned directly, but it is mentioned in passing as we are shown a rock formation connected to Bluff Rock. This guide is interested in the future — and all the important sites are out this way anyway. It is a wonderful experience. Colonialism is put into perspective as just one group of people who came here — people who really didn't know much about the foods available or how the land worked. Aboriginal people were killed but there is still a strong Aboriginal presence, and languages are being relearnt and opportunities being invented. I know this delight is fragile. I know it's 'just' a tourist attraction, not an absolution. I also know that this enormous feeling of calm and place is entirely dependent on Aboriginal generosity and that that is a much exploited thing. These are 'cultural' tours, not Historical ones, but the histories they invent and the cultures they create make a place for me. They let me live. Thank you.

And then

Months later I am sent a photograph of the memorial to the massacre, which has been recently erected. Most of the text is very familiar, but it is the final words and Indigenous unveilers that remind me that this story doesn't end.

> Unveiled in memory of the Aboriginals killed in this
> area during settlement by
>
> George Binge & Bertha Daley

ACKNOWLEDGEMENTS

This book has emerged because I have had the luck to have friends who challenge, inspire and sustain me. Thank you all. For the constancy of their intellectual engagement and friendship may I thank in particular Penny Rossiter, Jan Schlunke, Linnell Secomb, Stephen Muecke, Wendy Holland, Jane Hobson, John O'Carroll, Elizabeth Mars, Nathalie O'Carroll, Fiona Nicoll, Carolyn Williams, Virginia Watson, Sally Edith, Pip Nicholson, Penny Paul, Catherine Robinson, Jane Goodall and Justine Lloyd — none of whom have ever let me settle.

It is also a book that has a particular institutional birthplace; the New Humanities Program at the University of Western Sydney, Hawkesbury. Now that that chaotic, nomadic, badly housed and wonderfully staffed entity has been finally restructured out of existence it is remembered as an island of intel lectual curiosity and generous friendly collegiality with the finest administrative staff in the country (and the most patient!). I must thank Bob Hodge for saying hardly anything as the prose got wilder and the ideas more splenetic, except 'write it in' which has become a kind of mantra for me. David Phillips added the necessary humour, the much needed restraint and he never let me forget that books are written to be read. Ruth Barcan ordered my prose, Sara Knox whipped particular words to show me that the reader should see the blood beneath but also be able to eat them with strawberries. And in its half formed state Jane Goodall read it when she didn't have to and thought it readable and Lindsay Barrett told me, when I had anxiously forgotten all about it, that it could be a good book.

Much later Julie Marcus simply did not let me forget the project when all I could imagine was getting through the next class. At that same time Will Letts, Sharon Pickering and Michael Gard kept alive a play of ideas and Brett Hartmann made certain I didn't jump off a cliff. And meandering in and out of these times were Lyn Hughes who gave me tough pep talks about the cost of caring for the 'baby' and Sarah Gardner who thinks up and puts into place pleasures that please the brain and the heart.

For the final spurt I have to thank Sarah Shrubb my clever, surgical editor, Pru Black for final clarifications to the introduction (but also for the best of puddings), Stephen Muecke for textual triage (but also the best sauerkraut this side of the Rhine) and the entire Clarke family: Rolley, Joey and Ireni but Robbie in particular, for being such valuable thinkers and aesthetic trouble-shooters. And steering in and about the publishing process has been Margaret Whiskin of Curtin University Books who has been able to be simultaneously a wonderful storyteller, a hard nosed sales pragmatist, a sensitive reader and an academic provocateur — many thanks.

To Susan who has been with me on so many steps of these stories and who has seen me go up and come down with a startling lack of grace but who always lightens those clumsy landings with her love — a continuous thanks. I hope the trace of all these affections are in the book.

NOTES

1   Halliday, K (1988) *Call of the Highlands; The Tenterfield Story*, Toowoomba: Southern Cross Printery. p. 147; Irby, E and L (1908) *Memoirs of Edward and Leonard Irby*, Sydney: William Brooks & Co., p. 52.

2   Irby, E and L (1908) *Memoirs of Edward and Leonard Irby*, Sydney: William Brooks & Co., pp. 77, 90.

3   Thomas, JF (b. 1882, d. 1941) Papers. Miscellaneous Historical Subjects, vol. 2, Tenterfield. Microfilm CY1524 (location A2539-2540 Mitchell Library, Sydney).

4   Tenterfield District Historical Society Records, vols 1 and 2, University of New England Archives, No. 2821.

5   Leaflet, Tenterfield Tourist Information Office, Rouse Street, Tenterfield.

6   Condie, T (2001) 'Massacre site remembered with memorial', *The Koori Mail*, 18 April, p. 12.

7   Delbridge, A et al. (1992) *The Macquarie Dictionary* (Second Edition), Sydney: Macquarie Library, p. 763.

8   Pitcher, W (1993) *The Nature and Origin of Granite*, London: Blackie Academic & Professional, p. 29.

9   Baker, RT (1915) *Building and Ornamental Stones of Australia*, Sydney: Government Printer.

10 *Proceedings of the Workshop on Geological Disposal of Radioactive Waste, In Situ Experiments in Granite* (1983) Stockholm: Nuclear Energy Agency (OECD), p. 9.

11 Morris, M (1993) 'At Henry Parkes Motel', in Frow, J and Morris, M (eds) *Australian Cultural Studies: A Reader*, Sydney: Allen & Unwin, p. 269.

12 Thomas, JF (b. 1882, d. 1941) Papers. Miscellaneous Historical Subjects, vol. 2, Tenterfield. Microfilm CY1524 (location A2539-2540 Mitchell Library, Sydney).

13 Irby, E and L (1908) *Memoirs of Edward and Leonard Irby*, Sydney: William Brooks & Co., p. 88.

14 Newbury, G (1986) *Mother of Ducks with Echoes on the Wind*, Glen Innes: McMahon Graphics.

15   ibid., p. 86.

16   Carter, P (1987) *The Road to Botany Bay*, London: Faber & Faber.

17   Newbury, G (1986) *Mother of Ducks with Echoes on the Wind*, Glen Innes: McMahon Graphics, p. 126.

18   ibid., p. 121.

19   Morris, M (1993) 'At Henry Parkes Motel', in Frow, J and Morris, M (eds) *Australian Cultural Studies: A Reader*, Sydney: Allen & Unwin, p. 264.

20   Tyler, SA (1987) *The Unspeakable: Discourse, Dialogue, and Rhetoric in the Postmodern World*, Madison: University of Wisconsin Press, p. 136.

21   Abish, W (1983) *How German Is It?*, London: Faber & Faber.

22   *Manchester Guardian* (World Edition) (1998), 1 February, p. 3.

23   Thomas, JF (b. 1882, d. 1941) Papers. Miscellaneous Historical Subjects, vol. 2, Tenterfield. Microfilm CY1524 (location A2539-2540 Mitchell Library, Sydney).

24   Glasson, WR (n.d.) *Our Shepherds*, Molong: Australian Medical Publishing.

25   Anderson, R (1967) *On the Sheep's Back*, Adelaide: Rigby, p. 35; Hughes, W (1852) *The Australian Colonies*, London: Longman, Brown, Green & Longmans, p. 130.

26   Butlin, NG (1994) *Forming a Colonial Economy: Australia 1810–1850s*, Melbourne: Cambridge University Press, p. 216.

27   Blacklock, A (1841) *A Treatise on Sheep (with Remarks on the Management of Sheep in Australia)*, London: R Tyas, p. 230.

28   ibid., p. 231.

29   Abbott, GJ (1971) *The Pastoral Age: A Re-Examination*, Melbourne: Macmillan, p. 163.

30   Indyk, I (1993) 'Pastoral and priority: the Aboriginal in Australian pastoral', *New Literary History*, 24, p. 838.

31   Irby, E and L (1908) *Memoirs of Edward and Leonard Irby*, Sydney: William Brooks & Co., p. 43.

32   Boyd AJ (1974) *Old Colonials* (Facsimile Edition), Sydney: Sydney University Education Press, p. 15.

33   Blacklock, A (1841) *A Treatise on Sheep (with Remarks on the Management of Sheep in Australia)*, London: R Tyas, p. 230.

34   Coghlan, TA (1892) *The Wealth and Progress of New South Wales* (6th Issue), Sydney: Charles Potter, Government Publisher, p. 350.

35   Said, EW (1993) *Culture and Imperialism*, London: Chatto & Windus, p. xvi and a critique, Carter, P (1987) *The Road to Botany Bay*, London: Faber & Faber.

36   Armstrong and Campbell (1882) *Australian Sheep Husbandry: A Handbook of the Breeding and Treatment of Sheep and Station Management*, Melbourne: Robertson, p. 237.

37   ibid., p. 2.

38   Windeyer, R (1842) 'On the Rights of the Aborigines of Australia' (manuscript), Windeyer Papers: Mitchell Library, Sydney.

39   Douglas, M (1984) *Purity and Danger: An Analysis of the Concepts of Pollution and Taboo*, London: Ark Paperbacks.

40   Ware, JR (c. 1900) *Passing English of the Victorian Era: A Heterodox English, Slang, and Phrase*, London: George Routledge & Sons, p. 160.

41   Delbridge, A et al. (1992) *The Macquarie Dictionary* (Second Edition), Sydney: Macquarie Library, p. 1140.

42   Bhabha, H (1994) *The Location of Culture*, London: Routledge, p. 67.

43   Read, P (1996) 'A rape of the soul so profound: some reflections on the dispersal policy in New South Wales', in Chapman, V and Read, P (eds) *Terrible Hard Biscuits: A Reader in Aboriginal History*, Sydney: Allen & Unwin, pp. 76–8; Goodall, H (1996) *Invasion to Embassy: Land in Aboriginal Politics in New South Wales, 1770–1972*, Sydney: Allen & Unwin in association with Blackbooks.

44   Tenterfield District Historical Society Records, vols 1 and 2, University of New England Archives, No. 2821.

45   ibid.

46   Thomas, JF (b. 1882, d. 1941) Papers. Miscellaneous Historical Subjects, vol 2, Tenterfield, Microfilm CY1524 (location A2539-2540 Mitchell Library).

47   Geertz, C (1973) *Interpretation of Cultures*, London: Fontana. pp. 412–42.

48   Tenterfield District Historical Society Records, vols 1 and 2, University of New England Archives, No. 2821.

49   There are many examples of this language now and previously, but see in particular, *Sydney Morning Herald*, 1 December 1997, pp. 1, 6.

50   Irby, E and L (1908) *Memoirs of Edward and Leonard Irby*, Sydney: William Brooks & Co., p. 65.

51   ibid., p. 94.

52   Tenterfield District Historical Society Records, vols 1 and 2, University of New England Archives, No. 2821.

53   Campbell, IC (1969) The relations between settlers and Aborigines in the pastoral district of New England, 1832–1860, BA thesis, University New England (69/4196).

54   Chomley, C (1903) *Tales of Old Times: Early Australian Incident and Adventure*, Melbourne: WT Pater and Co., p. 12.

55 Clerk of the Peace: Depositions re the Myall Creek Massacre (1838–), Archives Authority, NSW, AONSW 4/9090.

56 Thomas Foster's Evidence per Clerk of the Peace: Depositions re the Myall Creek Massacre (A.O.N.S.W. 4/9090) Archive Authority NSW.

57 George Anderson's Evidence per Clerk of the Peace: Depositions re the Myall Creek Massacre (A.O.N.S.W. 4/9090) Archive Authority NSW.

58 Milliss, R (1992) *Waterloo Creek: The Australia Day Massacre of 1838, George Gipps and the British Conquest of New South Wales*, Sydney: UNSW Press, p. 296.

59 Tenterfield District Historical Society Records, vols 1 and 2, University of New England Archives, No. 2821, Heading: 'Robert Bates'.

60 ibid.

61 Milliss, R (1992) *Waterloo Creek: The Australia Day Massacre of 1838, George Gipps and the British Conquest of New South Wales*, Sydney: UNSW Press; Walker, RB (1966) *Old New England: A History of the Northern Tablelands of NSW 1818–1900*, London: Sydney University Press; Campbell, IC (1969) The relations between settlers and Aborigines in the pastoral district of New England, 1832–1860, BA Thesis, University of New England (69/4196).

62 Tenterfield District Historical Society Records, vols 1 and 2, University of New England Archives, No. 2821, Heading: 'Holocaust of Blacks'.

63 ibid., Heading: 'Reprisals'.

64 ibid., Heading: 'An Outrage Revenged' (1941).

65 *The Jerusalem Bible*, Students' Paperback Edition (1971), London: Geoffrey Chapman, Mark 5:15.

66 Sebald, WG (1998) *The Rings of Saturn*, London: The Harvill Press, p. 67.

67 Newsome, C (1981) *The Green Tree Snake*, Stanthorpe: International Colour Productions, p. 12.

68 ibid., p. 13.

69 ibid.

70 Muecke, S (1992) *Textual Spaces; Aboriginality & Cultural Studies*, Sydney: UNSW Press, pp. 23–35.

71 Newsome, C (1981) *The Green Tree Snake*, Stanthorpe: International Colour Productions, p. 14.

72 ibid.

73 Barcan, R (1996) 'Big things: consumer totemism and serial monumentality', *LINQ*, vol. 23, No. 2, pp. 31–9.

74 Hughes, W (1852) *The Australian Colonies*, London: Longman, Brown, Green & Longman, pp. 311, 314.

75   Bhabha, H (1994) *The Location of Culture*, London: Routledge, p. 5.

76   Gray, Robert (1998) *New and Selected Poems* (2nd edition), Sydney: Duffy & Snellgrove, p. 119.

77   I am inspired by historian Greg Dening's goals of ethnographic history: 'to re-present what actually happened in its specificity, to re-present the systems of meaning in their manifold and processual character (and) to authenticate these re-presentations of the other by displaying their relationship to the author of them' (see Dening, G (1988) *The Bounty: An Ethnographic History*, Melbourne: History Department, University of Melbourne, pp. 109–10). A partial success like cultural anthropologist James Clifford's 'partial truths' (see Clifford, J and Marcus, G (1986) *Writing Culture: The Poetics and Politics of Ethnography*, Berkeley: University of California Press, pp. 2–26.) is what I hope to achieve.

78   Irby, E and L (1908) *Memoirs of Edward and Leonard Irby*, Sydney: William Brooks & Co., p. 15.

79   ibid., p. 55.

80   Digby, E (ed.) (1889) *Australian Men of Mark*, vol. 2, Sydney: Charles F Maxwell.

81   Irby, E and L (1908) *Memoirs of Edward and Leonard Irby*, Sydney: William Brooks & Co., p. 371.

82   ibid., p. 21.

83   ibid., p. 5.

84   ibid., p. 12.

85   ibid., p. 19.

86   ibid., p. 21.

87   ibid., p. 40.

88   ibid., p. 59.

89   ibid., p. 63.

90   ibid., p. 61.

91   ibid., p. 57.

92   ibid., p. 67.

93   ibid., p. 70.

94   ibid., p. 70.

95   Bassett, J (1989) 'Faithfull Massacre at Broken River, 1838', *Journal of Australian Studies*, vol. 24, pp. 18–34; French, M (1993) 'The Great Darkey Flat Massacre Mystery', *Journal of Australian Studies*, vol. 38, pp. 12–24.

96   See Milliss (below) for the most sustained look at Nunn's campaign.

97   Milliss, R (1992) *Waterloo Creek: The Australia Day Massacre of 1838, George Gipps and the British Conquest of New South Wales*, Sydney: UNSW Press.

98 Townsend, N (1985) 'Masters and men and the Myall Creek Massacre', *Push from the Bush*, vol. 20, April, pp. 4–32, p. 24.

99 There was a famous local bushranger called Black Tommy who was killed in 1880, apparently, and I wonder if they were the same person or connected in some way. See Newsome, C (1993) *Outlawed Bushranger, Black Tommy*, McMahon Graphics: Glen Innes.

100 Irby, E and L (1908) *Memoirs of Edward and Leonard Irby*, Sydney: William Brooks & Co., p. 80.

101 ibid., p. 79.

102 ibid., pp. 89–90.

103 ibid.

104 ibid., pp. 85–6.

105 ibid., p. 76.

106 Arendt, H (1994) *Eichmann in Jerusalem; A Report on the Banality of Evil*, New York: Penguin.

107 Macdonald, G (1838–) Report to Governor in Government Despatches (Gipps–Stanley), Microfilm: Macdonald, 1845: CY102, Mitchell Library.

108 Bhabha, H (1994) *The Location of Culture*, London: Routledge, p. 67.

109 Kercher, B (1995) *An Unruly Child: A History of Law in Australia*, Sydney: Allen & Unwin, p. 6.

110 Milliss, R (1992) *Waterloo Creek: The Australia Day Massacre of 1838, George Gipps and the British Conquest of New South Wales*, Sydney: UNSW Press, pp. 274–322.

111 Kercher, B (1995) *An Unruly Child: A History of Law in Australia*, Sydney: Allen & Unwin, p. 6.

112 Franklin, M (1974) [1936] *All That Swaggers 1879–1954*, Sydney: Angus & Robertson.

113 Irby, E and L (1908) *Memoirs of Edward and Leonard Irby*, Sydney: William Brooks & Co., p. 56.

114 ibid., p. 46.

115 Hoffman, E (1989) *Lost in Translation*, London: Minerva.

116 Ariès, P (1974) *Western Attitudes Toward Death from the Middle Ages to the Present*, Baltimore: Johns Hopkins University Press, pp. 55–85.

117 Irby, E (1842–) Transcription of original diary. Available upon request, 1844: October.

118 Brady, V (1996) *Can These Bones Live?*, Sydney: Federation Press, p. 66.

119 ibid., p. 67.

120 Kristeva, J (1982) *Powers of Horror: An Essay on Abjection* (trans. Leon S Roudiez), New York: Columbia University Press, p. 3.

121 Porter, D (1984) *The Night Parrot*, Wentworth Falls: Black Lightning Press, p. 16.

122 Newbury, G (1986) *Mother of Ducks with Echoes on the Wind*, Glen Innes: McMahon Graphics, p. 126.

123 Grosz, E (1995) 'Refiguring lesbian desire', in *Space, Time and Perversion: Essays on the Politics of Bodies*, New York: Routledge, p. 184.

124 Irby, E and L (1908) *Memoirs of Edward and Leonard Irby*, Sydney: William Brooks & Co., pp. 88–9.

125 Victor Windeyer, in his pamphlet, identifies this property as 'Wallibah' but seems to be using the same diary source which identified it to me as 'Juandah'. See Windeyer, V (1977) *Charles Windeyer, 1780–1855, and Some Events of His Time*, Sydney: Haldane Publishing, pp. 40–1.

126 Ariès, P (1974) *Western Attitudes Toward Death from the Middle Ages to the Present*, Baltimore: Johns Hopkins University Press.

127 Windeyer, A (1838–91) Diary of Archibald Windeyer, University of New England Archives, A479 & A16, entry: 25 July 1839.

128 ibid., entry: 25 February 1846.

129 ibid., entry: 15 October 1846.

130 ibid., entry: July 1845.

131 Walker, RB (1966) *Old New England: A History of the Northern Tablelands of NSW 1818–1900*, London: Sydney University Press, p. 28.

132 ibid., p. 30.

133 Colonial Secretary Correspondence 45/3041.

134 Baudrillard, J (1983) *Simulations*, New York: Semiotext(e) Inc., p. 10.

135 Irby, E and L (1908) *Memoirs of Edward and Leonard Irby*, Sydney: William Brooks & Co., p. 88, October 1844.

136 Windeyer, A (b. 1838, d. 1891) Diary of Archibald Windeyer, University of New England Archives, A479 & A16.

137 ibid.

138 Irby, E and L (1908) *Memoirs of Edward and Leonard Irby*, Sydney: William Brooks & Co., p. 36.

139 Robertson, RR (1842–45) Journals and notebooks, University of New England Archives, A178, p. 17.

140 Irby, E and L (1908) *Memoirs of Edward and Leonard Irby*, Sydney: William Brooks & Co., p. 92, 15 October 1844.

141 Irby, E (1842–) Transcription of original diary. Available upon request, 1844: October.

142 Frankenberg, R (1993) *White Women, Race Matters: The Social Construction of Whiteness*, London: Routledge.

143 Halperin says this of queer: 'there is nothing to which it necessarily refers', but see Halperin, D (1995) *Saint Foucault: Towards a Gay Hagiography*, New York: Oxford University Press.

144 Chow, R (1991) 'Violence in the other country: China as crisis, spectacle and woman', in Mohanty, CT, Russo, A and Torres, L (eds) *Third World Women and the Politics of Feminism*, Bloomington: Indiana University Press, pp. 81–100.

145 Ang, I (2001) *On Not Speaking Chinese*, London & New York: Routledge.

146 Windeyer, A (b. 1838, d. 1891) Diary of Archibald Windeyer, University of New England Archives, A479 & A16.

147 Pratt, MB (1984) 'Identity, skin, blood, heart', in Bulkin, E *Yours in Struggle: Three Feminist Perspectives on Anti-Semitism and Racism*, New York: Long Haul Press, p. 18.

148 See Levinas on 'distance' and 'domination', and for cases particularly to do with takes on ethnographic knowing, see Rabinow, P (1986) 'Representations are social facts: modernity and post-modernity in anthropology' and Tyler, SA (1986) 'Post-modern ethnography: from document of the occult to occult document', both in Clifford, J and Marcus, G *Writing Culture: The Poetics and Politics of Ethnography*, Berkeley: University of California Press; Probyn, E (1993) *Sexing the Self: Gendered Positions in Cultural Studies*, London & New York: Routledge, p. 81.

149 Jackie Huggins is an Indigenous author, academic and activist, widely known and respected for her work on language and her contributions to Indigenous and feminist debates.

150 Deleuze, G (1994) 'He stuttered', in Boundas, CV and Olkowski, D (eds) *Gilles Deleuze and the Theater of Philosophy*, New York: Routledge; Chambers, R (2004) *Untimely Interventions: AIDS Writing, Testimonial and the Rhetoric of Haunting*, Ann Arbor: University of Michigan Press, pp. 102–47.

REFERENCES AND
WORKS CITED

Abish, W (1983) *How German Is It?*, London: Faber & Faber.

Abbott, GJ (1971) *The Pastoral Age: A Re-Examination*, Melbourne: Macmillan.

Anderson, R (1967) *On the Sheep's Back*, Adelaide: Rigby.

Anderson, B (1991) *Imagined Communities*, London & New York: Verso.

Ang, I (1995) 'I'm a feminist but. "Other" women and postnational feminism', in Caine, B and Pringle, R (eds) *Transitions*, Sydney: Allen & Unwin.

Ang, I (2001) *On Not Speaking Chinese*, London & New York: Routledge.

Arendt, H (1994) *Eichmann in Jerusalem: A Report on the Banality of Evil*, New York: Penguin.

Armstrong, AS (1882) *Australian Sheep Husbandry: A Handbook of the Breeding and Treatment of Sheep and Station Management*, Melbourne: George Robertson.

Ariès, P (1974) *Western Attitudes Toward Death from the Middle Ages to the Present*, Baltimore: Johns Hopkins University Press.

Ashcroft, B, Griffiths, G and Tiffin, H (eds) (1995) *The Post-Colonial Studies Reader*, London: Routledge.

Attwood, B and Arnold, J (1992) *Power, Knowledge and Aborigines: Special Edition of* Journal of Australian Studies, Bundoora: La Trobe University Press.

Barber, L (1993) *Massacre at Myall Creek*, Port Macquarie: L Barber.

Barcan, R (1996) 'Big things: consumer totemism and serial monumentality', *LINQ*, vol. 23, no. 2, pp. 31–39.

Barker, D (1958) 'The origins of Robertson's Land Act', *Historical Studies*, vol. 8, pp. 166–82.

Baker, RT (1915) *Building and Ornamental Stones of Australia*, Sydney: Government Printer.

Bassett, J (1989) 'Faithfull Massacre at Broken River, 1838', *Journal of Australian Studies*, vol. 24, pp. 18–34.

Baudrillard, J (1983) *Simulations*, New York: Semiotext(e) Inc.

Bean, CEW (1963) *On the Wool Track*, Sydney: Angus & Robertson.

Beckett, J (1988) *Past and Present: The Construction of Aboriginality*, Canberra: Aboriginal Studies Press.

Benterrak, K, Muecke, S and Roe, P (1984) *Reading the Country: Introduction to Nomadology*, Fremantle: Fremantle Arts Centre Press.

Bhabha, H (1992) 'The other question', in Merck, M (ed.) *The Sexual Subject: A Screen Reader in Sexuality*, New York: Routledge.

Bhabha, H (1994) *The Location of Culture*, London: Routledge.

Blacklock, A (1841) *A Treatise on Sheep (with Remarks on the Management of Sheep in Australia)*, London: R Tyas.

Blomfield, G (1981) *Baal Belbora: The End of the Dancing*, Sydney: Alternative Publishing Co-op.

Bohemia, J and McGregor, W (1992) 'A massacre on Christmas Creek Station', *Journal of Australian Studies*, vol. 33, pp. 26–40.

Boyd AJ (1974) *Old Colonials* (Facsimile Edition), Sydney: Sydney University Education Press.

Brady, V (1996) *Can These Bones Live?*, Sydney: Federation Press.

Bulkin, E (1984) *Yours in Struggle: Three Feminist Perspectives on Anti-Semitism and Racism*, New York: Long Haul Press.

Butler, J (1991) 'Imitation and gender insubordination', in Fuss, (ed.) *inside/out: lesbian theories, gay theories*, New York & London: Routledge, pp. 13–31.

Butler, J (1993) *Bodies that Matter; On the Discursive Limits of 'Sex'*, New York & London: Routledge.

Butler, J (1990) *Gender Trouble: Feminism and the Subversion of Identity*, New York: Routledge.

Butlin, NG (1994) *Forming a Colonial Economy: Australia 1810–1850s*, Melbourne: Cambridge University Press.

Campbell, IC (1969) The relations between settlers and Aborigines in the pastoral district of New England, 1832–1860, BA thesis, University New England (69/4196).

Campbell, IC (1971/4) 'Social backgrounds and relations with the Aborigines in New England', *Armidale and District Historical Society: Journal and Proceedings*, vols 14–16, pp. 1–11.

Cannon, M (1978) *Life in the Country: Australia in the Victorian Age 2*, Melbourne: Thomas Nelson.

Carter, P (1987) *The Road to Botany Bay*, London: Faber & Faber.

Chambers, I and Curti, (eds) (1996) *The Post-Colonial Question*, London: Routledge.

Chambers, R (2004) *Untimely Interventions: AIDS Writing, Testimonial and the Rhetoric of Haunting*, Ann Arbor: University of Michigan Press.

Chapman, V and Read, P (1996) *Terrible Hard Biscuits: A Reader in Aboriginal History*, Sydney: Allen & Unwin.

Chomley, C (1903) *Tales of Old Times: Early Australian Incident and Adventure*, Melbourne: WT Pater & Co.

Chow, R (1991) 'Violence in the other country: China as crisis, spectacle and woman', in Mohanty, C, Russo, A and Torres, L (eds) *Third World Women and the Politics of Feminism*, Bloomington: Indiana University Press, pp. 81–100.

Cleary, T (1993) *Poignant Regalia: 19th Century Aboriginal Breastplates and Images*, Sydney: Historic Houses Trust.

Clerk of the Peace: Depositions re the Myall Creek Massacre (1838–), Archives Authority, NSW, AONSW 4/9090.

Clifford, J and Marcus, G (1986) *Writing Culture: The Poetics and Politics of Ethnography*, Berkeley: University of California Press.

Clifford, J (1988) *The Predicament of Culture: Twentieth Century Ethnography, Literature and Art*, Cambridge MA: Harvard University Press.

Coetzee, J (1983) *Duskland*, Melbourne: Penguin.

Coghlan, TA (1892) *The Wealth and Progress of New South Wales* (6th Issue), Sydney: Charles Potter, Government Publisher.

Collaroy Collection. Letters and Documents relating to Dr RJ Traill, Mitchell Library, Manuscript.

Condie, T (2001) 'Massacre site remembered with memorial', *The Koori Mail*, 18 April, p. 12.

Couldry, N (1996) 'Speaking about others and speaking personally', *Cultural Studies*, vol. 10, no. 2, pp. 315–33.

Crawford, N (c. 1940) Tenterfield Historical Records, University of New England Archives.

Cryer, T (1992) *One in the Eye*, Castleford: Yorkshire Art Circus.

Delbridge, A et al. (1992) *The Macquarie Dictionary* (Second edition), Sydney: Macquarie Library.

Deleuze, G and Guattari, F (1987) *A Thousand Plateaus: Capitalism and Schizophrenia*, Minneapolis: University of Minnesota Press.

Deleuze, G (1994) 'He stuttered', in Boundas, CV and Olkowski, D (eds) *Gilles Deleuze and the Theater of Philosophy*, New York: Routledge.

Dening, G (1988) *The Bounty: An Ethnographic History*, Melbourne: History Department, University of Melbourne.

Dening, G (1993) *Mr Bligh's Bad Language: Passion, Power and Theatre on the Bounty*, Melbourne: Cambridge University Press.

Dening, G (1995) *The Death of William Gooch: A History's Anthropology*, Melbourne: Melbourne University Press.

Dening, G (1996) *Performances*, Melbourne: Melbourne University Press.

Digby, E (ed.) (1889) *Australian Men of Mark, vol. 2*, Sydney: Charles F Maxwell.

Doty, A (1993) *Making Things Perfectly Queer: Interpreting Mass Culture*, Minneapolis: University of Minnesota Press.

Douglas, M (1984) *Purity and Danger: An Analysis of the Concepts of Pollution and Taboo*, London: Ark Paperbacks.

Driscoll, W (1982) *Documents on Myall Creek Massacre*, Armidale: Armidale College of Advanced Education (ACAE) Publications.

Dyer, R (1988) 'White', *Screen*, vol. 29, no. 4, pp. 44–64.

Dyer, R (1997) *White*, London & New York: Routledge.

Elder, B (1988) *Blood on the Wattle: Massacres and Maltreatment of Australian Aborigines Since 1788*, Sydney: Child & Associates.

Emerson, R et al. (1995) *Writing Ethnographic Fieldnotes*, Chicago: University of Chicago Press.

Falzon, C (1994) 'Nomad', in Horton, D (1994) *The Encyclopaedia of Aboriginal Australia, vol. M–Z*, Canberra: Aboriginal Studies Press.

Flood, J (1990) *The Riches of Ancient Australia: A Journey into Prehistory*, St Lucia: University of Queensland Press.

Foucault, M (1995) *Discipline and Punish: The Birth of the Prison*, New York: Vintage Books.

Frankenberg, R (1993) *White Women, Race Matters: The Social Construction of Whiteness*, London: Routledge.

'Frederick' (1842) 'Religious instruction in the bush', *Sydney Morning Herald*, 20 April (under subheading 'Original correspondence').

French, M (1993) 'The Great Darkey Flat Massacre Mystery', *Journal of Australian Studies*, vol. 38, pp. 12–24.

Frith, G (1992) 'Embodying the nation: gender and performance in women's fiction', *New Formations*, pp. 98–113.

Frow, J (1988) 'Discipline and discipleship', *Textual Practice*, vol. 2, no. 3, pp. 307–23.

Frow J and Morris, M (1993) 'Introduction', in Frow, J and Morris, M (eds) *Australian Cultural Studies: A Reader*, Sydney: Allen & Unwin.

Fuss, D (1991) *inside/out: lesbian theories, gay theories*, New York & London: Routledge.

Gatens, M (1983) 'A critique of the sex/body distinction', in Patton, P and Allen, J (eds) *Beyond Marxism*, Sydney: Intervention Publication.

Geertz, C (1973) *Interpretation of Cultures*, London: Fontana.

Gibbons, PJ (1986) 'A note on writing, identity and colonisation in Aotearoa', *Sites*, vol. 13, pp. 32–8.

Giroux, H (1997) 'White squall: resistance and the pedagogy of whiteness', *Cultural Studies*, vol. 11, no. 3, pp. 377–88.

Glasson, WR (n.d.) *Our Shepherds*, Molong: Australian Medical Publishing.

Glendinnen, I (1998) *Reading the Holocaust*, Melbourne: Text Publishing.

Goodall, H (1996) *Invasion to Embassy: Land in Aboriginal Politics in New South Wales, 1770–1972*, Sydney: Allen & Unwin, in association with Blackbooks.

Grace, H (ed.) (1996) *Aesthesia and the Economy of the Senses*, Sydney: PAD Publications.

Graham, C and Hughes, J (eds) (1989) *Australian Words and Their Origins*, Melbourne: Oxford University Press.

Graham, D (1994) *Being Whitefella*, Perth: Fremantle Arts Centre Press.

Greenhalgh, AJ (1940) History of New England, MEc thesis, Armidale: University of New England.

Grosz, E (1993) *Volatile Bodies*, Bloomington: Indiana University Press.

Grosz, E (1995) 'Refiguring lesbian desire', in *Space, Time and Perversion: Essays on the Politics of Bodies*, New York: Routledge.

Guardian, 1 February 1998.

Gunn, A (1961) *We of the Never-Never*, Sydney: Angus & Robertson.

Halliday, K (1988) *Call of the Highlands: The Tenterfield Story*, Toowoomba: Southern Cross Printery.

Halliday, K (n.d.) *Tenterfield: Reflections 1 & 2*, Glen Innes: McMahon Graphics.

Halliday, K (n.d.) Tourist leaflet: available from Tenterfield Tourist Information Centre.

Harrison, P (1995) 'The return of the native: modernity, difference and postcolonialism', *Social Science Monographs*, no. 4, Carseldine: Queensland University of Technology.

Hennessy, R (1994) 'Queer visibility in commodity culture', in Nicholson, L and Seidman, S *Social Postmodernism: Beyond Identity Politics*, Cambridge: Cambridge University Press.

Hodge, B and Mishra, V (1990) *The Dark Side of the Dream*, Sydney: Allen & Unwin.

Hodge, B (1995) 'Monstrous knowledge: doing PhDs in the new humanities', *The Australian Universities Review*, vol. 38, no. 2, pp. 35–9.

Hoffman, E (1989) *Lost in Translation*, London: Minerva.

Horton, D (1994) *The Encyclopaedia of Aboriginal Australia, vol. M–Z*, Canberra: Aboriginal Studies Press.

Howard, J (1997) 'Native title plea', *Sydney Morning Herald*, 1 December.

Huggins, J (1993). 'Pretty deadly Tidda business', in Gunew, S and Yeatman, A (eds) *Feminism and the Politics of Difference*, Sydney: Allen & Unwin.

Hughes, W (1852) *The Australian Colonies*, London: Longman, Brown, Green & Longman.

Human Rights and Equal Opportunity Commission (1997) *Bringing Them Home: National Inquiry into the Separation of Aboriginal and Torres Strait Islander Children from Their Families*, Sydney: Sterling Press.

Indyk, I (1993) 'Pastoral and priority: the Aboriginal in Australian pastoral', *New Literary History* 24, pp. 837–55.

Irby, E and L (1908) *Memoirs of Edward and Leonard Irby*, Sydney: William Brooks and Co.

Irby, E (1842–) Transcription of original diary. Available upon request.

Isaac, R (1997) 'Stories and constructions of identity: folk tellings and diary inscriptions in revolutionary Virginia', in Hoffman, R, Sobel, M and Teute, F (eds) *Through a Glass Darkly*, Chapel Hill: University of North Carolina Press.

Isaac, R (1987) 'A diary and the performances in it', unpublished seminar paper, Wilson Centre, Washington DC, 5 May.

Jagose, A (1996) *Queer Theory*, Melbourne: Melbourne University Press.

Jagose, A (1994) *Lesbian Utopics*, New York & London: Routledge.

Kercher, B (1995) *An Unruly Child: A History of Law in Australia*, Sydney: Allen & Unwin.

Kristeva, J (1987) 'Talking about polylogue', in Moi, T (ed.) *French Feminist Thought: A Reader*, Oxford: Basil Blackwell, pp. 110–17.

Kristeva, J (1982) *Powers of Horror: An Essay on Abjection* (trans. Leon S Roudiez), New York: Columbia University Press.

Kulick, D and Willson M. (1995) *Taboo: Sex, Identity and Erotic Subjectivity in Anthropological Fieldwork*, New York: Routledge.

Lane, C (1995) *The Ruling Passion: British Colonial Allegory and the Paradox of Homosexual Desire*, Durham: Duke University Press.

Lang, DM (1967) History of New England 1832–1861, Honours Thesis, Armidale: University of New England.

Langford Ginibi, R (1994) *My Bundjalung People*, St Lucia: University of Queensland Press.

Lattas, A (1993) 'Essentialism, memory and resistance: Aboriginality and the politics of authenticity', *Oceania*, 63, pp. 240–67.

Lowell, R (1965) *Selected Poems*, London: Faber & Faber.

Macdonald, G (1838–) Report to Governor in Government Despatches (Gipps–Stanley), Mitchell Library, microfilm.

McDonald, R (1998) 'Darker hearts', *Australian Review of Books*, Dec/Jan, pp. 6–9.

Maras, S and Rizzo, T (1995) 'On becoming: an interview with Moira Gatens', *Southern Review*, vol. 28, no. 1, pp. 53–68.

Marcus, J (1993) *First in Their Field: Women and Australian Anthropology*, Melbourne: Melbourne University Press.

Marcus, J (1990) 'Anthropology, culture and post-modernity', in Marcus, J (ed.) *Writing Australian Culture; Text, Society and National Identity*, Social Analysis, April, no. 27 (special issue), pp. 3–16.

Marcus, J (ed.) (1990) *Writing Australian Culture; Text, Society and National Identity*, Social Analysis, April, no. 27 (special issue).

Matthews, B (1987) *Louisa*, Melbourne: McPhee Gribble/Penguin Books.

Milliss, R (1992) *Waterloo Creek: The Australia Day Massacre of 1838, George Gipps and the British Conquest of New South Wales*, Sydney: UNSW Press.

Moreton-Robinson, A (1998) 'White race privilege: nullifying Native Title', in *Bringing Australia Together: The Structure of Racism in Australia*, Woolloongabbba: Foundation for Aboriginal and Islander Research Action (FAIRA), pp. 33–38.

Moreton-Robinson, A (2000) *Talkin' Up to the White Woman: Indigenous Women and Feminism*, St Lucia:University of Queensland Press,

Moreton-Robinson, A (ed.) *Whitening Race; Essays in Social and Cultural Criticism*, Canberra: Aboriginal Studies Press

Morris, B (1992) 'Frontier colonialism as a culture of terror', in Attwood, B and Arnold, J (eds) *Power, Knowledge and Aborigines*, Bundoora: La Trobe University Press, pp. 72–87.

Morris, M (1993) 'At Henry Parkes Motel' in Frow, J and Morris, M (eds) *Australian Cultural Studies: A Reader*, Sydney: Allen & Unwin.

Muecke, S (1992) *Textual Spaces; Aboriginality & Cultural Studies*, Sydney: UNSW Press.

Muecke, S (1997) *No Road (Bitumen All the Way)*, Fremantle: Fremantle Arts Centre Press.

Muecke, S (2004) *Ancient and Modern*, Sydney: UNSW Press.

Mudrooroo (1995) *Us Mob; History, Culture, Struggle: An Introduction to Indigenous Australia*, Sydney: Angus & Robertson.

n.a. (1842) Letter to *Sydney Morning Herald* re 'Situation in NE', 8 July.

n.a. (1842) Letter to *Hunter River Gazette* re 'New England', 12 February.

Newbury, G (1986) *Mother of Ducks with Echoes on the Wind*, Glen Innes: McMahon Graphics.

Newsome, C (1981) *The Green Tree Snake*, Stanthorpe: International Colour Productions.

Newsome, C (1991) *Bushman's Holiday*, Glen Innes: McMahon Graphics.

Nicoll, F (2001) *From Diggers to Drag Queens: Configurations of Twentieth Century Australian National Identity*, Sydney:Pluto Press.

Nicoll, F (2002) 'De-facing terra nullius and facing the secret of Indigenous sovereignty in Australia', *Borderlands*, December (www.borderlandsjournal.adelaide.edu.au

Norton, A (1902) Reminiscences During the Fifties, Read before the Royal Society of Queensland, Manuscript Mitchell Library.

Ogilvie, EO (1841) Letter to *Sydney Morning Herald* re 'The Natives', 25 October.

Parker, A and Sedgwick, EK (1995) *Performativity and Performance*, London: Routledge.

Parker, K (1995) 'Very like a whale: post-colonialism between canonicities and ethnicities', *Social Identities*, vol. 1, no. 1, pp. 155–73.

Pearn, J et al. (1988) 'An early colonial pharmacopoeia: a drug list and its *materia medica* for an Australian convict settlement', *Medical Journal of Australia*, vol. 149, 5/19 December, pp. 630–34.

Phillips, G and Pearn, J (1996) 'A convict and colonial pharmacopoeia: two centuries' changes', in History, Heritage and Health: Proceedings of the Fourth Biennial conference of the Australian Society of the History of Medicine, Norfolk Island, 2–9 July 1995, Brisbane: Australian Society of the History of Medicine, pp. 89–92.

Pitcher, W (1993) *The Nature and Origin of Granite*, London: Blackie Academic and Professional.

Porter, D (1984) *The Night Parrot*, Wentworth Falls: Black Lightning Press.

Porter, D (1989) *Driving Too Fast*, St Lucia: University of Queensland Press.

Pratt, MB (1984) 'Identity, skin, blood, heart', in Bulkin, E *Yours in*

Struggle: Three Feminist Perspectives on Anti-Semitism and Racism, New York: Long Haul Press.

Price, M (1973) *The Restoration and the Eighteenth Century,* New York: Oxford University Press.

Probyn, E (1993) Sexing the Self: Gendered Positions in Cultural Studies, London & New York: Routledge.

Probyn, E (1996) *Outside Belongings,* London & New York: Routledge.

Proceedings of the Workshop on Geological Disposal of Radioactive Waste, In Situ Experiments in Granite (1983) Stockholm: Nuclear Energy Agency (OECD).

Prosser, J (1995) 'No place like home: the transgendered narrative of Leslie Feinberg's *Stone Butch Blues', Modern Fiction Studies,* vol. 41, nos 3–4, pp. 483–514.

Read, P (1996) 'A rape of the soul so profound: some reflections on the dispersal policy in New South Wales', in Chapman, V and Read, P (eds) *Terrible Hard Biscuits: A Reader in Aboriginal History,* Sydney: Allen & Unwin.

Read, HH (1957) *The Granite Controversy,* London: Thomas Murby & Co.

Reece, RHW (1974) *Aborigines and Colonists: Aborigines and Colonial Society in New South Wales in the 1830s and 1840s,* Sydney: Sydney University Press.

Reid, G (1982) *A Nest of Hornet: The Massacre of the Fraser Family at Hornet Bank Station,* Melbourne: Oxford University Press.

Reynolds, H (1981) *The Other Side of the Frontier,* Townsville: James Cook University.

Reynolds, H (1987) *The Law of the Land,* Melbourne: Penguin.

Roberts, D (1995) 'Bell Falls massacre and Bathurst's history of violence: local tradition and Australian historiography', *Australian Historical Studies,* vol. 26, no. 105, pp. 615–33.

Roberts, L (1959) 'Bandjalang tribal memories', *Mankind,* vol. 5, no. 9, July 1960.

Roberts, S (1935) *The Squatting Age in Australia 1835–1847,* Melbourne: npl.

Robertson, RR (1842–45) Journals and notebooks, University of New England Archives (A178).

Said, EW (1993) *Culture and Imperialism,* London: Chatto & Windus.

Sebald, WG (1998) *The Rings of Saturn,* London: The Harvill Press.

Seidman, S (ed.) (1996) *Queer Theory/Sociology,* Cambridge: Blackwell.

Sharpe, M (1988) *An Introduction to the Bundjalung Language and Its Dialects,* Armidale: ACAE Publications.

Southey, T (1840) *A Treatise on Sheep,* London: Smith & Elder.

Steedman, C (1986) *Landscape of a Good Woman: A Story of Two Lives*, London: Virago.

Tanoch-Bland, J (1998) 'Identifying white race privilege', in *Bringing Australia Together: The Structure of Racism in Australia*, Woolloongabbba: FAIRA, pp. 33–8.

Tenterfield District Historical Society Records, vols 1 and 2, University of New England Archives, No. 2821.

Tenterfield & District Visitors Guide, Tenterfield and District Visitors Association, Rouse Street, Tenterfield.

Tenterfield Star (1907–09) Tenterfield Public Library.

Tenterfield Courier (1907–09) Tenterfield Public Library.

Tenterfield Tourist News (1983?) vol .1, no. 4, Account of Bluff Rock Massacre.

The Jerusalem Bible (Students' Paperback Edition) (1971) London: Geoffrey Chapman.

Thieberger, N and McGregor, W (1994) *Macquarie Aboriginal Words*, Sydney: Macquarie Library.

Thomas, JF (1882–1941) Papers. Miscellaneous Historical Subjects, vol. 2, Tenterfield. Microfilm CY1524 (location A2539–2540 Mitchell Library, Sydney).

Tonkinson, M (1994) 'Thinking in colour', in Graham, E (ed.) *Being Whitefella*, Fremantle: Fremantle Arts Centre Press, pp. 162–76.

Totter, S, Parsons, W and Charny, I (1997) *Century of Genocide: Eyewitness Accounts and Critical Views*, New York: Garland Publishing.

Tourle, P (1845–) Letters of Mr Tourle, vol. 2, University of New England Archives.

Townsend, N (1985) 'Masters and men and the Myall Creek Massacre', *Push from the Bush*, vol. 20, April, pp. 4–32.

Tucker, M (1977) *If Everyone Cared*, Melbourne: Grosvenor.

Tyler, SA (1986) 'Post-modern ethnography: from document of the occult to occult document', in Clifford, J and Marcus, G *Writing Culture: The Poetics and Politics of Ethnography*, Berkeley: University of California Press.

Tyler, SA (1987) *The Unspeakable: Discourse, Dialogue, and Rhetoric in the Postmodern World*, Madison: University of Wisconsin Press.

Walker, E (1972) *Queensland's Granite Belt in Colour*, Stanthorpe: Walklee Publications.

Walker, RB (1966) *Old New England: A History of the Northern Tablelands of NSW 1818–1900*, London: Sydney University Press.

Ware, JR (n.d.) *Passing English of the Victorian Era: A Heterodox English,*

Slang and Phrase, London: George Routledge & Sons.

Watson, GL and Kopachevsky, JP (1996) 'Interpretations of tourism as commodity', in Apostolopoulos, Y, Leivadi, S and Yiannakis, A (eds) *The Sociology of Tourism: Theoretical and Empirical Investigations*, London: Routledge, pp. 281–95.

White, R (1981) *Inventing Australia*, Sydney: Allen & Unwin.

Williams, C (1997) 'Feminism and queer theory: allies or antagonists?',in *Australian Feminist Studies*, vol. 12, no. 26, pp. 293–98.

Windeyer, A (b. 1838, d. 1891) Diary of Archibald Windeyer, University of New England Archives, A479 & A165.

Windeyer, R (1842) 'On the Rights of the Aborigines of Australia' (manuscript), Windeyer Papers: Mitchell Library, Sydney.

Windeyer, T (1845–) Station Diary of Thomas Windeyer. Incorrectly listed under Archibald Windeyer. University of New England Archives V2202.

Wright, J (1977) *Collected Poems 1942–1970*, Sydney: Angus & Robertson.

Wright, J (1981) *The Cry for the Dead*, Melbourne: Oxford University Press.

Wright, J (1959) *The Generations of Men*, Melbourne: Oxford University Press.

Wright, J (1991) *Born of the Conquerors: Selected Essays*, Canberra: Aboriginal Studies Press.

Wyschogrod, E (1985) *Spirit in Ashes: Hegel, Heidegger and Man-Made Mass Death*, New Haven: Yale University Press.

Young, R (1990) *White Mythologies: Writing History and the West*, New York: Routledge.

INDEX